G-ACSS

CLASSIC LIGHT

AIRCRAFT

AN ILLUSTRATED LOOK
1920s TO THE PRESENT

RON SMITH

Schiffer Publishing Ltd®

4880 Lower Valley Road • Atglen, PA 19310

Library of Congress Control Number: 2015937547

Designed by Justin Watkinson
Cover by John Cheek
Type set in Univers LT Std/Minion Pro

ISBN: 978-0-7643-4896-9
Printed in China

Published by Schiffer Publishing, Ltd.
4880 Lower Valley Road
Atglen, PA 19310
Phone: (610) 593-1777; Fax: (610) 593-2002
E-mail: Info@schifferbooks.com

For our complete selection of fine books on this and related subjects,
please visit our website at www.schifferbooks.com.
You may also write for a free catalog.

This book may be purchased from the publisher.
Please try your bookstore first.

We are always looking for people to write books on new and related subjects.
If you have an idea for a book, please contact us at
proposals@schifferbooks.com.

Schiffer Publishing's titles are available at special discounts for bulk purchases
for sales promotions or premiums. Special editions, including personalized
covers, corporate imprints, and excerpts can be created in large quantities for
special needs. For more information, contact the publisher.

CONTENTS

INTRODUCTION
004

ACKNOWLEDGMENTS
005

CLASSIC LIGHT AIRCRAFT
A TO Z
006

BIBLIOGRAPHY
409

INDEX
410

INTRODUCTION

The world of aviation encompasses a multitude of aircraft types designed for specific roles. Perhaps the most familiar are the commercial airliners that provide holiday and business transport for millions – the long range jets of Boeing and Airbus, and the shorter range products from Embraer and Bombardier.

More dramatic and exotic are the high performance military aircraft such as the Typhoon, F-22 and B-2 and their less glamorous support aircraft in transport and training roles, such as the Hercules, C-17, Hawk and Tucano. The helicopter serves worldwide in utility, transport, search and rescue, and fire-fighting roles, with the products of AgustaWestland, Bell, Eurocopter, Mil and Sikorsky being among the most numerous.

The aircraft mentioned above are examples of the current types that perform these roles. However, there is a heritage of aircraft going back to the early days of aviation designed to provide many of these capabilities (with the exception of the helicopter, which came to the fore largely after the Second World War).

Far more numerous and varied and, to many, less familiar are the light aircraft used for training and pleasure flying throughout the world. This book seeks to illustrate a range of 'classic' light aircraft that are likely to be seen when visiting smaller airports and airfields across the globe.

Of course, 'classic' is a subjective term and is taken here to include major products, built in the thousands by the most significant manufacturers such as Beechcraft, Cessna, De Havilland and Piper. It also includes lesser-known but significant types, built in hundreds, rather than thousands. Finally, a selection of older aircraft that continue to be flown and cherished is included; in this case, 'classic' is used in much the same sense as describing a classic car. All these definitions are in themselves flexible, rather than rigid; in effect, the light aircraft presented are simply those that the author feels merit inclusion.

The content cannot be comprehensive with new types being introduced worldwide. Certain types that might be considered to fall under the description 'light aircraft' have been excluded. These include balloons, gliders, agricultural aircraft and one-off homebuilt aircraft. Also, executive jets and most larger turboprop aircraft have been excluded, where these are seen to have a primarily commercial transport or business market, rather than being sold for private ownership. Warbird fighters and bombers are not included, but military trainers, such as the Harvard, many of which are in private hands, are deemed to fall within the scope of this work.

The emphasis is on photographs of the aircraft, with brief information on the types being augmented by captions. Each of the 'Major' manufacturers is also accorded an introduction to describe the firm's history and outline its product range. The aim is to provide a representative snapshot of the products of each company, rather than to include every sub-variant of each type.

The author is an aeronautical engineer, aircraft owner and pilot. His long interest in aviation was sparked by cycling to the airfields around his school in Surrey and photographing all the aircraft that he couldn't initially recognize. This naturally led to an interest in older and more obscure light aircraft. Hopefully, the reader will excuse the inclusion of a few such relatively obscure types to add interest to the mix.

Key references used to prepare this material include various copies of *Jane's All The World's Aircraft*; *The Aircraft of the World* by William Green (1965) and by Green & Pollinger (1953 and 1955); *Airlife's General Aviation* by Rod Simpson (1991); the author's own five volume series *British Built Aircraft*; *British Civil Aircraft since 1919* by A.J. Jackson; *U.S. Civil Aircraft* (eight volumes) by J.P. Juptner; *The Vintage and Veteran Aircraft Guide* by J.W. Underwood; *Les Avions Français* (two volumes) by Pierre Gillard, and appropriate material from Wikipedia. See the Bibliography for more details.

ACKNOWLEDGMENTS

The majority of the photographs included are from the author's own collection (these are not individually credited). I must, however, give particular thanks to my twin brother Jim Smith for the use of a number of images from his collection. Other key contributors include Peter Davison, Johan Visschedijk, Rod Simpson and Jeff Jacobs, who I thank for their help, support and encouragement. All other contributors are individually credited where their images appear and I greatly appreciate the difference that their willing offers of help have made to the quality of the final work.

CLASSIC LIGHT

AIRCRAFT

A TO Z

Presentation throughout this volume is in alphabetical order by manufacturer. Where, over time, a family has evolved under the control of different organizations, all the related types are usually presented under the initial originating firm (for example, related products from, Aeronca, Champion and Bellanca are presented under Aeronca in section A). Similar considerations apply to Aero Commander and American Aviation, for example.

Aircraft built by the Czech state aircraft industry were marketed to the west by a sales organization called Omnipol. This sold products from a number of companies, including Aero, LET, and Zlin. The products of these firms are presented under each individual company's name.

The Percival Prentice is presented in section A under Aviation Traders, who were responsible for civil conversions of the type.

Spanish-built examples of the Bucker Jungmann and Jungmeister are included in the Bucker entry in section B.

Jodel, Centre Est and Robin:

    (i) Jodel aircraft from the D.9 to D.150 Mascaret through to the DR1051-M1 Sicile Record are presented under section J, irrespective of their actual manufacturer (Jodel, Alpavia, CEA, SAN, Wassmer or amateur built).

    (ii) Centre Est aircraft in the DR.200 series are presented in section C.

    (iii) Pierre Robin aircraft in the DR.300 and DR.400 series and later models are presented in section R.

All varieties of the Erco Ercoupe design are discussed under Erco in section E.

The entry for the Fieseler Storch in section F also covers the French-built Morane 500 series.

Monnett and Sonex are both described under Monnett in section M.

All variants of the CP301 Emeraude are discussed under Piel, in section P.

Although introduced by Taylor Aircraft, the E-2 Cub is the true progenitor of the Piper series of light aircraft and is therefore included in the Piper entry in section P.

The Robin entry in section R covers the DR300 and DR400 series, and later models. The DR200 series aircraft are discussed under Centre Est in section C.

Scintex developments of the Piel Emeraude are included under Piel in section P; SAN-built Jodel aircraft are included under Jodel in section J.

The Rallye series of aircraft that originated with Morane Saulnier are discussed under SOCATA in section S, as is the Gardan GY80 Horizon.

Sportavia-Putzer and Slingsby developments of aircraft designed by René Fournier are discussed in section S

All variants of the Victa Airtourer aircraft are covered in section V.

Adam RA-14 Loisirs F-PEVV photographed at Brienne-le-Chateau, France.

Adam

The Adam RA-14 is a French two-seat light aircraft that first flew in March 1946. In the 1950s, plans for the type were distributed by Maranda in Canada as the Falconar AMF-S14. Some forty aircraft were built in France, with around fifty homebuilt in Canada. In June 2014, eleven Adam RA-14 and two RA-15-1 (a higher-powered version known as the Adam Major) appeared on the French civil register.

Aermacchi Lockheed

The Aermacchi Lockheed AL60 utility aircraft was a Lockheed design manufactured under license in Mexico and Italy. At total of 145 were built, forty-four of these in Mexico.

This Aermacchi AL60B N1047L was photographed at Merrill Field, Anchorage, Alaska in May 1983.

1956 Super Aero 45 G-APRR photographed at Wroughton, Wiltshire.

Aero (Czechoslovakia)

Aircraft built by the Czech state aircraft industry were marketed to the west by a sales organization called Omnipol. This sold products from a number of companies, including Aero, LET, and Zlin. The products of these firms are presented under each individual company's name. The light aircraft products of the Aero Vodochodny concern included the twin engine Aero 45 and its developments, the Super Aero 45 and Aero 145 and Super Aero 145. These aircraft have a fully faired cockpit enclosure under a side-hinged canopy and are powered by different versions of the four-cylinder in-line Walter Minor engine. Some 200 Aero 45 were built with 105hp Walter Minor 4-III engines, the type flying for the first time in 1947. The Super Aero 45 was an upgraded model;

228 were built. The Aero 145 used two more powerful 140hp Walter M332 engines; 162 were built. All variants are externally very similar. The later models (Super Aero 45 and Aero 145) were built by LET.

Aero Boero

Aero Boero is an Argentinian company that has built a family of high wing light aircraft for private ownership, and flying club use. Many are also used as glider tugs.

Aero Boero AB95. The first model to be built was the Aero Boero AB 95, seating three, with the pilot ahead of a bench seat for two. The type resembles a Piper Cub with a more angular tail fin and was first flown in March 1959. About forty were built powered by a 95hp C-90 (AB95), or a 100hp O-200 (AB95A).

Aero Boero 95 LV-IZU at the Argentine National Aeronautical Museum, Morón in October 2012.
Peter Davison

Aero Boero AB115 PP-GRB at Campinas, Sao Paulo, Brazil in October 2012. *Peter Davison*

Aero Boero AB115. The AB115 is a more powerful version of the AB95, with metal-skinned flaps and ailerons and (AB115BS) an increased wingspan and a swept fin. The type was sold in both Brazil and Argentina. Related types include the AB150 and the four-seat AB180. The numerical part of the designation indicates installed power in horsepower. Various references disagree on numbers built, but the total for the whole family is believed to be in excess of 400.

Aero Commander
(and successor companies)

The Aero Commander family has its origins in a company founded by the well-known designer Ted Smith called The Aero Design and Engineering Company. The first product was the L.3805 of 1948, which went into production as the Aero Commander 520. This was the start of a large family of twin-engine high wing cabin light business aircraft that was to remain in production in its various guises into the mid-1980s.

During the long life of the company, ownership passed successively to North American Rockwell and then to Gulfstream American/Gulfstream Aerospace, under whom the product range continued to evolve. In addition to the main twin-engine family, it eventually included single-engine private aircraft, agricultural aircraft and the Jet Commander executive jet. The main products of the company are summarized below

Single-engine private aircraft.
This group includes the Aero Commander 100 Darter, Lark Commander, Aero Commander 200 and the Aero Commander/Rockwell 112 and 114.

Aero Commander 100. This is a high wing single-engine machine derived from the Volaire 10 and introduced by Rockwell from 1965. 335 were built.

The Aero Commander 100 was a version of the Volaire 10. Recognizable by its unswept fin, the type was sold as the Darter Commander. This aircraft was photographed at Oshkosh, Wisconsin.

1968 Lark Commander N3605X is a 180hp version of the Aero Commander 100 with a swept fin and other improvements.

Aero Commander Lark Commander. The Lark Commander is an upgraded Aero Commander 100 with swept fin and 180hp engine. 212 were built.

Aero Commander 112. A Rockwell-designed low wing retractable undercarriage monoplane with a mid-set tailplane and a spacious cabin. Powered by a 200hp Lycoming IO-360, the type was produced in five models with a total of 526 being built.

The Commander 112 was developed by Rockwell and featured a particularly roomy cabin and wide track undercarriage. N9AC is seen at its home base of Henstridge in Somerset.

Commander 114B demonstrator photographed on display at the Farnborough Air Show.

Aero Commander 114. An uprated Aero Commander 112 with increased maximum weight and 260hp Lycoming IO-540 engine. The two main versions were the 114 and 114A, of which 428 were built by Rockwell, together with a single 114B. The 112 and 114 models were produced between 1971 and 1979. A new company Commander Aircraft put the 114B back into production from 1990.

Aero Commander 200. A four-seat low wing aircraft with retractable undercarriage developed from the Meyers 200, a type that was first flown in 1953. Meyers were taken over by Rockwell in 1965 and the type joined the Aero Commander product line as the Aero Commander 200D. About forty aircraft were built by Meyers, followed by some ninety by Aero Commander.

The Aero Commander 200D was developed from the Meyers 200. N34380 is one of just eleven Meyers 200A built. It is seen at the EAA Convention, Oshkosh, Wisconsin.

The first production Aero Commander was the 520, which can readily be identified by its unswept tailfin. This is one of a small number supplied as the U-4 to the US Air Force. *Jim Smith*

Twin Commander series. The Aero Commander series of twin engine aircraft was developed progressively to include models with different installed power and cabin size, together with pressurized and turbo-prop variants. Some of the main models are listed below, with comments on distinguishing features.

Aero Commander 520. This was the first production version, with an unswept fin and two 260hp Lycoming engines, 150 were built.

Aero Commander 560. An uprated 520 with swept tail and 270hp engines. Later models after 1960 (e.g. 560F) featured a change of undercarriage to retract into a nacelle with a tapered, flattened trailing edge. Weight, wingspan and power were increased during development (to 350hp engines for 560F). The total production of the 560 series comprised 345 aircraft.

An immaculate Aero Commander 560A photographed at Hicks Field, outside of Fort Worth, Texas.

Aero Commander 560F G-ARDK photographed from the viewing area at London's Gatwick Airport. The revised engine nacelle shape of this model can clearly be seen. *Jim Smith*

The Aero Commander 500 remained in production for a number of years. This is a late model 500S Shrike Commander with pointed nose, squared-off fin tip and vestigial winglets. VH-DZC was photographed at Tocumwal, Australia in April 2013

Aero Commander 500. The model 500 is a lower power version of the 560E with two 250hp engines. Later models were the 500A (260hp), 500B (290hp), 500S and 500U Shrike Commander (with a pointed nose and squared-off fin). The total production of 500 series was 789 aircraft.

N39BA is a Texas-based Aero Commander 680E.

Aero Commander 680. A more powerful version of the 560 with 340hp supercharged engines. Later models (680F, 680FP) respectively with 380hp fuel injected engines; and cabin pressurization. Total production of these models was 506 aircraft.

Aero Commander 680FL Grand Commander. The Grand Commander featured a stretched fuselage with four cabin windows and eleven seats. The 680FL(P) offered cabin pressurization. A total of 194 were built.

N78348 is a stretched Aero Commander 680FL Grand Commander. It was photographed at Biggin Hill and is fitted with a tail-mounted geological survey sensor.

The Turbo Commander 690 continued the development of the Turbo Commander series. This aircraft was photographed at McCarran International Airport, Las Vegas, Nevada.

Aero Commander 680T Turbo Commander. This is basically a 680FL(P) adapted for 605hp Garrett TPE-331 turboprop engines. It was first flown in December 1964 as the Turbo Commander and formed the basis for all subsequent development of this family. Later models include the 680V, 680W, 681 and 681B. Total production for these models was 210 aircraft. The Turbo Commander 690 was an upgraded Turbo Commander 681 with engines moved further outboard,

using two 717hp Garrett TPE331-5-251K turboprops. Later developments were the 690A and 690B. A total of 541 were built.

Commander 685. This is basically a twin piston model marrying the pressurized airframe of the Commander 690 to two 435hp Continental GTSIO-520K geared and supercharged piston engines, sixty-six were built.

N6525V is an Aero Commander 685. This example was photographed at Blackbushe, Hampshire. *Jim Smith*

Jetprop series. The final production models were sold as the Jetprop 840 (690C), Jetprop 900 (690D), Jetprop 980 (695), and the Jetprop 1000 and 1000B (695A and 695B). These aircraft featured increased span, changes in powerplant and different cabin and cabin window arrangements. 369 aircraft were built in this series.

The importance of the Aero Commander concern and its successors is clear from the total number of aircraft produced. The figures above (which do not include a number of lesser types, or the agricultural aircraft and the Jet Commander) indicate a total production well in excess of 5,000 aircraft.

690C Jetprop 840 G-RNCO landing at its home base on the Badminton Estate.

VH-PJC is a 695B Jetprop 1000B, photographed at Fairoaks airfield, the last variant of the Aero Commander Twin Commander family.

G-BUSR is a 1995 Aero Designs Pulsar, photographed taking off from Henstridge, Somerset.

Aero Designs

The Aero Designs Pulsar is a two-seat side-by-side low wing composite homebuilt monoplane aircraft developed from the Starlite SL-1. The type was introduced in 1985 and has been built in many countries. In June 2014, twenty-eight were registered in the UK, six in Canada, eight in France and 129 listed on the U.S. civil register.

Aeromot

The Aeromot AMT-100 Ximango and AMT-200 Super Ximango are two-seat side-by-side motorgliders. They have been built under licence in Brazil, being developments of the Fournier RF-10.

G-CECJ is an Aeromot AMT-200 Super Ximango, photographed at Lasham, Hampshire.

Aeronca (and successor companies)

The name Aeronca stems from the company's full title, The <u>Aeron</u>autical <u>C</u>orporation of <u>A</u>merica. The company's first products were the very small and lightweight Aeronca C-2 and C-3, referred to as 'flivvers,' and being inspired, like the French Pou de Ciel (or Flying Flea), by the aim of bringing affordable flying to the many.

The C-2 was a single-seat high wing monoplane based on a one-off design by Jean Roche. Power was provided by a two cylinder air-cooled engine of Aeronca's own design, producing just 26hp. The type was developed into the two-seat C-3 Collegiate (initially open cockpit but subsequently with an enclosed cabin as the C-3 Master). This later type was also produced under license in Great Britain. Production comprised 112 Aeronca C-2, 205 C-3 Collegiate, 290 C-3 Master in the U.S. and a further twenty-three in the UK, where the type was known as the Aeronca 100.

Aeronca's first production aircraft the Aeronca C-2 exhibited at the Seattle Museum of Flight. *Jim Smith*

The two-seat C-3 Collegiate with open cockpit and 'razorback' fuselage photographed at Oshkosh, Wisconsin.

The Aeronca C-3 was license-built in Great Britain as the Aeronca 100; G-AEFT is a 1936 example photographed at Thruxton, Hampshire.

Pre-war production continued with the Aeronca L low wing monoplane (65 built) and the Aeronca K, which was a more powerful development of the C-3 powered by a number of types of 40hp-50hp engine. No less than 498 Aeronca Ks were built. The availability of the 50hp and 65hp Continental flat four engines led to the Aeronca 50C Chief (initially the Aeronca KCA) and the Aeronca 65C Super Chief. 195 50C and 1,060 65C were built. Somewhat confusingly, the same model names were later to be used for the post-war Aeronca 11AC and 11CC.

The Aeronca K was an evolutionary development of the C-3 and led on to the Aeronca Chief. G-ONKA was photographed at Abingdon, Oxfordshire.

The pre-war Aeronca 65C was known as the Super Chief. The post-war 11AC and 11CC reintroduced the names Chief and Super Chief. Aeronca 65CA D-EFEL was photographed at Cranfield, Bedfordshire.

With war approaching, there was an increasing need for training aircraft for the civilian pilot training program. A tandem seat aircraft was required and to meet this need Aeronca produced a new design the Aeronca 65T, which was available with a number of different engine types. Most numerous was the Aeronca 65TC Defender with Continental A-65-7 engine. This aircraft was modified with extended cockpit glazing to become the O-58 (L-3) Army cooperation aircraft. Some 900 civilian machines were built, with 1,414 being delivered for service use.

The tandem seat Aeronca 65TC Defender was the basis of the wartime O-58B. NC31751 was photographed at Oshkosh, Wisconsin.

The O-58B served as an Army co-operation aircraft during the Second World War.

Post-war production picked up the pre-war threads with a family of tandem seat aircraft (based around the model 7AC, developed from the O-58) and aircraft with side-by-side seating developed from the pre-war Chief. Most important was the 7AC Champ and its derivatives, that had a bewildering range of letter suffices indicating design changes and different engine choices. The closely related 7ECA Citabria and its own derivatives were also built in large numbers with the 8KCAB Super Decathlon remaining in current production. In 1954, design rights passed to Champion

Aircraft Corporation until it, in turn, was bought by Bellanca Aircraft in 1970. Bellanca closed down in 1980, rights eventually passing to American Champion Aircraft (ACA), with whom production continues. The main types are summarized below.

7AC Champion. The 65hp Champ is a tandem two-seat high wing aircraft. 7,200 were built, with 609 of a military version, the L-16A and L-16B built. Bellanca built seventy-one aircraft with designation 7ACA with a Franklin engine and sprung steel undercarriage.

Aeronca's most successful design was the Aeronca 7AC, subsequently also produced by Champion Aircraft and Bellanca. G-ATHK was photographed at Compton Abbas, Wiltshire.

A 1971 Bellanca-built 7ACA Champ with spring steel undercarriage.

A Champion 7DC with the larger tail fin that was introduced with this model (although subsequently fitted to some examples of the earlier 7AC).

7DC Champion. The 7DC was a civil version of L-16B with larger fin (many 7AC also have been modified with this type of fin, meaning that it cannot be relied on to distinguish between models). 184 were built. The 7EC Traveler is similar to the 7DC with higher maximum weight and a 90hp Continental C-90; 773 were built.

7FC Tri-Traveler. The 7FC is a nosewheel equipped 7EC; many have subsequently been converted back to tailwheel configuration. 472 7FC were built.

The 7FC Tri-Traveler is a nosewheel version of the Champion 7EC Traveler. G-ARAP was photographed landing at Compton Abbas, Wiltshire.

The Champion 7GCB Challenger was a three-seat derivative with a 140hp engine.

7GC, GCA and GCB Challenger. These aircraft are three-seat variants with increased power (140hp or 150hp). A combined total of 762 of these aircraft were built.

7ECA Citabria (name advertised as 'Airbatic' spelt backward). The Citabria is a 7EC with extended glazing and a new fin shape. The type was initially flown with 100hp, but production aircraft used a 115hp engine. Development continued with the 7GCBC (150hp) and 7KCAB (also 150hp) with inverted fuel system and revised wing section. Bellanca developed a Utility version, the 8GCBC Scout with 180hp and a beefed-up airframe. More than 5,000 aircraft of the Citabria family (Citabria, Scout and Decathlon) have been built.

N575H is a float-equipped Champion 7GCBC Citabria at Lake Hood Airstrip, Anchorage, Alaska in May 1983.

The Champion 7KCAB was a predecessor of the aerobatic Bellanca 8KCAB Decathlon (see below).

The American Champion 8GCBC Scout offered 180hp and a strengthened airframe. N233SF was photographed at Arlington, Texas.

2003 American Champion Bellanca 8KCAB Super Decathlon G-IGLZ taking off from Henstridge, Somerset in August 2014.

8KCAB Decathlon. This model was intended for aerobatics, having a reduced wingspan, closer rib spacing and a full inverted fuel and oil system. ACA produced a further improved version, the Super Decathlon with metal wing spars and 180hp.

Chief and Super Chief. The side-by-side Chief was revised and put into production post-war as the 11AC Chief. One prototype and 1,960 production 11AC were built with the 65hp Continental A-65-8. The 11BC (181 built) had 85hp and was followed by 277 Aeronca 11CC Super Chief with aerodynamically balanced elevators and enlarged fin. As with the 7AC, many 11AC have also been fitted with the larger fin, making fin size unreliable in distinguishing between models.

The post-war Aeronca 11AC Chief was a descendant of the pre-war Aeronca 65C. G-BJEV was built in 1946 and photographed landing at the Badminton House airstrip.

The Aeronca 11CC Super Chief has an enlarged fin and aerodynamically balanced elevator.

The four-seat Aeronca 15AC Sedan, seen here at Lake Winnebago, Wisconsin, was the last Aeronca design.

Sedan. The final model to be produced in any significant numbers was the Aeronca 15AC four-seat high wing monoplane. Power was provided by a 145hp Continental O-145 and 562 examples were built.

The importance of the Aeronca concern and its successors is clear from the total number of aircraft produced. The figures above (which do not include a number of lesser types) indicate a total production well in excess of 22,000 aircraft.

G-BKPB is a 1985 Aerosport Scamp photographed at Cranfield, Bedfordshire.

Aerosport

The Aerosport Scamp is a single-seat open cockpit biplane with a tricycle undercarriage and T-tail. The type was first flown in August 1973 and a substantial number of sets of plans were sold. In June 2014, three Scamps were registered in the UK, with sixteen listed on the U.S. civil aircraft register.

AISA

Aeronáutica Industrial S.A. is a Spanish concern that manufactured a number of light aircraft designs.

AISA I-11B Peque. Comparatively little known outside Spain, the two-seat C-90 powered I-11B Peque was flown in 1953. 206 were built.

AISA I-11B Peque on display at the Spanish Air Force Museum at Cuatro Vientos, Madrid.

Alpi Pioneer 200 G-CGLI was photographed at Henstridge, Somerset in August 2014.

Alon A2 Aircoupe
All varieties of the Erco Ercoupe design are discussed under Erco.

Alpi
The Italian Alpi Pioneer 200 is a two-seat side-by-side low wing monoplane that is supplied as a kit for home construction, or as a ready-to-fly aircraft. The Pioneer 200 has a fixed tricycle undercarriage and is designed to meet Light Sport aircraft (LSA) requirements. In June 2014, eleven Pioneer 200s were registered in the UK.

The Alpi Pioneer 300 is a two-seat side-by-side retractable undercarriage low wing monoplane. The type is designed to meet LSA certification requirements and is supplied in kit form for home building. In June 2014, forty-seven Pioneer 300s were registered in the UK.

Alpi Pioneer 300 G-PION landing at its home base of Henstridge, Somerset in May 2011.

An AA-1 Yankee at Dahlemer-Binz, the home airfield of German agents Sportavia Putzer Gmbh, in 1971. The author was working there at the time.

American Aviation
(and successor companies)

The designer Jim Bede was responsible for the Bede BD-1, a somewhat stubby low wing monoplane with tricycle undercarriage, which was first flown in 1963. American Aviation initiated production of a modified version of the design, The AA-1 Yankee. This type was powered by the 115hp Lycoming O-235 engine, rather than the limited 65hp of the BD-1. It also featured larger overall dimensions. One notable feature was the use of metal bonding in construction, with many of the panels being stabilized by a bonded honeycomb substrate, rather than using a traditional frame and stringer construction. The result was a dramatic reduction in parts count, cost and assembly man-hours. A series of variants followed, which are summarized below.

AA-1 Yankee. The AA-1 is the two-seat base model, of which 461 were built.

AA-1A and AA-1B Trainer. These aircraft were fitted with dual controls, the AA-1B offering an increase in maximum weight. A total of 1,150 were built. The AA-1C Lynx is a revised version of the AA-1B; 211 were built.

G-BEXN is a 1977 AA-1C Lynx.

G-AZMJ is an early example of the AA-5 Traveler, photographed at Henstridge, Somerset.

AA-5 Traveler and AA-5A Cheetah. The AA-5 is a four-seat development of the AA-1 series with a 150hp Lycoming O-360. The AA-5A featured longer rear cabin windows and modified fin geometry. A combined total of 1,731 were built.

AA-5B Tiger. The AA-5B is a more powerful (180hp) AA-5A with increased maximum weight. Also designated GA-5B after American Aviation was sold to Grumman, becoming Grumman American Aviation and later Gulfstream Aviation. Finally became the AG-5B under the ownership of American General Aircraft Co. At least 1,323 AA-5B were built.

Grumman American GA-5 Tiger landing at Henstridge, Somerset.

1979 Gulfstream American GA7 Cougar taking off from Popham, Hampshire in July 2014.

The last product (of Grumman American) was the light twin-engine Grumman GA-7 Cougar. This four-seat aircraft was, in effect, a twin-engine derivative of the AA-5A, with two 160hp Lycoming O-320 engines. 115 were built.

The AA-1 and AA-5 were affordable types offering comparatively high performance and were justifiably popular. Some pilots found that care was needed in landing to avoid porpoising onto the flexible fibreglass nosewheel leg, which could result in the propeller striking the ground. While not being comparable to the output of Cessna or Piper, nearly 5,000 aircraft of this family were built.

American Eagle

American Eagle, set up by Edward Porterfield, designed and built a number of light aircraft in the 1920s and early-1930s. Notable types included the OX-5 powered A-1 and A-101 biplane (more than 500 built); A-129 (one of a number of versions of the A-101 powered by different engines, in this case 100hp Kinner – more than 100 built); and the Eaglet 230 parasol monoplane, of which ninety were built.

American Eagle Eaglet NC548Y is a rare survivor of some ninety built and is seen at Oshkosh, Wisconsin.

1978 Anderson Kingfisher N47170 was photographed at Lake Hood Airstrip, Anchorage, Alaska.

Anderson

The Anderson Kingfisher is a two-seat side-by-side amphibian flying boat powered by a pylon mounted engine above the wing center section driving a tractor propeller. Eleven Anderson Kingfisher aircraft were listed on the U.S. civil register in June 2014.

Andreasson

Designed by Björn Andreasson, the BA-4B is an aerobatic single-seat all-metal biplane, based on the designer's pre-war wooden BA-4. The type was first flown in 1966 and was built as the Crosby BA-4B in the UK and marketed as the Canary Hawk in the U.S. In June 2014, six BA-4Bs were registered in the UK, with a single Canary Hawk listed on the U.S. register.

1972 Andreasson (Crosby) BA-4B G-AYFV photographed at Cranfield, Bedfordshire.

The ANEC II Monoplane is a rare survivor from the 1924 Air Ministry Light Aeroplane Trials. It is preserved at The Shuttleworth Trust, Old Warden, Bedfordshire.

ANEC

The Air Navigation & Engineering Co. Ltd. (ANEC) has its origin in the British arm of Louis Blériot, having gone through several name changes before becoming ANEC in August 1919. The company built the ANEC I and II monoplanes for the 1923 and 1924 motor glider and light aircraft competitions at Lympne. These were followed by three large ANEC III biplanes for use in Australia and the ANEC IV, which was a graceful I-strutted biplane for the 1926 Light Aeroplane Competition.

Antonov

The Russian Antonov Design Bureau is not a name widely associated with light aircraft, the majority of their products being large transport aircraft. A notable exception is the Antonov An-2 built in huge numbers as a civil and military utility aircraft for the Eastern Bloc, a few An-2 aircraft operate in private hands for joy riding and display purposes.

Antonov An2 HA-MKF is seen at its Popham base. *Jim Smith*

Arctic Tern N70AT photographed operating on 'tundra tires' in Alaska in May 1983.

Arctic Aircraft

Arctic Aircraft manufacture an updated version of the Interstate Cadet at Anchorage, Alaska as the Arctic Tern. Upgraded to 150hp, the Tern is visually very similar to The Interstate design. Some thirty-two Arctic Terns were built, the first having flown in 1977.

Arion

The Arion Lightning is a high performance composite homebuilt aircraft that meets LSA certification requirements. The Lightning was first flown in March 2006 and it is reported (Wikipedia) that 150 had been built by 1992. In June 2014, twenty-six were listed on the U.S. civil register.

Arion Lightning 19-7380 photographed at Temora, NSW, Australia in April 2011. *Jim Smith*

The diminutive Arrow Active. This is the sole survivor of two built, seen taking off from Cranfield, Bedfordshire.

Arrow Aircraft (UK)

Arrow Aircraft of Leeds, West Yorkshire built two examples of a small fighter-like aerobatic biplane, the Arrow Active in 1931 and 1932. One, G-ABVE, still survives, the first aircraft G-ABIX having been destroyed in an accident.

Arrow Aircraft and Motors (U.S.)

The Arrow Sport was a dual control two-seat side-by-side biplane. Some 100 were built powered by either a 60hp or 90hp Le Blond radial engine. A number of examples remain in the U.S., most of these being held in museum collections.

1929 Arrow A2-60 Sport G-AARO photographed at Biggin Hill, Kent after rebuild in the UK. This aircraft is now on display at the Steven F. Udvar-Hazy Center, Chantilly, Virginia. *Jim Smith*

1937 Arrow Sport F (or Sport V-8) NC18722 photographed at San Francisco Airport, California.

Arrow Sport F or Sport V-8. The Sport F is a two-seat side-by-side low wing monoplane using a modified Ford V-8 car engine. The type first flew in 1934 and a total of 103 were built.

ARV Aviation Ltd.

ARV was set up in December 1983 by Richard Noble, holder of the World Land Speed Record to manufacture a new low-cost light aircraft, the ARV Super 2. The type first flew in March 1985, but encountered some reliability issues with its new Hewland AE75 three-cylinder two-stroke engine. About twenty-eight aircraft were built before production stopped in mid-1988, and twenty aircraft remained registered in the UK in December 2013. A number of other concerns have since tried to relaunch the design, with no lasting success.

ARV Super2 G-ERMO seen at Netherthorpe, South Yorkshire.

Auster I/Taylorcraft Plus D LB312 G-AHXE climbing away after a short takeoff at Popham, Hampshire.

Auster Aircraft Ltd.
and Taylorcraft Aeroplanes (England) Ltd.,
Beagle-Auster Aircraft Ltd.

Taylorcraft Aeroplanes (England) Ltd. was set up in 1938 to undertake license production of the U.S.-designed Taylorcraft Model B. The anglicized design entered production as the Taylorcraft Plus C, of which twenty-three were built prior to the outbreak of the Second World War. This was followed by the Plus D with a 90hp Cirrus Minor engine. Nine were completed pre-war, followed by 100 aircraft for Army cooperation use as the Auster AOP. Mk.I. A range of derivative models followed for Army use, the name Auster becoming so well known that the company was re-named Auster Aircraft Ltd. in March 1946. The list below summarizes the main Auster and Beagle Auster models. (Beagle-Auster Aircraft Ltd. was formed in September 1960, later being fully absorbed into Beagle Aircraft Ltd., whose products are described separately). The full list is diverse and numerous. More complete details can be found in the author's *British Built Aircraft, Volume 4, Central and Eastern England.*

Auster I and Taylorcraft Plus D. A derivative of the Taylorcraft Plus C with 90hp Cirrus Minor. One hundred were built for Army cooperation duties. Civilian aircraft are known as the Taylorcraft Plus D. Nine aircraft pre-war plus 100 Auster AOP Mk.I.

Auster III. This is an AOP aircraft with a 130hp Gipsy Major I, with extended cockpit glazing; 458 were built.

Auster III VH-SNI (A33-1) was photographed at Echuca, Victoria in April 2013.

The Auster IV and V were powered by the Lycoming O-290. G-APBW is an Auster 5 Alpha seen at Eggesford, Devon.

Many Auster V have been modified with increased power for roles such as glider towing. G-AKWS has been re-engined with a 160hp Lycoming O-320-B.

Auster IV, V and Auster 5 Alpha. AOP aircraft powered by 130hp Lycoming O-290. Production comprised 253 Auster IVs; 790 Auster Vs; and fourteen new-build Auster 5 Alphas. Many aircraft were civilianized post-war.

Auster 5C and 5D. This type is an Auster V with 130hp Gipsy Major I engine; one 5C and twenty-five Auster 5Ds were built.

A small number of Auster Vs were re-engined with the Gipsy Major as the 5C or 5D. G-AKSZ was photographed at Brienne le Chateau in France.

The three-seat Cirrus Minor-powered J/1 Autocrat was Auster's most successful design for the civil market. 1945 G-AGTO was photographed at Shoreham Airport, West Sussex.

Auster J/1 Autocrat. A post-war three-seat design with 100hp Blackburn Cirrus Minor; 414 were built.

Aiglet J/1B. A Gipsy Major-powered development of the Autocrat, similar to J/1N Alpha. Eighty-six were built, most being exported to Australia and New Zealand.

The J/1B Aiglet is essentially an Autocrat with Gipsy Major engine and an enlarged aerodynamically balanced rudder. G-AMKU was photographed at Eggesford, Devon.

VH-SAH is a J/1N Alpha at Echuca, VIC, Australia. The J/1N is similar to the J/1B Aiglet. In addition to new-build examples, a number of Autocrats were converted to this model.

Alpha J/1N Alpha. Gipsy Major conversions of the Autocrat plus forty-three new-build aircraft and one built-up from spares. The J/1N has a larger fin with aerodynamically balanced rudder, and is very similar in specification to the J/1B Aiglet.

Workmaster J/1U. The J/1U is an agricultural/aerial work development with 180hp Lycoming O-360. First flown in 1958, a total of ten were built.

The J/1U Workmaster was developed for agricultural use for Crop Culture Aerial Ltd. G-APMH was photographed at Leicester.

The two-seat Auster J/2 was powered by the Continental A-75 engine. G-BEAH was photographed at Eggesford, Devon.

Arrow J/2. The J/2 is a two-seat aircraft with 75hp Continental A75 and can readily be identified by the exposed engine cylinder heads. Forty-five were built.

Archer J/4. The J/4 was developed from the J/2 with a 90hp Cirrus Minor. Twenty-six were built.

The Auster J/4 is a Cirrus Minor-powered J/2; G-AIPR is seen here at Cranfield, Bedfordshire.

The Auster J/5 Adventurer is Gipsy Major-powered Autocrat (like the J/1B and J/1N), but lacks the aerodynamically balanced rudder. VH-KSL was photographed at Caboulture, Queensland.

Auster J/5 Adventurer. Similar to the J/1N Alpha, but without the aerodynamically balanced rudder. Fifty were built, most being exported to Australia, where they are known as the Adventurer.

Autocar (J/5B, J/5G, J/5P, J/5V). Four-seat development with widened fuselage and raised cabin roof line. Model types are distinguished by their different engine types. J/5B Gipsy Major I, eighty-two built; J/5G 155hp Cirrus Major 3, ninety-four built; J/5P 145hp Gipsy Major 10-2, twenty-four built; J/5V 160hp Lycoming O-320, only one built.

The Autocar is a four-seat Auster variant with a wider and deeper rear fuselage. This is a Gipsy Major I-powered J/5B at Eggesford, Devon.

G-AOBV is a 1955 J/5P Autocar photographed at Stapleford Tawney, Essex.

G-AOIY is a 1956 J/5G Autocar with 155hp Cirrus Major 3. It was photographed at Dunkeswell, Devon.

Last of the Autocars is the sole J/5V 160 G-APUW, seen here at Biggin Hill, Kent.

Auster J/5F Aiglet Trainer VH-BTQ photographed at Echuca, Victoria in April 2013.

G-AMMS is the sole J/5K Aiglet Trainer with 155hp Cirrus Major 3. It was photographed at Eggesford, Devon.

The Auster J/5L is an Aiglet Trainer powered by a 145hp Gipsy Major 10-2 photographed at Cranfield, Bedfordshire.

Aiglet Trainer (J/5F, J/5K. J/5L, J/8L). The Aiglet Trainer is a clipped wing version of the Aiglet for aerobatic training. J/5F had 130hp Gipsy Major I; ninety-two were built. J/5K had 155hp Cirrus Major 3; only two built, one later converted to J/8L with 145hp Gipsy Major 10-1 engine. J/5L 145hp Gipsy Major 10-1 or 10-2, twenty-seven built.

The Auster Alpine married the Autocar wing to the Aiglet Trainer fuselage. This is a J/5Q with Gipsy Major I engine seen at Popham, Hampshire.

G-ANXC, seen here at Dunkeswell, Devon, is a J/5R Alpine with 145hp Gipsy Major 10-1.

Alpine (J/5Q, J/5R). An Aiglet Trainer fuselage with Autocar wings and Aiglet Trainer ailerons. J/5Q had a 130hp Gipsy Major I, four were built. J/5R had 145hp Gipsy Major 10-1, one J/5L conversion and six new build.

Auster AOP. Mk6 and T7 and 6A Tugmaster. Army cooperation and training aircraft for the RAF. The type was also sold to Canada, South Africa, Belgium, Iraq, Jordan and Australia. 383 AOP. Mk.6 and eighty-three T.7 were built. Civilian conversions for glider towing (as Auster 6A) and, on retirement from the services, as Beagle Terrier 1 and 2.

The Auster AOP6 and T7 were replacements for the earlier Auster Mks I to V in Army/RAF service. This is an Auster 6A (civilianized AOP6) at Compton Abbas. The AOP6 was later to be the basis of the Beagle Terrier.

The last military Auster was the AOP9, powered by the 172hp Cirrus Bombardier 203 engine. XR241 (G-AXRR) was photographed at Eggesford, Devon.

The 1954 Auster 9M G-AVHT was a one-off cleaned-up adaptation of the Auster AOP9 with 180hp Lycoming O-320-A1D.

AOP. Mk.9. A 1954 Army cooperation model with 172hp Bombardier 203 engine; 167 were built.

D4/108. A new two-seat design flown in 1960. Six were built in UK with parts for more aircraft to be assembled in Portugal. Power was provided by a 108hp Lycoming O-235. The total built was around forty.

G-ARLG is an Auster D4/108. The type was also assembled in Portugal. G-ARLG is seen at Dunkeswell, Devon.

The Beagle Auster D5/160 and D5/180 Husky were built in Portugal and in the UK. This 1965 D5/180 was photographed at Henstridge, Somerset.

D5/160 & D5/180 Husky. Designed for license production in Portugal by OGMA. First flown in 1960 with160hp Lycoming O-320-A2A. Twenty-five were completed at Rearsby and parts for more than 100 were supplied for assembly in Portugal. D5/180 Husky: A rugged STOL utility aircraft using the 180hp Lycoming O-360-A2A. Five were built in Portugal and sixteen in the UK.

D6/180. An Autocar derivative with 180hp Lycoming O-360. Three were built plus one D6/160 later upgraded to D6/180.

The D-series aircraft, although designed by Auster were produced after the company was taken over by Pressed Steel Co. Ltd. in 1960 to form Beagle-Auster Ltd. The following additional types are described under the Beagle Aircraft Ltd. entry – A61 Terrier, AOP. Mk.II, A.109 Airedale. The additional products that were wholly developed by Beagle were the Beagle B121 Pup, Beagle 206 Basset twin and the Beagle Bulldog (later taken over by Scottish Aviation).

Last of the Auster series was the Beagle Auster D6/180, three were built plus a D6/160 later converted to D6/180. G-ARCS was built in 1960 and photographed at Henstridge, Somerset.

The Avia (or Lombardi) FL3 was first flown in 1939. 400 were built up to 1942, with additional production after the end of the war.

Avia

Avia was set up pre-war by Francis Lombardi and built 338 L3 trainers for the Italian Air Force and ten more for Croatia. Many of these aircraft flew post-war with civilian clubs. The company was reorganized as the Francis Lombardi Co. and the type was put back into production as the FL3, 53 of which were built. Limited production of other models was undertaken.

AviaMilano

This Italian company built fifty examples of a two-seat side-by-side low wing training monoplane, the Aviamilano P.19 Scricciolo, the first example flying in December 1959. The company was one of a number that built aircraft designed by the talented designer Stelio Frati. His best known designs include the F.8L Falco (discussed under Laverda), the F.15 Picchio (under Procaer) and the F.250 (under SIAI-Marchetti). Aviamilano built a prototype and ten production examples of the F.14 Picchio, which was, in effect, a four-seat derivative of the F.8 Falco.

This elegant Aviamilano F.14 Nibbio G-OWYN was photographed at Henstridge, Somerset.

1948 Aviation Traders Prentice G-APPL taxiing at Cranfield, Bedfordshire.

Aviation Traders (Engineering) Ltd.

Aviation Traders was formed in 1949 and specialized in civilian conversions of ex-military aircraft, notably the Handley Page Halifax and the Percival Prentice. The Percival Prentice was built as an intermediate trainer for the RAF. When retired from service, some 252 aircraft were purchased by Aviation Traders (Engineering) Ltd. for conversion to civil use. The conversion was normally configured with five-seats. Power was provided by a 250hp Gipsy Queen 30.

Some twenty-eight aircraft were eventually to appear as civil aircraft.

Avid

Avid Flyer. The Avid Flyer is a light two-seat side-by-side high wing STOL monoplane, similar in concept to the Denney Kitfox. First flown in 1983, more than 2,000 kits have been sold and in June 2014 some 400 were listed on the U.S. civil register.

Avid Flyer Model C N316BM photographed at North Las Vegas, Las Vegas, Nevada.

AV Roe & Co. Ltd.

More usually associated with bomber aircraft such as the Lancaster, Lincoln and Vulcan, AV Roe built a number of lighter aircraft, including the Avro Avian, Tutor, Avro 626, Prefect and Cadet. The Avian was one of relatively few designs to compete with the De Havilland Moth; 396 Avian were built, with limited additional production in Canada and the USA.

1927 Avro Avian VH-UFZ was photographed at Cranfield Bedfordshire. This aircraft is currently registered in the U.S. as N7083.

Although the Avro 621 Tutor was designed for use as a military trainer, around twenty received British civilian registrations, together with a similar number of the closely-related Avro Prefect. A combined total of nearly 1,000 Tutors, Avro 626s and Prefects were built.

The Avro Cadet was a smaller version of the Avro Tutor designed for private and club use. Six versions of the Avro Cadet were built, including thirty-five Cadet, fifteen Club Cadet and sixty-one Cadet II.

Avro Cadet A6-17 (VH-AGH) is believed to be the only example of the type currently flying. It was photographed in April 2013 at Echuca, VIC, Australia.

1933 Avro Tutor G-AHSA is preserved in flying condition at The Shuttleworth Trust, Old Warden, Bedfordshire.

Beagle Aircraft Ltd.

In January 1960, the Pressed Steel Co. Ltd. took over Auster Aircraft Ltd. and launched a new company Beagle-Auster Aircraft Ltd. The name Beagle was a shortened version of British Executive and General Aviation Ltd. Beagle took over the Auster production facilities at Rearsby and also opened facilities at Shoreham to produce new products of its own design.

Initially, Beagle-Auster built the Auster D-series of aircraft (described under the Auster entry) and marketed civilian conversions of the Auster AOP6, T7 and T10 as the Beagle Terrier. Eighteen Terrier 1s were converted, followed by forty-five Terrier 2s with increased maximum flap deflection and enlarged tail surfaces. A single Terrier 3 was converted by apprentices of British European Airways, powered by a 160hp Lycoming O-160-B2B.

A single improved Auster AOP9 was built as the Beagle E.3 or AOP. Mk.11 with a 260hp Rolls-Royce Continental IO-470-D. The final high wing design to be built was the Beagle A.109 Airedale, a four-seat aircraft intended to compete with the Cessna series. First flown in April 1961, a total of forty-three were built up to August 1964.

In 1962, the company was renamed Beagle Aircraft Ltd. and concentrated its development efforts at Shoreham, West Sussex on two wholly new designs, the single-engine Beagle B121 Pup and the twin engine Beagle 206.

The prototype 100hp Pup 1 flew in April 1967, followed by the 150hp Pup 2 in October 1967. Orders were received for some 400 aircraft, but only 176 had been built when the company ceased trading at the end of 1969. A military training derivative, the Bulldog, was flown in May 1969 and was subsequently manufactured by Scottish Aviation at Prestwick.

The Beagle 206 was intended as a twin-engine executive, air taxi and military communications aircraft, in which guise, it was ordered by the RAF as the Basset CC.1. Built in a number of versions, production totaled two prototypes, seventy-five production B.206, two RAF evaluation aircraft and twenty Basset CC.1 and two prototype B.206 Srs.3 with an enlarged cabin and deeper rear fuselage.

The company was nationalized in December 1966 but entered receivership in December 1969 following the withdrawal of government funding.

Beagle Terrier 2 G-AYDW, photographed at Blackbushe airfield, Hampshire.

The sole Beagle Terrier 3 G-AVYK at Cranfield, Bedfordshire; it was built in 1957

XP254/G-ASCC is the Beagle E.3 or Auster AOP. Mk.11 prototype, built in 1962.

VH-UEH is a Beagle A.109 Airedale photographed in its original manufacturer's color scheme at Illawarra, NSW.

G-AXEV is a Beagle Pup 150, a popular type well known for its excellent handling. It was photographed at the hilltop airfield of Compton Abbas, Wiltshire.

A Beagle 206 Basset CC.1 XS770/G-HRHI in non-standard RAF colors at an event to celebrate the sixtieth anniversary of Shoreham Airport, West Sussex, with which the type has a deep association.

N469JH is a 1975 Bede BD-4 photographed at Oshkosh, Wisconsin.

Bede

The designer Jim Bede first came to prominence with his BD-1 design. This two-seat monoplane was originally intended for home construction, but became the basis of the American Aviation AA-1 and AA-5 series. His next successful design was the Bede BD-4 which was a two or four-seat side-by-side high wing cantilever monoplane, with either tailwheel or tricycle undercarriage. The type is distinguished by a resolutely rectangular fuselage section with few curved surfaces. First flown in 1968, several hundred have been built, 100 appearing on the U.S. register in June 2014.

Bede BD-5 and BD-5J. Bede's most famous design is the Bede BD-5 and its jet powered counterpart, the BD-5J. The diminutive and fighter-like BD-5 was offered as a kit plane with very high performance on limited engine power. In the event, large numbers of kits were sold, but engine supply problems prevented many from being completed. The BD-5 was first flown in September 1971.

Left: N777KH is a Bede BD-5B photographed at Oshkosh, Wisconsin.

Right: Coors 'Silver Bullet,' a 1976 Bede BD-5J N21AP taxying at Oshkosh, Wisconsin.

The BD-5J was a jet-powered version using the 250lbst (250 pounds static thrust) Micoturbo engine, with around twenty being built. Several of these were used as airshow performers. Both types suffered from relatively poor accident records. In June 2014, seven BD-5Js were listed on the U.S. civil register, together with around 50 BD-5B.

Beech Aircraft Corporation

The Beech Aircraft Corporation was formed by Walter Beech in 1932 and produced a range of quality aircraft that could fairly be described as products for the wealthy private owner. The designs were known as Beechcraft, the line beginning with one of the company's most famous products, the powerful, high performance Beechcraft 17 'Staggerwing' biplane, which featured a retractable undercarriage and reverse wing stagger, with the upper wing mounted aft of the lower wing.

A number of the company's subsequent products were highly successful and the subject of long production runs in a multitude of sub variants. A top level summary of the various products is given below, some of the most famous designs being the Beechcraft 18 'Twin Beech,' the Bonanza, Twin Bonanza, Baron, Queen Air and King Air.

With its focus on private aircraft, this work does not cover products exclusively intended for commercial or corporate operation, including the later models of King Air; the Beechcraft 99 and 1900; and the various executive jets latterly produced by the company.

The production numbers given below for certain of the types included in this volume are approximate rather than exact, but hopefully give an indication of the importance of the company, which sits alongside Cessna and Piper as the pre-eminent producers of American light aircraft. Where possible, the information given has been taken from the Hawker Beechcraft data to be found at: http://www.beechcraft.com/customer_support/technical_publications/docs/nontechnical/serializationList.pdf

The Beech 17. The Beech 17 'Staggerwing' is a high performance four or five-seat biplane. The initial three aircraft were fitted with a fixed undercarriage, thereafter a retractable undercarriage was used. Production aircraft used a range of radial engines from the 225hp Jacobs to the 450hp Pratt & Whitney R-985. Total production was 785 aircraft between 1933 and 1945.

Beech D17S NC18028 is based at Popham, Hampshire and is every inch a luxury means of transport.

Beech 18. The Beech 18 is a six- to eight-seat light commercial transport powered by two 450hp Pratt & Whitney R-985 engines. Its long production run extended from 1937 to 1970 including the AT-11 Kansan navigation trainer. Post-war production aircraft featured extended squared-off wingtips, stretched fuselage and nosewheel undercarriage (Super H18). Most of the surviving aircraft are now in private ownership. Total production of the family was in excess of 9,000 aircraft.

1952 Beech D18S N15750 was a rare visitor to London's Heathrow Airport in the early-1970s.

N508MH is a rare Beech AT-11 navigation trainer variant of the Beech 18. It was photographed at Merrill Field, Anchorage, Alaska in May 1983.

G-TAMS is a Beech A23-24 Musketeer Super III manufactured in 1967. It was photographed at Dunkeswell, Devon in August 2013.

Beech 23 Musketeer. the Musketeer is a four-seat low wing aircraft designed to compete with the Piper Cherokee and Cessna 172. The aircraft was offered with a range of engines including the 160hp O-320, 180hp O-320 (C23 Sundowner 180) or 200hp IO-360B (A23-24 Musketeer Super III). A two-seat version intended primarily for training was sold as the Beech 19 Musketeer Sport. Total production of all variants was around 3,600 aircraft between 1963 and 1983.

Beech 24R Sierra. Originally produced as the Musketeer Super R, this is in essence a retractable undercarriage Musketeer. It was subsequently marketed as the Sierra and was powered by a 200hp Lycoming IO-360 engine. 744 Sierra were built between 1970 and 1983.

VH-WEI is a 1980 Beech C24R Sierra, photographed at Echuca, Victoria, Australia in April 2013.

Beech 33 Debonair/Bonanza. The Beech 33 is a four-seat retractable undercarriage high performance light aircraft. The Debonair was a derivative of the Beech 35 Bonanza (see below), with conventional tail surfaces replacing the V-tail empennage of the Bonanza. Initially known as the Debonair (Beech 33 to C33), it was subsequently marketed alongside the Beech 35 as the Bonanza (E33 to G33). Various engines were fitted from the 225hp Continental IO-470 to the 285hp IO-520-B. Total production of all variants was 3,150.

VH-DHL is a 1960 Beech 33 Debonair, this early model being distinguished by the comparative lack of cabin glazing, photographed at Temora, NSW, Australia. *Jim Smith*

1987 Beech F33A Bonanza G-HOSS taking off from Henstridge, Somerset. This was the most successful variant of the Beech 33.

G-APVW is a 1947 Beech 35 Bonanza, photographed at Jersey in the Channel Islands.

Beech 35 Bonanza. The revolutionary Beech 35 Bonanza with its V-tail and retractable undercarriage was first flown in 1945 and was far ahead of its contemporaries in performance. During its long production run the type was produced in many variants up to the V35B and remained in production until 1981. The prototype was powered by a 165hp Continental E-185 engine, power increasing in late-production models to a 285hp Continental IO-520. Total production of all models was in excess of 10,500 aircraft. The type delivered high performance, long range and good load capacity, but was regarded by some as difficult to handle in turbulence in instrument conditions. This criticism led to the development of the similar Beech 33 with conventional tail surfaces (see above).

Beech 36 Bonanza 36. The Beech 36 Bonanza 36 was a stretched E33 (conventional tail configuration) Bonanza designed for normal operation as a six-seat aircraft and first flown in 1968. The most popular model was the A36 with a 300hp Continental IO-550-B engine. Nearly 4,000 Beech 36s had been built up to the end of 2012. These figures give a total for the Beech 33/35/36 family of more than 17,500 aircraft.

Beech A36 Bonanza G-KSHI landing at Compton Abbas, Wiltshire. The lengthened fuselage and conventional tail surfaces are readily apparent.

N836TP is a turboprop conversion of a Beech 36, photographed taking off from Henstridge Airfield, Somerset in September 2013.

Beech T-34 Mentor N34825 at the EAA Convention at Oshkosh, Wisconsin.

Beech 45 Mentor. Although essentially built as a military basic training aircraft, significant numbers of Beech T-34 Mentor aircraft are privately owned, being popular as an 'entry-level' warbird. Power is provided by a 225hp Continental O-470. Some 950 Mentors were built, serving with the USAF, U.S. Navy and export customers, particularly in Latin America.

The final version of the Twin Bonanza was the J50; this is VH-BRH, a 1962 example, photographed at Avalon, VIC, Australia in March 2009.
Jim Smith

Beech 50 Twin Bonanza. First flown in November 1949, 994 examples of the six-seat Twin Bonanza were produced before production ceased in 1961. Early models were powered by two 260hp Lycoming GO-435 engines, the final production model, the J50, using two 340hp Lycoming IGSO-480 engines.

Beech 60 Duke. First flown in December 1966, the high performance six-seat pressurized Beech Duke was produced between 1968 and 1983, 593 being built in three models.

Power and high performance characterize the Beech 60 Duke. This winglet-equipped example was photographed at Blackbushe, Hampshire.

Beech 65 Queen Air. The Queen Air is a light transport aircraft based on the combination of Twin Bonanza components with a large passenger fuselage. The type was first flown in August 1958 and remained in production until 1977. The first model had an unswept tail fin, sweep being introduced with the A65 model. Later versions were the 65-70, 65-80, A80, B80 and 65-88. This final model has a pressurized fuselage and can be recognized by its circular cabin windows. Power for the initial Beech 65 was provided by two 340hp Lycoming IGSO-480 engines. Subsequent aircraft used the 380hp Lycoming IGSO-540 engines. A total of 930 Queen Air aircraft were built.

The first production model of the Beech 65 Queen Air featured an unswept tail fin. F-BNAT is a 1961 example at St Cyr, France.

VH-EYG is a 1967 Beech 65-B80 Queen Air photographed at Parafield, South Australia.

The clean lines of the Beech King Air pressurized twin turboprop. The type has been hugely successful and the subject of a fifty-year production run.

Beech 65-90 King Air. The King Air is a turbo-prop powered version of the Beech 65-88 Queen Air. The type was hugely successful and versions continue in production in 2013, fifty years after the aircraft's first flight. The larger models of the King Air, the A100 and the T-tail Super King Air 200, are not discussed here as they (and the Beech 99, 1900 and 1900D) are considered to fall outside the scope of this work. Various models of the PT6A engine were used for most of these aircraft, the C90GT version being powered by two 750hp PT6A-135A engines de-rated

to 550hp each. Well over 2,500 of the smaller King Air models have been built.

Beech 76 Duchess. The Beech 76 Duchess is a four-seat light twin engine aircraft for the private owner that is also commonly used in the twin engine training role. First flown in September 1974, the Beech 76 remained in production until 1982, a total of 437 being built. Power is provided by two 180hp Lycoming O-360 engines.

1979 Beech 76 Duchess G-BGHP on the approach to Blackbushe Airport, Hampshire in August 2006.

Beech Skipper OO-GVE photographed at Balen Keiheuvel, Belgium in May 1989.

Beech 77 Skipper. The two-seat Beech 77 Skipper was designed to compete with the Piper PA-38 Tomahawk to which it has more than a passing resemblance. First flown in September 1978, the Skipper had only modest success, 312 being built before production was completed in 1981. Power is provided by a 115hp Lycoming O-235 engine.

Beech 95 Travel Air. The Beech 95 Travel Air is a four/five-seat light twin derived from the Beech Bonanza, fitted with two 180hp Lycoming O-360 engines. The type is readily recognized by its unswept tailfin, which came from the Beech T-34 Mentor. First flown in August 1956, 720 were built in a production run that continued until 1968.

The Beech 95 Travel Air is readily distinguished from the Baron by its unswept fin. VH-FDX is a 1960 example, photographed at Avalon, VIC, Australia. *Jim Smith*

Beech 95-55 Baron. The Beech 95-55 Baron was a development of the Travel Air fitted with a swept fin that immediately made the aircraft look much more up to date than the earlier type. The Baron had a long and successful production run, with the Baron G58 remaining in production in 2013, fifty-three years after the type's first flight. Initial production ran from the 95-55 through the A55 to E55, the most numerous model being the B55, of which nearly 2,000 were built.

The Beech 95-55 Baron is, in essence, a Travel Air with a swept fin and increased power. G-SUZI was built in 1973 and is a 95-B55, the most numerous variant, seen at Henstridge Airfield, Somerset, UK.

An American-registered Baron 58 photographed at Henstridge Airfield, Somerset, UK.

Bellanca CH-300 Pacemaker CF-ATN in the Canadian Aviation & Space Museum, Ottawa. *Jim Smith*

Bellanca Aircraft Corporation (and successors)

The Bellanca Aircraft Corporation's notable early products were utility and transport aircraft, which were particularly successful in 'bush operations' supporting the development of aviation in northern Canada and Alaska. These were the Bellanca Pacemaker and Skyrocket family. Some 118 Pacemaker and Senior Pacemaker aircraft were built in a number of variants. The six-seat Skyrocket and Senior Skyrocket (with 420hp) were more powerful and can be regarded as precursors of such aircraft as the Cessna 206, Beaver and Otter that continue to perform similar roles to this day.

Another product was the unusually configured Bellanca K, which was produced in small numbers as the P-100 and P-200 Airbus, and as the Bellanca Aircruiser. This single-engine high wing transport aircraft had a large W-shaped subsidiary lifting surface that ran from the lower fuselage down to the undercarriage and then up to the underside of the wing as a tapered triangular-planform strut. A combined total thirteen were built.

There followed a series of three and four-seat light aircraft developed from the 1937 Bellanca 14-7 Junior. This aircraft was a low wing monoplane with a retractable undercarriage. It featured a low set tailplane with small elliptical endplate fins. Some fifty-nine were produced pre-war as the 14-9 Junior and, with 120hp Franklin, the 14-12-F3 Crusair.

After the war, production was re-started with the designation 14-13 Cruisair Senior. *U.S. Civil Aircraft* indicates that the prototype and some 325 aircraft were built in 1946, with 198 Bellanca 14-13-2 in 1947 followed by sixty-two Bellanca 14-13-3 in 1948. The 1949 model was the 14-13-4.

The next product was the more powerful 1949 Bellanca 14-19 Cruisemaster powered by a 190hp Lycoming O-435-A. Some ninety-seven were built before production ceased in 1951. Thereafter, aircraft derived from the Cruisemaster were produced by a bewildering series of companies including Northern Aircraft Inc.; Downer Aircraft Industries; International Aircraft Manufacturing; Bellanca Sales Manufacturing Inc.; Miller Aviation; Bellanca Aircraft Corporation; Viking Aviation; and Bellanca Inc. *Note*: Bellanca production of Champion models is discussed under the entry for Aeronca.

In 1956, Northern Aircraft put the Cruisemaster back into production as the 14-19-2, followed in 1958, under the Downer brand, by the 14-19-3 Bellanca 260 with a tricycle undercarriage and 260hp Continental IO-470. Production figures are not entirely clear, but one source suggests a combined figure of 686 for the 14-19-2 and 14-19-3.

The next main change was the adoption of a swept fin and elimination of the tailplane endplate fins. This aircraft was produced by International Aircraft and marketed as the Miller Bellanca 260A. An increase in power to the 300hp Continental IO-520 resulted in the Model 17-30 Viking 300. This was a very successful design and was produced in a number of variants, the most successful being the 17-30A Super Viking, 684 of which were built. *Jane's All the World's Aircraft for 1985-86* indicates total production of 1,598 Viking series aircraft by January 1979.

1949 Bellanca 14-13-2 Cruisair Senior HB-DUN, photographed at Stauning, Denmark.

1974 Bellanca 17-30A Super Viking N14703 at North Las Vegas airfield, Las Vegas, Nevada.

N520DJ is one of a small number of Bellanca Aries to be built.

Bellanca Aries. The Bellanca T250 Aries 250 is a high performance low wing monoplane with a T-tail and a 250hp Lycoming O-540 engine. Only five were built.

Binder Smaragad

All variants of the CP301 Emeraude are discussed under Piel.

Blackburn

The British pioneer Robert Blackburn began experimenting in 1909 and founded a company bearing his name the Blackburn Aeroplane and Motor Company, later Blackburn Aircraft Ltd. The company is best known for a range of naval aircraft, including the Shark, Baffin, Firebrand and the Buccaneer naval

strike aircraft. The company built aircraft for the private owner before the First World War and in the 1930s, as discussed below.

The first successful type was a Blackburn monoplane that was flown successfully at Filey on 8 March 1911. This aircraft was followed by the series of Mercury monoplanes, production comprising a single example of the Mercury I, two Mercury IIs, followed by six Mercury III. These aircraft were flying at Filey, Brooklands and Hendon from mid-1911 until mid-1912. Other early machines included a single-seat design of 1912 for Mr Cyril Foggin – this aircraft surviving in flying condition with The Shuttleworth Trust at Old Warden, Bedfordshire.

The Blackburn 1912 Monoplane, which is normally resident at The Shuttleworth Trust, Old Warden, photographed at Farnborough, Hampshire.

Blackburn Bluebird and B.2. The first Blackburn Bluebird side-by-side two-seat biplane had its origins as an intended entry in the 1924 Lympne two-seat light aeroplane trials. The design began to gain acceptance after it was fitted with the Genet engine, flying in this form in June 1926. Thirteen wooden Bluebird IIs and seven Bluebird IIIs were built before the type was redesigned with an all-metal structure as the Bluebird IV. The prototype Bluebird IV was flown in 23 February 1929. Fifty-eight were built, but by the time that the Bluebird had reached this fully developed state, the de Havilland Moth was too firmly established to be displaced. The Blackburn B-2 was a side-by-side, all metal, biplane training aircraft first flown in 10 December 1931 – forty-two were built. The one preserved example, G-AEBJ, is still capable of smooth and graceful aerobatics as testimony to the fine handling of the type.

1932 Blackburn B2 G-AEBJ photographed at Farnborough, Hampshire in July 2014.

Mike Beach's excellent 1982 Blériot replica G-LOTI seen at Cranfield, Bedfordshire shortly after its first flight.

Blériot

The name Louis Blériot is famous in aeronautical history for making the first flight across the English Channel on 25 July 1909 in his Blériot XI monoplane. He later took over the Deperdussin company, renaming it SPAD, which became an almost equally famous name during the First World War. The Blériot XI was built in significant numbers and widely copied as a design. Two original 1909 machines remain in flyable condition, one at The Shuttleworth Trust in the UK, and the other at Old Rheinbeck, New York. A 1918 Swedish built Thulin A was also restored to flying condition in 2010. A number of replica aircraft have been built and can be seen in Museums, with relatively few being flying examples.

Boeing (Stearman Aircraft Division of Boeing Aircraft Co, Wichita)

The Stearman 75 Kaydet two-seat training biplane was flown for the first time in 1934 and ordered by the U.S. Army as the PT-13 in 1936. The aircraft became the standard primary trainer for the U.S. services, being ordered in large quantities, with production finally being completed in February 1945. Since the war, the aircraft has been extremely popular with private owners. The type is a popular performer at airshows and, given its maneuverability and robust construction, has also been modified in some numbers for agricultural work.

The main individual models, which are primarily distinguished by different powerplants, are as follows:

PT-13 U.S. Army — 220hp Lycoming R-680-5 radial engine
PT-17 U.S. Army — 220hp Continental R-670-5
PT-18 U.S. Army — 225hp Jacobs R-755-7
PT-27 RCAF (as PT-17 with enclosed cockpit canopy, cockpit heating)
N2S-1 and N2S-4 U.S. Navy — as PT-17
N2S-2 U.S. Navy — as PT-13A, 220hp Lycoming R-680-8
N2S-3 U.S. Navy — as PT-17A, Continental R-670-4
N2S-5 U.S. Navy — as PT-13D, Lycoming R-680

While the complete breakdown of production figures is unclear, *Jane's All the World's Aircraft* 1945 states that 'production of the Kaydet was completed in February 1945, after 10,346 had been built.' One other source quotes a total of 8,584 complete aircraft and the equivalent of 2,242 aircraft in spares.

The Boeing Stearman is a popular display aircraft and is much associated in the UK with wing-walking displays. 1944 Boeing A75N1 N54922 was photographed at an airshow at Badminton House.

This 450hp Stearman with roll-over pylon and modified rudder is representative of many modified aircraft for agricultural and fire bombing work. N58219 was operated by Willows Flying Service, a pioneer of the use of aircraft in the fire tanker role; it was photographed at Pima County Air Museum, Tucson, Arizona.

OO-KLO is a B.610L, the most numerous variant of the Boisavia Mercurey, photographed at Balen Keiheuvel in Belgium in May 1989. A total of forty-six Mercurey were built.

Boisavia

Boisavia Mercurey. Boisavia produced a series of four-seat high wing aircraft in France called the Boisavia B.60 Mercurey, developed from an earlier two-seat design, the B.50.

Bölkow
(and Messerschmitt-Bölkow-Blohm)

The first aircraft manufactured under the name Bölkow was an updated version of the Klemm Kl.107, a clean two-seat low wing monoplane of all wood construction. The Klemm design stemmed from the pre-war Kl.35 and Kl.105 monoplanes. After some twenty-five Kl.107B had been built, Bölkow took over production and further development, building another thirty aircraft as the Kl.107C. In 1960, Bölkow produced an enlarged four-seat version, the Bölkow 207 of which ninety-one were built. Powered by a 180hp Lycoming O-360 engine, the 207 retained the clean lines and plywood stressed skin fuselage of its predecessor.

The next design had Swedish origins. In October 1958, the designer Björn Andreasson flew a prototype two-seat monoplane with a shoulder-mounted forward swept wing called the BA-7. This aircraft subsequently entered production in Sweden as the Malmo MFI-9 Junior with a 100hp Continental O-200 engine.

In 1962, Bölkow took out a license for the manufacture of this aircraft, building 186 as the Bölkow Bo.208 Junior (some sources indicate that 200 or 210 were built; the figure given here is given in *Airlife's General Aviation*, where it is supported by a listing of the construction numbers allocated to the aircraft built).

The final light aircraft to be constructed by Bölkow (now part of MBB – Messerschmitt-Bölkow-Blohm) was the Bölkow Bo.209 Monsun, 102 of which were built. Unusually, the aircraft was offered with either a fixed, or retractable, nosewheel. Power was either provided by a 150hp Lycoming O-320-E1C, or 160hp O-320-E1E.

1961 Bolkow 207 G-EFTE photographed at Popham, Hampshire in July 2014.

1966 Bölkow Bo.208C1 Junior G-ATXZ at Leicester Airport, in May 2009.

Bölkow Bo.209 Monsun 150FV D-EGHW taking off from Henstridge, Somerset, UK.

Bowers Fly Baby G-UPID takes off from Henstridge, Somerset in May 2014.

Bowers

The Bowers Fly Baby is a successful single-seat homebuilt low wing monoplane. Designed by Pete Bowers and first flown in 1962, the Fly Baby is simple to build and fly, with the result that it has become a popular type with 155 listed on the U.S. civil register in May 2014. Aircraft have flown with significant modifications, including two-seat side-by-side versions, biplane variants and aircraft adapted as replica First World War aircraft.

HB-YDW is a Brandli BX-2 Cherry photographed at Cranfield, Bedfordshire in July 1999.

Brandli

The Brandli BX-2 Cherry is a retractable undercarriage two-seat side-by-side low wing homebuilt aircraft. The type was first flown in April 1982 and more than 100 have been completed.

British Aircraft Manufacturing Co. Ltd.

Some 27 Klemm L.25 monoplanes were imported into England from 1929 onward, leading to the formation of the British Klemm Aeroplane Co. in 1933. British Klemm began license manufacture of a British version of the design, the Swallow, powered by a Pobjoy geared radial engine. After the construction of twenty-eight Swallow 1s, the improved Swallow 2 was announced, and the company changed name to British Aircraft Manufacturing. 105 Swallow 2 were built, advertising emphasizing the slow landing speed, ample control at low speed and folding wings. The company's next product was the BA Eagle touring monoplane with a retractable undercarriage. First flown in early 1934, forty-three were built. Contemporary advertising offered a cruise speed of 130mph and a top speed of 150mph. Single examples of two unsuccessful designs, the BA Cupid and Double Eagle were built.

Long-winged 1937 Swallow 2 G-AFGE at Shoreham, celebrating the airfield's sixty years as a Municipal Airport.

1934 BA Eagle VH-UTI at Echuca, VIC, Australia in April 2013.

1953 MB.72 Pipistrelle F-PYQV photographed at Brienne le Chateau, France.

Brochet

Brochet Pipistrelle. Maurice Brochet designed a number of light aircraft. The Pipistrelle family includes the single-seat, parasol wing, open cockpit MB.50 first flown in 1947; the MB.70 and MB.80 series that seat two in tandem beneath a high wing; and the three-seat MB.100 and MB.101 models. Sub-variants mainly differ in engine choice. In February 2014, the French register listed thirty-five Pipistrelles, as follows: one MB.50, two MB.72s, eleven MB.80s and MB.83s, six MB.100s and fifteen MB.101s, many of the latter being based in Africa. One MB.50 is registered in the UK.

1988 Brugger MB-2 Colibri G-BKRH at Cranfield, Bedfordshire.

Brugger

The Brugger MB-2 Colibri is a Swiss design and is a very popular single-seat, plans-built, wooden low-wing monoplane. The prototype flew in May 1970 and the type is flying in many European countries, including France, Switzerland, Sweden and the UK. Forty-five appeared on the French register in February 2014, with fourteen registered in the UK. The MB-3 is an all-metal derivative.

Brunner-Winkle (and successors)

The Brunner-Winkle company built a series of three-seat biplanes with the generic model name Bird. The company later changed its name to Bird Aircraft Corporation. These aircraft can be readily identified by their undercarriage, with one of the diagonal cross-members passing through an aperture in the opposite bracing strut. They also have an upper wing of significantly greater area than the lower wing – sometimes called a sesquiplane configuration. The pilot sat in a rear cockpit, with two passengers side-by-side in the forward cockpit. The first model was the Curtiss OX-5 powered Bird A of 1928, of which some eighty were built and which was highly rated in the Guggenheim Safety Airplane competition. Later models included the Bird B and C series, with various air-cooled radial engines, the most successful being the Kinner-powered Bird BK and the four-seat CK. Some 140 Bird B and Bird C were built, production ending in 1932.

OX-5 powered Bird A at the Flying Tigers Warbird Restoration Museum, Kissimmee, Florida. The difference in area of the upper and lower wings is readily apparent.

1930 Bird CK NC847W – the undercarriage arrangement is clearly seen in this photograph.

Bücker (factory and license-built)

Regarded by many as the some of the World's finest-handling aerobatic aircraft, the most famous products of Bücker Flugzeugebau were the Bü.131 Jungmann and the Bü.133 Jungmeister. Two other products were the Bü.180 Student and the Bü.181 Bestmann.

The Bü.131 Jungmann is a two-seat training biplane that first flew in April 1934. It was selected as a the basic trainer for the German Luftwaffe and produced in large numbers, both in Germany and under license in several other nations, including Spain (CASA I-131), Switzerland (Dornier), Czechoslovakia (Aero and Tatra) and Japan (Kokusai, Kyushu). Aircraft were also exported from Germany, notably to Yugoslavia (up to 400 aircraft), South Africa, Hungary, Bulgaria, Rumania, Brazil, Uruguay, Chile, Sweden, Austria, Finland, France, The Netherlands, Poland and Portugal.

A number of aircraft have also been built recently in Poland (SSH Janusz Karasiewicz). Total production numbers are not known, but it is thought that some 3,000 to 4,000 were built in Germany. The most significant license manufacturers were in Japan (Kokusai 1,037 and Kyushu/Hitachi 339), Czechoslovakia (more than 300), Spain (more than 200), Switzerland (97).

The Bü.133 Jungmeister single-seat biplane was optimized for advanced training, aerobatic competition and display flying. The main production variant was the Bü.133C with a Siemens Sh.14A radial engine. The prototype flew for the first time in 1935 and the type was immediately successful in many aerobatic competitions. License production was undertaken in Switzerland (Dornier) and Spain (CASA I-133), amounting to some fifty aircraft in each country. German production records were lost during the war but it is believed that around 200 were built there. A number of aircraft have been re-engined, particularly in the United States, with engines such as the 180hp Lycoming IO-360. As with the Jungmann, the Jungmeister is renowned for its exceptional handling qualities.

The Bü.181 Bestmann low wing side-by-side trainer was flown in February 1939 and selected by the Luftwaffe as a primary trainer and built in large quantities in Germany (2,730), The Netherlands (Fokker – 708), Sweden (Hägglunds AB – 125), Czechoslovakia (Zlin 181 and Zlin 381-393 total). The type was also produced post-war in Egypt as the Heliopolis Gomhouria (some 300 built in six main variants).

Spanish-built Jungmann (CASA I-131E) sideslips to land at Cranfield, Bedfordshire.

Swiss-built Bu.133C Jungmeister G-AXMT at Cranfield, Bedfordshire.

Bucker Bu.181 Bestmann preserved at The Shuttleworth Trust, Old Warden, Bedfordshire.

1933 Buhl LA-1 Bull Pup NC348Y at the EAA Convention at Oshkosh, Wisconsin.

Buhl

The Buhl LA-1 Bull Pup is a small single-seat shoulder-wing monoplane offering comparatively high performance on the modest power of its three cylinder 45hp Szekely SR-3 engine. First flown in late 1930, at least 100 were built in a short production run lasting until the end of 1932. Thirteen remained listed on the U.S. civil register in June 2014.

N14LB is a retractable gear Midget Mustang built by Jim Butler and flown in 1973. It has been a twice winner of the Grand Champion Homebuilt Award at the EAA Convention at Oshkosh, Wisconsin.

Bushby Long

The single-seat Midget Mustang was designed by David Long and first flew in 1948, being intended for use as a midget racer. Its performance was not totally competitive, but it was an attractive aircraft with superb handling. The rights were bought by Robert Bushby after David Long's death and plans were marketed for home construction. Most aircraft have a fixed, sprung-steel main undercarriage, but a few have been built with retractable gear. The type is currently marketed by Mustang Aeronautics. In June 2014, sixty-three Midget Mustang aircraft were listed on the U.S. civil register.

Bushby Mustang II. Robert Bushby designed a two-seat derivative of the Midget Mustang known as the Mustang II. The first prototype N1117M flew for the first time in 1966, rights passing to Mustang Aeronautics in 1992, that market the aircraft in kit form and indicate that more than 400 have been completed. The Mustang II is similar in style, concept and performance to the Thorp T18. Individual builders have produced tricycle undercarriage and retractable undercarriage variants. In June 2014, 161 Mustang II aircraft were listed on the U.S. civil register.

Swiss-built Mustang II HB-YBT photographed at Brienne-le-Chateau, France in 1984.

Butler

Butler Blackhawk. The Blackhawk is a three-seat biplane flown in 1930 by the Butler Manufacturing Co./Butler Aircraft Corp. of Kansas City. A total of eleven were built.

NX299N is a 1930 Butler Blackhawk photographed at Lakeland, Florida. *Jim Smith*

CAARP

CAARP (Cooperatives des Ateliers Aéronautiques de la Region Parisienne) began producing the Scintex CP.1310-C3 Super Emeraude in 1965

CAARP developed a series of designs that were progressively evolved from the Emeraude into a range of capable aerobatic training and competition machines. After two prototypes – the CP-100 and the CAP-10 – production centered on the CAP-10B with 180hp Lycoming IO-360 with inverted fuel and oil systems. As well as the extra power, the CAP-10B featured an enlarged canopy and a much larger rudder. A later variant, the CAP-10C introduced a carbon fiber main wing spar. At least 275 CAP-10B have been built.

The single-seat CAP-20 was flown in July 1969 with a 200hp AIO-360 and was followed by the CAP-20L and LS, which were lighter weight variants. Some forty examples of the various models of the CAP-20 were built.

CAP-10B G-CDIF landing at Henstridge, Somerset in June 2013.

The next development was the CAP-21, first flown in June 1980, with a straight taper wing and sprung steel undercarriage. Eighteen CAP-21s were built.

The final competition aerobatics variant was the CAP-230, first flown in July 1994, with power increased to 300hp with the Lycoming AEIO-540 engine and a revised fin shape. Additional production variants were the CAP-231, -231EX and -232, with a number of structural modifications. About forty CAP-230, CAP-231 and CAP-232s have been built.

F-BPXU is the prototype CAP-20, previously F-WPXU.

G-BLZZ is CAP-21 c/n12, seen when competing in an aerobatic competition at Dunkeswell, Devon.

F-WZCH is the prototype CAP-230 photographed at the World Aerobatic Championships at South Cerney, Gloucestershire in August 1986.
Jim Smith

CAP 232 OH-SKA photographed at Dunkeswell, Devon in January 2014.

Homebuilt GY201 Minicab 28-0825 operating on the Recreational Aircraft register in Australia. *Jim Smith*

CAB

Constructions Aéronautiques de Béarn (CAB) produced the CAB GY20 Minicab and GY30 Supercab two-seat light aircraft designed by Yves Gardan (who had previously designed the similar Sipa 90 series and went on to design the GY80 Horizon).

The GY20 was a low wing monoplane with a tapered wing and a forward-hinged one piece cockpit canopy, powered by a 65hp Continental A-65 engine. The prototype was flown in February 1949 and CAB produced twenty-two examples before making plans available for amateur constructors. The type was subsequently extensively built by homebuilders around the world. The Barritault JB01 was a variant of the

Minicab fitted with a 90hp Continental C-90 and first flown in May 1960. It is probable that at least 100 Minicabs have been built. In September 2013, twenty were listed on the British civil register, thirty-nine in France; five in Australia; and one in the USA. A total of fifteen have been registered in New Zealand, although not all are still active.

The GY30 Supercab featured a retractable undercarriage, slotted flaps and an increase in power to the 90hp Continental C-90. This offered exceptional performance for its relatively low power, but a total of only seven were built.

1954 GY30 Supercab G-BHLZ photographed at Middle Wallop, Hampshire.

1947 Callair A-3 N2901V photographed at Oshkosh, Wisconsin.

Callair

The Call Aircraft Company was established by the Call brothers at Afton, Wyoming (elevation 6,200 ft) in 1939. They designed and flew a prototype, the 80hp Callair A in 1940.

The initial production model was the A-1 with a 100hp Lycoming O-235; four were built. The model A was a two or three-seat low wing cabin monoplane with an externally braced wing. Production was interrupted by the Second World War and resumed with the A-2 (125hp Lycoming O-290-A), A-3 (125hp Continental C-125-A), and A-4 (135hp Lycoming O-290-D2). These aircraft established a reputation for rugged construction and good performance.

Production comprised one Model A; four A-1s; sixteen A-2s; fifteen A-3s; and sixty-five A-4s, for a grand total of 101 aircraft.

The type was developed into a new role as series of agricultural aircraft, the A-5 to A-9. In 1956, the company was purchased by the Intermountain Manufacturing Company (IMCO), who continued development and production of the agricultural variants. These agricultural aircraft fall outside the scope of this work.

CASA

Spanish-built examples of the Bücker Jungmann and Jungmeister are included in the Bücker entry.

This homebuilt example of the Cassutt IIIM, G-BFMF was photographed at its then home base of Henstridge, Somerset.

Cassutt

The Cassutt Special single-seat racing aircraft was first flown in 1954. Initially flown with a rectangular wing planform, the later 'taperwing' variants featured a thinner tapered wing of increased span. Three aircraft were built by Tom Storey in the UK and sold as the Airmark Cassutt IIIM, together with a number of homebuilt examples. In June 2014, 127 were listed on the U.S. civil register, with twelve in the UK.

Caudron

Société des Avions Caudron produced aircraft from before the First World War through to the Second World War. The range of light aircraft included:

C.109 parasol monoplane;

C.163 low wing monoplane (1929, six built);

C.270 – C.278 Luciole biplane (more than 700 built the main version being the C.275, 1931);

C.280 Phalène and C.286 Super Phalène high wing monoplane (nearly 300 built, including military variants (C.400, C.410), 1932);

C.450 and C.460 single-seat racing aircraft (six built, 1934)

C.480 three-seat high wing monoplane (twenty-seven built, 1935)

C.510 Pelican high wing monoplane (an improved Phalène, sixty-two built, 1934);

C.600 Aiglon two-seat low wing monoplane (203 built; 1935)

C.635 Simoun four-seat cabin monoplane (main production version the C.635M for military communications of which 489 were built; production of other versions was approximately eighty aircraft).

A number of Caudron machines are displayed at the French Musée de L'Air et de L'Espace at Le Bourget, Paris. Relatively few examples are still flying.

British-registered 1932 Caudron C.270 Luciole G-BDFM at its then home base, Compton Abbas, Dorset.

Celerity N5104X photographed at Oshkosh, Wisconsin in 1985.

Celerity

The Celerity light aircraft, is a two-seat low wing monoplane of mixed wood and composite construction and was designed by Larry Burton and first flown in May 1985. In appearance, the type has some similarity to a tailwheel K & S Cavalier with a retractable undercarriage, or to a cleaned-up Bearn (CAB) Supercab with a swept fin. Plans were marketed by Tucson-based Mirage Aircraft. A fixed landing gear variant is known as the Mirage Marathon. Three Celeritys and one Mirage Marathon were listed on the U.S. register in June 2014.

Centre Est

Centre Est Aéronautique (CEA) is one of the companies that built and developed aircraft of the Jodel type, before transitioning to become Avions Pierre Robin. The aircraft family from Jodel through Centre Est to Robin comprises a wide range of very successful machines. Many of the aircraft in this series are externally similar to each other and the photographic coverage presented here is therefore representative, rather than exhaustive.

For the purposes of this work, the author is making the following sub-division of content:

(i)   Jodel aircraft from the D.9 to D.150 Mascaret thru to the DR1051-M1 Sicile Record are presented under Jodel, irrespective of their actual manufacturer (Jodel, Alpavia, CEA, SAN, Wassmer or amateur built).

(ii) Centre Est aircraft in the DR.200 series are presented in this chapter.

(iii) Pierre Robin aircraft in the DR.300 and DR.400 series and later models are presented under the entry for Robin.

CEA was set up in 1959 and initially produced the DR.100 and DR.1050 Ambassadeur and DR.1051 Sicile and DR.1051-M1 Sicile Record. Subsequent development led to the types described here. These were the four-seat 160hp DR.250 Capitane, first flown in April 1965 and lower-powered two-seat developments including the 105hp DR.220 2+2 and the 115hp DR.221 Dauphin. These aircraft were progressively developed in a series of nosewheel variants, whose appearance coincided with a change of company name to Avions Pierre Robin in 1969. First of these was the DR.253 Regent, which married an enlarged DR.250 fuselage to a nosewheel undercarriage and 180hp Lycoming O-360 engine. Production comprised 100 DR.250, eighty-three DR.220, sixty-two DR.221, and 100 DR.253. Development continued under Robin with the DR.300 and DR.400 series.

1965 Centre Est DR250-160 Capitaine G-BYEH takes off from Popham, Hampshire in July 2014.

Centre Est DR.220 2+2 F-BNVB photographed in 1983 at Brienne le Chateau, France.

1967 Centre Est DR.221 Dauphin G-BHRW at Dunkeswell, Devon.

1968 Centre Est DR.253 Regent photographed at Bembridge, IOW, from the author's Jodel D.120A G-BIEN.

1973 Cerva Guepard 456/LM photographed at Brienne le Chateau, France.

Cerva

The Cerva CE43 Guepard is a four/five-seat low wing monoplane and is an all-metal derivative of the Wassmer 4/21. First flown in May 1971, a total of forty-four were built, twenty-three of these being purchased by the French Government. Sixteen were listed on the French civil register in June 2014.

Cessna

The Cessna Aircraft Company is the World's most successful manufacturer of light aircraft, with a most extensive product range. Rod Simpson in *Airlife's General Aviation* comments that the company has delivered over 164,000 aircraft since the end of the Second World War.

The company's product range includes a number of aircraft that fall outside the scope of this work, including those designed exclusively for commercial work (the Cessna 400 series of twins), agricultural operations (the Cessna Agwagon), an extensive range of executive jets (the Citation family) and the T-37 military jet trainer.

Cessna's most notable pre-war products were high wing cantilever monoplanes, the Cessna AW and the Cessna Airmaster series (C-34, -37, -38, -145 and -165) whose design is to a degree reflected in the later

Cessna 195. Product highlights of the later range include the immensely successful Cessna 150 training aircraft; the four-seat Cessna 172 Skyhawk, the more powerful Cessna 182 Skylane, the 180 and 185 Skywagon STOL utility aircraft, and the larger six-seat Cessna 205 and 206 Super Skywagon and Super Skylane which may be seen widely dropping parachutists or operating on floats.

The most notable twin-engine machine for the private owner is the ground-breaking Cessna 310, produced from 1953 to 1981. Others in this category are the Cessna 340 and the Cessna T303 Crusader. Further innovation was shown by the twin engine 'push-me-pull-you' Cessna 336 Skymaster and 337 Super Skymaster, featuring a fuselage pod with front and rear-mounted engines and twin tailbooms.

Rather than list all the products together in this preamble, the Cessna family is presented below with a brief description of each type, including role, number built and length of production, etc., immediately before a photograph or photographs of the type in question.

Cessna AW. A four-seat cabin high wing cantilever monoplane built from 1928 with a variety of engines, reflected in the product designation AA, AC, AF, AS, and AW. Most significant were the Anzani-powered

Cessna AW NC4725 at Oshkosh, Wisconsin.

AA (fourteen built) and the Warner-powered AW (forty-eight built). Thirteen examples of the similar BW with a Wright engine were built, giving a combined total for these models of eighty-three aircraft. Six Cessna AWs were listed on the FAA Register in September 2013.

Cessna Airmaster series. The Cessna Airmaster appeared as the C-34 in 1934 (forty-two built), being developed via the C-37 (forty-six built) and C-38 pre-war (sixteen built). Post-war, the type re-entered production as the C-145 and C-165; the designations indicate the installed engine power (145hp or 165hp). A combined production total of 228 is quoted.

The clean lines of the 1940 Cessna Airmaster NC21911 (later G-BTDE), photographed at Wroughton, Wiltshire.

A colorful Cessna Bobcat N58542 photographed in 1990 at Vancouver, Washington. *Jim Smith*

Cessna T-50 Bobcat. The Cessna Bobcat (or 'bamboo bomber') was a twin engine low wing monoplane powered by two radial engines (either 295hp Lycoming R-680, or 245hp Jacobs R-775). Used widely as a wartime navigation trainer (Crane 1 RCAF, or USAF AT-8, AT-17 or UC-78) no less than 5,401 were built, surviving aircraft operating with private owners across the USA. Sixty-three were listed on the FAA register in September 2013.

Cessna 120 and 140. The Cessna 120 and 140 are high wing two-seat monoplanes powered by the Continental C-85 engine and sold in direct competition to the somewhat similar Luscombe 8A. The Cessna 120 and 140 are similar in appearance, although the Cessna 140 is fitted with flaps, this providing a distinguishing feature. A combined total of just over 7,600 were built between 1946 and 1952.

1947 Cessna 140 G-ALOD (with flaps lowered) landing on the airstrip at Badminton House.

1965 Cessna 150E G-ATEF photographed at Blackbushe, Hampshire, showing the omni-vision rear window and unswept fin. Later models have the more familiar swept fin. *Jim Smith*

Cessna 150 (all models). First flown in 1957, the Cessna 150 became one of the World's most successful primary trainers. Early aircraft had an unswept fin and limited rearward vision. The fuselage was cut down to the rear with the C150D to introduce an 'omni-vision' rear window. A swept tail fin was introduced in 1966 with the Cessna 150F. Total production of all models was nearly 24,000, including aircraft built in France and Argentina.

Cessna 170. The 1948 Cessna 170 was a four-seat 145hp development of the Cessna 140, retaining this aircraft's fabric-covered untapered wing. The Cessna 170A introduced a metal skinned wing with a rectangular center section and tapered tips, and a new fin similar to that of the contemporaneous Cessna 195. The Cessna 170B introduced wing dihedral and an improved slotted flap system. 5,174 Cessna 170 were built and the type is a direct ancestor of the Cessna 172.

1952 Cessna 170B G-AORB photographed at Popham, Hampshire, UK.

1973 Cessna F172M G-BBDH was built in France by Reims Aviation and is seen at its Henstridge home base.

Cessna 172 Skyhawk. Cessna's greatest product and probably the world's most successful light aircraft, the Cessna 172 is, in effect, a nosewheel Cessna 170B. When first produced, the type had an unswept fin. The 1960 172C introduced a swept fin (the 'Flight Sweep' fin). A cut-down rear fuselage and 'omni-vision' rear window was introduced with the 1963 172D. Production continued from 1956 to the 1985 172Q, being re-started in 1996 with the 172R and 172S. Well over 40,000 Cessna 172 aircraft have been built.

Cessna 172RG Cutlass or Skyhawk RG. The Cutlass is a 180hp retractable undercarriage version of the Cessna 172 produced from 1980 to 1985. A total of 1,192 were built.

1981 Cessna 172 Cutlass RGII VH-ODF at Goulburn, NSW, Australia in April 2013.

Cessna 175C G-ARWM tied down at Henstridge, Somerset. The raised thrust line of the geared engine is evident.

Cessna 175 Skylark. The Cessna 175 is a Cessna 172 with a geared engine, the 175hp GO-300. Produced between 1958 and 1963, a total of 2,190 were built. The raised thrust line of the geared engine is reflected in a cowling centerline bulge on most Cessna 175, providing a useful identification feature.

Cessna 177, Cardinal and Cardinal RG. The Cessna 177 Cardinal was initially intended as a Cessna 172 replacement. The basic Cessna 177 had a fixed undercarriage, cantilever wing and a stabilator (or all-moving tailplane). From 1970, a retractable undercarriage version was produced as the Cardinal RG. 2,750 fixed gear models were produced, together with 1,545 Cardinal RG, 177 being FR177RG, built by Reims Aviation in France. Production ran from 1968 to 1978.

N34974 is a 1974 Cessna 177B photographed in 1990 at Culpeper County Airpark, Virginia. *Jim Smith*

1957 Cessna 180A VH-MTF at Echuca, Victoria, Australia in April 2013.

Cessna 180. The Cessna 180 was a more powerful (225hp or 230hp) derivative of the Cessna 170 first flown in May 1952. A tall squared off fin reflected the increased power. Highly rated as a utility aircraft, large numbers continue to operate in remote and backcountry areas. A total of 6,193 were built, between 1953 and 1982.

Cessna 182 Skylane. The Cessna 182 is in effect a nosewheel Cessna 180. First flown in 1955, it initially retained the unswept fin of the earlier model. A swept fin was introduced with the Cessna 182C in 1960. An 'omni-vision' rear window and cut down fuselage was also introduced. The Cessna 182 was hugely successful and remains in production (Cessna 182T and T182T). Over 23,000 have been built.

1957 Cessna 182A N3921D on the approach to Hicks Field, Texas. The Cessna 180 origins are apparent in this early model with its unswept fin.

1999 Cessna 182S VH-PGC at Echuca, VIC, Australia in April 2013.

1983 Cessna R182 Skylane RG G-OZOI at Henstridge, Somerset in September 2013. Nosewheel doors, lack of wheel fairings and fuselage apertures for wheel retraction distinguish this model.

Cessna R182 Skylane RG. A retractable undercarriage variant of the Cessna 182, the Skylane RG was manufactured between 1976 and 1985; some 2,108 were built, sixty-seven of these in France.

Cessna 185. The six-seat Cessna 185 utility aircraft is a more powerful (260hp to 285hp) development of the Cessna 180. The increased power leads to a larger dorsal fin. The Cessna 185 was produced from 1961 until 1978, 3,978 being built.

N53079 is a Cessna A185F on floats at Lake Hood, Anchorage, Alaska in May 1983.

Cessna 195B N999MH takes off from its Henstridge, Somerset home base in April 2011.

Cessna 190 and 195. The C190 and C195 are five-seat high wing cantilever monoplanes powered by radial engines and are very much the successors to the Cessna Airmaster series. The first C190, powered by a 240hp Continental W670 engine, flew in December 1945. The Cessna 195 was powered by the Jacobs R755 (245hp-300hp) engine. Production ran in parallel from 1947 to 1954 and comprised around 1,180 aircraft.

Cessna 205 and 206 Super Skywagon, Super Skylane and Stationair. These types form a family of six-seat utility aircraft which are very similar to each other. These aircraft have good power, performance and load carrying capacity and are widely operated as parachute drop aircraft and on skis or floats in remote areas. Developed from the Cessna 210, the 260hp Cessna 205 entered production in 1963. It was replaced in production from 1964 by the Cessna 206, which continued to be built until 1986. Power for the Cessna 206 ranged from 285hp to 310hp, dependent on model. Total production extended to more than 7,850 aircraft, of which 576 were Cessna 205s.

VH-KFI is a 1980 Cessna U206G Stationair, the final production model of the C205 and C206 series.

1970 Cessna 207 G-AYTJ photographed at Cranfield, Bedfordshire, UK.

Cessna 207 Stationair 7 and Stationair 8. The Cessna 207 is a stretched development of the 206, with seven seats. The C207 is powered by a 300hp Continental IO-520 engine. An extra seat is provided in the Stationair 8. 626 Cessna 207 were built between 1969 and 1984; relatively few are in private ownership.

Cessna 210 Centurion. First flown in 1957, the Cessna 210 is a four to six-seat high performance retractable undercarriage development of the Cessna 182. The type was produced from 1957 to 1986 in a range of variants including both turbocharged and pressurized models. A cantilever wing was introduced on the 1967 model 210G. A total of 9,240 Cessna 210 of all models were built.

Cessna T210L N71WT on the approach to Hick's Field, near Fort Worth, Texas.

1983 Cessna T303 G-PUSI climbs away from its home base of Henstridge, Somerset, UK in April 2012.

Cessna T303 Clipper/Crusader. Flown for the first time on 17 October 1979, this is a six-seat cabin-class aircraft powered by two 250hp turbocharged Continental TSIO-520 engines, driving counter-rotating propellers. A total of 315 Cessna T303 was built in a relatively short production run from 1982 to 1984.

Cessna 305 Birddog. The Cessna O-1 Birddog is a military observation aircraft, seating two crew in tandem. Developed from the Cessna 170, it was first flown in December 1949. 3,431 examples of the rugged STOL aircraft were built and it is popular with private owners seeking an entry-level warbird.

Rob Fox's 1953 ex-Vietnam Air Force Cessna Birddog VH-FXY at Echuca, VIC, Australia in April 2013.

VH-REK is a 1957 Cessna 310B, photographed at Goulburn, NSW, Australia in April 2013.

Cessna 310. The fighter-like high performance five to six-seat Cessna 310 was first flown in 1953 and remained in production until 1981. More than 5,700 were built in a wide range of variants from the basic Cessna 310 to the T310R.

Cessna 320 Skynight. The Cessna 320 Skynight was a six-seat turbocharged development of the Cessna 310. 577 were built in six models between 1962 and 1968, before being supplanted by later versions of the Cessna 310 with similar capacity and performance.

1962 N5783X was photographed at Manassas, Virginia in December 1989. *Jim Smith*

1964 Cessna 336 Skymaster VH-GKY at Moorabbin, VIC, Australia.

1968 Cessna 337C Super Skymaster N2657S on the Approach to Hicks Field, Texas, with rear engine stopped and its propeller feathered.

Cessna 336 and 337 Skymaster and Super Skymaster. The innovative six-seat Cessna 336 Skymaster appeared in 1961. Powered by two engines in a push-pull configuration, with twin tail booms, the type was instantly recognizable. Only 195 examples of the fixed undercarriage Skymaster were built before production switched to the retractable gear Cessna 337 Super Skymaster. This was produced between 1965 and 1980, with high performance turbocharged and pressurized models being included in the family.

The type was also license-built in France by Reims Aviation. Including French production, some 3,160 Cessna 337 were built.

Cessna 340. The Cessna 340 is an entry-level cabin class pressurized twin produced from 1972 to 1985. The externally similar Cessna 335 is an unpressurized variant. 1,298 Cessna 340s and sixty-five Cessna 335s were built.

VH-CIO is an upgraded 1976 RAM Series VII Cessna 340. It was photographed at Archerfield, QLD, Australia in November 2008. *Jim Smith*

1996 Streak Shadow G-BWPS climbs steeply from Henstridge, Somerset in June 2013.

CFM (Cook Flying Machines)

The CFM (Cook Flying Machines) Shadow was designed by David Cook and more than 400 have been built in a number of variants, including the high performance Streak Shadow. This offers a 121 mph maximum speed, and climb to 10,000 feet in eight minutes and thirty-six seconds, all on 64hp. It has also been flown to a 27,000-foot altitude. The Shadow and Streak Shadow have been sold in more than thirty-six countries, and have completed many notable flights, including from England to Australia.

Chilton

The Chilton DW1 Monoplane was a delightful single-seat monoplane of clean lines and sparkling performance. The first aircraft G-AESZ flew in April 1937. The Chilton performed well in air races, winning the 1939 Folkestone Trophy at 126mph on 44hp. Five aircraft were built, all of which survived the war.

The restored Chilton Monoplane prototype G-AESZ photographed at the Shuttleworth Trust, Old Warden, Bedfordshire.

1948 Chrislea Super Ace G-AKVF photographed at its then home base at Bourne Park, Hampshire.

The last flying Chrislea Skyjeep, 1951 G-AKVR takes off from Henstridge, Somerset in April 2014.

Chrislea

The Chrislea CH3 Ace first flew in September 1946. This four-seat high wing type had a tricycle undercarriage and (after initial flying with a single fin), twin fins. The Ace had a novel control system with no rudder bar, all controls being provided by a steering wheel control mounted from the dashboard. A universal joint allowed control inputs to be provided in all axes. Thirty-three aircraft were built, comprising the Ace, twenty-seven Super Aces, and five Skyjeep utility aircraft, with tailwheel undercarriage and conventional stick and rudder controls.

Christavia

The Christavia comprises a series of Canadian-designed high wing aircraft for homebuilding from plans. The Christavia Mk.I seats two in tandem, the Mk.II seats two side-by-side and the Mk.IV seats four occupants. The Mk.I was first flown in 1983 and 350 were reported to have been flown by 2002. As a design, the Mk.I strongly resembles the similarly powered Aeronca 7AC Champ. In June 2014, forty-three Christavia aircraft were listed on the U.S. civil register, forty-two in Canada and one in the UK.

2007 Christavia Mk I G-MRED takes off from Henstridge, Somerset in April 2012. This was the sole example flying in Britain at that time.

1980 Christen Eagle II G-EGIL (previously N21SB) taxying at Compton Abbas airfield, Wiltshire.

Christen (later Aviat)

The Christen Eagle is a two-seat aerobatic aircraft designed by Frank Christensen. It is, in essence, a competitor to the Pitts S2. Sold as a complete kit of parts, or as a factory-assembled completed aircraft, the type has been very successful and it is reported that more than 350 examples were flying by 2011. The type flew for the first time in February 1977 and is now marketed by Aviat Aircraft Inc.

Christena

The Christena Minicoupe, which first flew in September 1970, is a single-seat all metal low wing monoplane with twin fins. The name reflects the generic similarity in the aircraft's configuration with that of the Erco 415 Ercoupe. In June 2014, seventeen were listed on the U.S. civil register, with single examples in Canada and the UK.

G-BDPJ is a 1984 Christena Minicoupe photographed at its home base of Popham, Hampshire.

N820CD is a 2002 Cirrus SR22 photographed at Henstridge, Somerset in April 2014.

Cirrus

The Cirrus SR22 is a high performance all composite four/five-seat low wing monoplane. The aircraft is powered by a 310hp Continental IO-550-N engine providing cruise speeds in excess of 200mph. turbocharged variants are available offering further increases in capability including operating altitudes up to 25,000 feet. The aircraft is fitted with a ballistic parachute system to enable the complete aircraft to descend by parachute in case of engine failure. In June 2014, more than 3,400 were listed on the U.S. civil register.

Clutton Tabenor

The Clutton-Tabenor FRED, Flying Runabout Experimental Design, is a basic parasol monoplane with a short span wing of thick section and high camber, designed for home-building. The first prototype, was designed by Mr E. Clutton and Mr E. Sherry, and flew on 3 November 1963. As the Clutton-Tabenor FRED Series 2, power is provided by a 1,500cc VW engine. The type is very popular with large numbers now flying. Some forty-eight have appeared on the UK register; twenty-five of these remaining registered in 2013.

Clutton FRED Srs 2 G-BMMF 'Thankyou Girl' at Henstridge, Somerset.

1984 Colomban MC15 Cri Cri G-SHOG flies past at East Pennard airstrip in June 2014.

Colomban

The Colomban Cri Cri is the world's smallest twin engine aircraft with two 15hp engines. First flown in 1973 the type has been homebuilt in France, the UK, the U.S. and elsewhere. The aircraft has a very respectable performance, despite its limited installed power, with a cruising speed in excess of 90kt. In June 2014, more than 100 were registered in France, with eight in the UK and four listed on the U.S. register.

Commonwealth (Rearwin)

The two-seat Skyranger was the last type to be built by Rearwin Aircraft. 82 aircraft were built between 1940 and 1942. Rearwin was purchased by Commonwealth Aircraft in 1942 and the Skyranger 185 was put back into production in 1945, around 296 being built by the end of 1946. The type offered a full electrical system, but failed to sell well in the face of competition from the Cessna 120 and 140 and the Luscombe Silvaire.

1946 Commonwealth Skyranger 185 NC93252 at Casa Grande in October 2013. *Peter Davison*

VH-WWY is a 1940 Commonwealth CAC-3 Mk II Wirraway photographed landing at Echuca, VIC, Australia in April 2013.

Commonwealth Aircraft Corporation (CAC) (Australia)

CAC was set up to provide Australia with a local capacity for military aircraft and engine manufacture. Its fighter products included the wartime CAC Boomerang and the CAC-16 and CAC-17 Mustang, followed post-war by the CAC-26 and CAC-27 Sabre. The company's training aircraft fall within the scope of this work. First was the CAC Wackett (202 built), which was a two-seat basic trainer powered by a Warner Scarab engine. One Wackett (VH-WKT) was listed on the Australian civil register in June 2014. The CAC Wirraway was derived from the North American NA-16 and was first flown in March 1939.

A total of 755 were built in seven different versions, its roles extending from training to dive-bombing and use as an emergency fighter. In June 2014, 9 CAC Wirraway appeared on the Australian civil register.

The Commonwealth CA-25 is a two-seat side-by-side basic trainer that is similar in appearance and concept to the Hunting Provost. The prototype Winjeel first flew in February 1951 and two prototypes (CA-22) and sixty-two production aircraft were built between 1955 and 1958. The type remained in RAAF service until 1977. In June 2014, 30 CA-25 aircraft were listed on the Australian civil register, where the type is a popular entry-level warbird.

VH-HFM (A85-440 '40') is a CA-25 Winjeel, photographed at Echuca, VIC, Australia in April 2013.

1932 Comper Swift G-ACTF photographed landing at Old Warden in October 2014.

Comper

The first Comper C.L.A.7 Swift G-AARX was flown in January 1930. The attractive Swift was noted for its racing and long distance flights, particularly those of Charles A. Butler whose flights included a record-breaking trip from England to Australia starting at the end of October 1931. A total of forty-one Comper Swift were built with a number of different engines, most commonly using the 75hp Pobjoy R geared radial engine.

Corben

The Corben Baby Ace (or Ace Baby Ace) is a plans-built single-seat parasol monoplane. More than 400 are believed to have been built and in June 2014, 108 were listed on the U.S. civil aircraft register. The origins of the design go back to 1929, but most that are still flying are homebuilts from the 1960s or later, the plans having been updated by the EAA in the 1950s.

N1141J is a 1977 Corben Baby Ace photographed at Oshkosh, Wisconsin.

VH-NEZ '04732' is a 2001 Corby CJ-1 Starlet photographed at Echuca, VIC, Australia in April 2013.

Corby

The Corby Starlet is an Australian homebuilt single-seat low wing monoplane. The first prototype flew for the first time in August 1967. Most aircraft are powered by converted Volkswagen engines, although Rotax and Jabiru engines may also be used. The type is popular in Australia, with examples also flying in both New Zealand and the UK. In June 2014, twenty-one Starlets were listed on the Australian Recreational Aircraft register with a further twenty on the main CASA register, with six in the UK and ten in New Zealand.

Cozy Aircraft

The Cozy is a derivative of the Rutan Long Eze with a widened fuselage to accommodate three (Cozy III) or four-seats (Cozy IV). The Cozy (now designated Cozy III) was first flown in 1981. Over 800 sets of plans were sold for the Cozy III. The four-seat Cozy IV has been even more successful in terms of plans sold. In March 2014, there were around 190 Cozy on the U.S. civil register, some 110 being Cozy IVs; at the same time, seven Cozys appeared on the UK register, only one being a Cozy IV.

VH-BRN is a Cozy IV photographed in March 2008 at Illawarra Regional Airport, NSW, Australia.

Croses

Emilien Croses was a French piano maker who established a range of aircraft based on an updated variant of the Mignet tandem wing configuration. These aircraft have an unusual control arrangement, with pitch control provided by a variable incidence front wing. No ailerons are fitted and roll is generated by the secondary effects of the rudder.

M. Croses died in 2006, at which time the RSA (French equivalent of the EAA) reported on their website that he had designed some fifteen types of aircraft and at that time around 200 had been flown.

The first design was the EC.1, the prototype F-WCZP flying in 1948. Next to fly, in June 1961, was the lightweight single-seat EAC.3 Pouplume, powered by a 232 cc 10.5hp engine. The most popular type has been the Continental C-90 powered EC.6 (and LC.6) Criquet two-seater. The first Criquet flew in July 1966. The LC.6 is an improved version with modifications introduced by Gilbert Landray.

Other designs include the three-seat EC.7 (Triplace or Tous Terrains), which is distinguished by its four-wheel main undercarriage and the somewhat rotund B-EC.9 Para-cargo. An all-composite version of the LC.6, the LC.10 Criquet F-PXKK was flown for the first time in July 1975; two were built. A single-seat version, the Croses-Flicot CF.1 Mini-Criquet F-PVQI was flown in August 1974 and is displayed in the French Musée de L'Air at Le Bourget, Paris. A further one-off variant is the Croses-Noel CN.01 F-PYHQ, which was flown in July 1980.

Ultralight derivatives include the very popular Rotax 503-powered Criquet Léger and the tandem two-seat Croses Airplume, which flew for the first time in October 1983.

A number of other Mignet and related tandem wing designs are described under Mignet.

F-PIHL is the second example of the initial Croses EC.1 design, powered by the Continental A-65 and photographed at Brienne le Chateau.

F-PYLI is a Croses LC.6 Criquet, one of the most successful variants of the Croses family.

The unique Croses EC.7 Tous Terrain is easily recognized by its four wheel main undercarriage.

The one-off Croses-Noel CN.01 F-PYHQ at the Brienne le Chateau RSA Rally.

The Croses Airplume is a two-seat ultralight design from Croses, first flown in 1983.

Culver

The Culver Aircraft Company began production of the two-seat, retractable undercarriage Culver Cadet in 1938. 357 were built before the U.S. entered the Second World War. The PQ-8 (201 built) was a drone version of the Cadet, followed by the single-seat PQ-14 target drone, nearly 2,600 of which were built for the U.S. services.

Culver LCA Cadet NC29261 photographed at Cranfield, Bedfordshire, UK.

The Culver V was a post-war development of the Culver Cadet, with a tricycle undercarriage, revised fuselage and wing tip dihedral; 393 were built. N80281 is a 1946 Culver V photographed at Oshkosh, Wisconsin.

Cunningham-Hall PT-6 NC692W on display at Palmer, Alaska. This aircraft is now preserved at Wasilla, Alaska.

Cunningham Hall

The Cunningham-Hall PT-6 is a six-seat cabin biplane, which was first flown in April 1929. Six aircraft were built, comprising two PT-6 and four PT-6F (a freighter variant). The sole surviving aircraft is PT-6F NC444 with the Golden Wings of Flying Museum at Anoka, Minnesota.

Currie

The Currie Wot is a small single-seat biplane designed pre-war by J.R. Currie and first flown in November 1937. Two aircraft were completed pre-war. Post-war, the type was revived by the Hampshire Aero Club and subsequently became popular with homebuilders. The type has flown with several different types of engine and forms the basis of the Isaacs Fury homebuilt. A two-seat derivative is known as the Turner Super Wot. A number of film replica SE5A aircraft have also been built as modifications of the design.

Currie Wot G-APNT 'Airymouse' was owned by Westland test pilot Harald Penrose and featured in his book of the same name. It was photographed at Dunkeswell, Devon, UK.

Few Curtiss JN-4 Jenny aircraft remain airworthy, although many can be seen in museums.

Curtiss and Curtiss-Wright

Aviation pioneer Glenn Curtiss began flying in 1908 and founded the Curtiss Aeroplane Company in 1910 and made many contributions to the development of aviation, including the development of practical flying boats. In 1929, the company was absorbed into the Curtiss-Wright Corporation. The Curtiss company went on to build a variety of civil and military aircraft including such notable types as the P-40 Warhawk fighter and the C-46 Commando transport. In addition, the company developed many different types of light aircraft, including the JN-4 Jenny, Curtiss Robin, Curtiss Fledgling, Curtiss-Wright Junior, Curtiss-Wight Sedan and various Travel Air models. A selection of these lighter Curtiss models are illustrated below.

The Curtiss JN-4 Jenny became the standard U.S. training aircraft during the First World War and, like its British counterpart, the Avro 504, became the preferred mount for barnstorming and joyriding in the 1920s. The JN designation resulted in the aircraft being generally known as the 'Jenny.' At least 6,500 were built, including more than 2,800 in Canada.

The Curtiss Robin was a utility aircraft that was used by bush pilots in Canada and Alaska. First flown in 1927, several variants were produced with different engines, including the Curtiss OX-5, Wright J-6-5 and Continental W-670. 769 Curtiss Robin were built in October 2013, forty-two were listed on the FAA Register.

1929 Curtiss Robin N76H operating on floats at Lake Hood, Anchorage, Alaska in May 1983.

The Curtiss-Wright Junior NC10967 camera ship for film work displayed at The Movieland of the Air, John Wayne Orange County Airport, Santa Ana, California. This aircraft is now part of the Kermit Weeks collection. Note the enlarged forward cockpit opening for the cameraman.

The 1930 Curtiss-Wright Junior was a light aircraft with a high wing behind an open tandem seat cockpit, driven by a pusher engine mounted at the wing trailing edge. Despite its low power and reputed poor engine reliability, 270 Curtiss-Wright Junior were built. Only a small number remain active.

CZAW

The CZAW SportCruiser is a Czech Light Sport Aircraft and homebuilt that has become a very popular design. The SportCruiser is a two-seat side-by-side all metal low wing monoplane. Some 400 are thought to be flying worldwide. In June 2014, seventy-three were registered in the UK and some 135 were listed on the U.S. civil aircraft register.

CZAW SportCruiser G-MUTT takes off from its home base of Henstridge, Somerset in May 2010.

Daphne SD-1A N961Z was first flown in June 1965. It was photographed at Oshkosh, Wisconsin.

Daphne Airplanes

The Daphne SD-1A (or Szaras SDS-1A) was first flown in October 1961 and is a two-seat high wing homebuilt light aircraft of similar design to the Wittman Tailwind or Nesmith Cougar, albeit with a somewhat thicker wing section. In June 2014, fourteen were listed on the U.S. civil aircraft register.

Dart Aircraft Co.

The Dart Aircraft Co. was formed in 1935 by Al Mooney and KK Culver to produce an elliptical wing low wing monoplane the Dart G, originally designed by Mr Mooney as the Lambert Monosport G. Power was provided by a small 90hp radial of either Lambert, Ken-Royce or Warner design, resulting respectively in the Dart G, GK and GW. The company was later reorganized and went on to produce the Culver Cadet. At least forty-seven examples were built, with a further ten Continental C85-powered examples built post-war.

Left: 1938 Dart GK N20994 seen taxying at Oshkosh, Wisconsin.

Right: 1939 Dart GW NC20390 re-engined with a Lycoming O-290.
Rod Simpson

The second Dart Kitten G-AEXT at an event celebrating Shoreham Airport's sixtieth anniversary as a municipal airport.

Dart Aircraft Ltd.

Dart Aircraft Ltd. was formed in March 1936 and produced a number of designs including the one-off Dart Pup and Dart Flittermouse. The final design was the Dart Kitten a delightful single-seat low wing monoplane. Two were built in 1937 and a third aircraft G-AMJP was flown in 1951.

Davis

The V-tailed Davis DA-2 low wing monoplane, has achieved some success as a homebuilt aircraft. The aircraft seats two side-by-side and has a somewhat inelegant appearance due to the use of single curvature fuselage skins to ease construction. Around fifty have been built, with examples flying in Canada, Australia, the UK and the USA. The DA-3A is a three-seat derivative; the DA-5 is a single-seater of the same general configuration. The range extends to the DA-6, DA-7, DA-8, DA-9 and DA-11. All models have a butterfly tail, but only the DA-2A has been built in any numbers.

Davis DA-2A G-BFPL photographed at Cranfield, Bedfordshire.

The third DH51 G-EBIR 'Miss Kenya' was exported to Nairobi in 1926. It survived until the mid-1960s, when it returned to England and was rebuilt for display at The Shuttleworth Trust, Old Warden. It is the oldest de Havilland machine still flying.

The de Havilland Aircraft Co. Ltd.

The De Havilland Aircraft Co. Ltd. had its origins in the Aircraft Manufacturing Co. (AIRCO) based at Hendon, north London. Geoffrey de Havilland was recruited from the Royal Aircraft Factory as Chief Designer from June 1914. AIRCO built many aircraft during the First World War, notable examples being the DH2 fighter, DH4 and DH9 bombers and the DH6 trainer. Derivatives of the DH4 and DH9 made an important contribution post-war to the development of early airmail and airline services, both in Britain and the USA, where the DH4 was built in large numbers. AIRCO was wound up in 1920, followed by the formation of The De Havilland Aircraft Co. at Stag Lane and later Hatfield

The company went on to design many notable military and civil aircraft including the Mosquito fighter-bomber, the Vampire and Venom jet fighters and the Comet, the world's first jet airliner. One of their final and most long-lived designs was the DH125 executive jet.

In the context of this work, De Havilland is the company that produced the first practical light aircraft, the DH60 Moth, which was manufactured in large quantities and sold all over the world. The success of the Moth led the company to concentrate on aircraft for the civil market between the wars, developing a wide range of Moth derivatives and other civil machines, many of these types being illustrated and briefly described below. Because of the light aircraft focus, most of the larger aircraft are not discussed, but some of the light twin engine machines that would fall within the modern term 'general aviation types' such as the Dragon, Dragon Rapide and Dove have been included.

DH51. The DH51 was a three-seat touring biplane; it was de Havilland's first aircraft built for private ownership, but was too large and expensive to operate. It nevertheless pointed the way to the De Havilland Moth. The prototype DH51 G-EBIM flew (in July 1924) with a 90hp RAF 1A engine, the second and third aircraft being powered by a 120hp Airdisco.

The prototype DH53 Humming Bird at The Shuttleworth Trust, Old Warden, Bedfordshire. It was badly damaged in an accident in 2012.

DH53. The prototype DH53 G-EBHX 'Humming Bird' (first flown in October 1923) and its sister aircraft G-EBHZ were entries into the 1923 Light Aeroplane competition, held at Lympne, Kent. The aim was to find the most economical light single-seat British aeroplane. The DH53 was a workmanlike strut-braced low wing monoplane, albeit with the low power of a 750cc Douglas motorcycle engine. Thirteen additional machines were built, the production aircraft being powered by the 698cc 26hp Blackburn Tomtit twin cylinder inverted V engine.

DH60 Cirrus Moth and Hermes Moth. The prototype DH60 Moth G-EBKT flew for the first time on 22 February 1925. The main variants were the Cirrus Moth and the DH60G Gipsy Moth (described separately). The Moth was immediately successful and was, effectively, the world's first affordable, practical and safe light aeroplane. From 1928, production switched to the DH60X, fitted with the 90hp Cirrus II or 105hp Cirrus Hermes I. The Cirrus Moth was widely exported with license manufacture in Australia and Finland. The type was succeeded in production by the DH60G Gipsy Moth, by which time some 403 had been built, the majority being DH60X Moths.

Only one Cirrus Moth remains flying, G-EBLV, rebuilt by The De Havilland Company and kept and flown at The Shuttleworth Trust, Old Warden, Bedfordshire. DH60X Hermes Moth G-EBWD also flies from Old Warden.

1930 DH60G Gipsy Moth G-AAJT landing at Woburn Abbey, Bedfordshire during the De Havilland Moth Club Rally in August 2014.

DH60G and DH60M Gipsy Moth. The DH60G Gipsy Moth (built from late 1928) was an improved version of the Cirrus Moth, making use of the 100hp de Havilland Gipsy I engine, or 120hp Gipsy II engine. The DH60M with a metal tube fuselage was built in parallel with the DH60G. Some 595 examples of the DH60G were built at Stag Lane, with a further eighty aircraft built under license in France, the United States and Australia. The DH60M was produced in similar numbers (approx. 550) to the DH60G, along with some sixty-three DH60T Moth Trainers; a military training version of the DH60M. The DH60M was also built in Canada (35), the United States (161) and Norway (10).

DH60GIII and Moth Major. The DH60GIII Moth used the de Havilland Gipsy III inverted engine, which allowed a cleaner, lower engine installation. The prototype DH60GIII flew for the first time in March 1932. An improved version of this engine, the Gipsy IIIA, was produced in large quantities as the 130hp Gipsy Major, which powered many types of light aircraft. Powered by this engine, the type became known as the Moth Major. A total of 154 DH60GIII aircraft were built with either the Gipsy III or Gipsy Major engine.

This DH60GIII Moth Major was photographed at Abingdon in a non-standard single-seat configuration with faired headrest.

1930 DH80A Puss Moth G-AAZP landing at Woburn Abbey, Bedfordshire during the De Havilland Moth Club Rally in August 2014.

DH80A Puss Moth. The prototype DH80 Puss Moth flew for the first time in September 1929. This aircraft had a flat-sided wooden fuselage. The production aircraft, the DH80A, had a fabric-covered steel tube fuselage. The Puss Moth was a high wing two-seat light aircraft offering long range and cabin comfort. A second passenger could be carried when desired. The wings could be folded to reduce hangar space. In addition to the prototype, 259 aircraft were built in the UK, with a further twenty-five built in Canada.

DH82A Tiger Moth. The Tiger Moth flew in October 1931. It was developed from the DH60T Moth Trainer using the inverted Gipsy III engine and a modified center section to allow the front seat occupant to escape more easily in emergencies, moving the center section forward of the front cockpit. Wing sweep was then used to restore the center of gravity position, with increased lower wing dihedral to improve tip clearance. These features distinguish the Tiger Moth from the Moth or Moth Major. The DH82A rapidly became the standard trainer for civilian and RAF use and was widely exported. Nearly 5,500 were built in the UK from a total of some 8,800 (including production in Australia, Canada and New Zealand, and license production in Portugal, Norway and Sweden).

DH82A Tiger Moth R5246 newly rebuilt at Henstridge in 2012, flying over the Somerset countryside.

1933 DH83 Fox Moth G-ACEJ takes off from Woburn Abbey, Bedfordshire at the De Havilland Moth Club Rally in August 2014.

DH83 Fox Moth. The DH83 Fox Moth flew in March 1932 and had an open cockpit for its pilot, located well aft on the fuselage. Ahead of the pilot and enclosed within the fuselage, there was a small cabin that could seat four passengers. The type was popular for passenger pleasure flights both pre- and post-war. Ninety-eight were built in the UK, and a further fifty-three in Canada and two in Australia. The Canadian examples (DH83C) were built post-war and were usually fitted with an enclosed sliding cockpit for the pilot.

DH84 Dragon. The DH84 Dragon twin engine six passenger biplane was very successful and attracted orders from many British regional airlines, particularly in Scotland. The first air service to be flown by the Irish airline Aer Lingus was by DH84 Dragon EI-ABI 'Iolar.' The Dragon first flew in November 1932. 115 DH84 were built at Stag Lane, with an additional eighty-seven in Australia. The Dragon offered profitable regional flying to the airlines and brought affordable passenger flying to many for the first time and opened up air services to outlying communities in Scotland. There are a number of survivors, but few flying examples.

DH84 Dragon 'G-ECAN' (ex-VH-DHX, VH-AQU) photographed at Abingdon, Oxfordshire.

The immaculate 1934 DH85 Leopard Moth G-AIYS at Woburn Abbey, Bedfordshire during the De Havilland Moth Club Rally in August 2014.

DH85 Leopard Moth. The first DH85 Leopard Moth flew for the first time in May 1933. Unlike the DH80 Puss Moth, the DH85 was designed from the outset to carry three occupants and featured a plywood, rather than steel tube fuselage construction. Externally, the two aircraft are similar, although the DH85 undercarriage legs attach at the engine bulkhead, rather than to the forward wing root fitting. The Leopard Moth wing also features straight leading and trailing edges, with the leading edge being gently swept back. 132 DH85s were built.

DH87 Hornet Moth. The Hornet Moth flew for the first time in May 1934. It combined a biplane configuration with the advantages of enclosed side-by-side seating. The initial production wing planform was a high aspect ratio tapered elliptical shape. In this form, the type was known as the DH87A. The tapered wing was prone to sudden tip stall and a new rectangular wing was introduced on the DH87B. Earlier aircraft were modified to this standard. 165 Hornet Moths were built, with approximately half of these exported.

1936 DH87 Hornet Moth G-ADMT landing at Woburn Abbey, Bedfordshire during the De Havilland Moth Club Rally in August 2014.

DH88 Comet G-ACSS 'Grosvenor House', winner of the 1934 MacRobertson Air Race, on display in October 2014.

DH88 Comet. The DH88 was produced for the 1934 MacRobertson Air Race from England to Australia. Three aircraft were ordered, the flying on 8 September 1934, six weeks before the start of the race. Two crewmen were seated in tandem behind three large fuel tanks providing a maximum range of nearly 3,000 miles. The three race entrants were the black and gold G-ACSP 'Black Magic'; green G-ACSP, and the red and white G-ACSS 'Grosvenor House' flown by Scott and Campbell Black. G-ACSS reached Melbourne in first place in just seventy hours and fifty-four minutes. G-ACSR came fourth and returned to England carrying newsreel film, completing the round trip in a record thirteen and a half days.

DH89 Dragon Rapide. The prototype DH89 Dragon Six flew in April 1934 and was essentially a scaled down version of the four engine DH86 Express. Production aircraft were known as the Dragon Rapide; the majority being DH89A, fitted with small trailing edge flaps. The type was immediately successful in both home and export markets, being operated by many British regional airlines. The type gained a new lease of life in the Second World War, as the Dominie in navigation training and communication roles. 728 DH89 Rapides and Dominies were built. Large numbers of Dominie aircraft were converted to civilian use post-war.

Newly-restored 1945 DH89A Dragon Rapide G-AHAG displaying at Woburn Abbey, Bedfordshire during the De Havilland Moth Club Rally in August 2014.

1936 DH90 Dragonfly G-AEDT seen at Henstridge, Somerset.

DH90 Dragonfly. The DH90 Dragonfly was effectively a scaled down and streamlined derivative of the DH89 Dragon Rapide aimed at the wealthy private owner. The Dragonfly flew in August 1935, powered by two 130hp de Havilland Gipsy Major I engines; sixty-seven were built. Only two examples remain, one in the UK and the other in New Zealand. Both surviving aircraft have been re-engined with 145hp Gipsy Major Mk.10 engines.

DH94 Moth Minor. The Moth Minor flew in June 1937; it was powered by a 90hp Gipsy Minor and sat two in tandem open cockpits. Nine aircraft were fitted with an enclosed cockpit canopy and were known as the Moth Minor Coupé. The aircraft had a conventional plywood and spruce fuselage, but the high aspect ratio wing was skinned with plywood, like the earlier Comet and Albatross. The wing could be folded from a point outside each undercarriage leg to minimize hangar space requirements. Due to its clean lines, the aircraft was fitted with a perforated airbrake installed between the undercarriage legs. Seventy-three aircraft were built in the UK before production was transferred in wartime to Australia, where a further forty were completed.

DH94 Moth Minor G-AFPN at Halton, Buckinghamshire in June 2008. *Rod Simpson*

Dove 7 JY-RYU photographed over the Hampshire countryside on a flight between Blackbushe and Thruxton.

DH104 Dove. The Dove was the first new commercial aircraft to fly in the UK after the end of the Second World War. It flew for the first time on 25 September 1945, the twenty-fifth anniversary of the De Havilland company. 544 Dove were built in a twenty-three-year production run. The aircraft was of a very elegant appearance, with clean lines and a sweeping dorsal fin reminiscent of that fitted to the DH103 Hornet fighter. The Dove 1 was powered by two 330hp Gipsy Queen engines. Power was increased progressively to 400hp for the final models, the Dove 7 and 8. Thirty-nine Dove 4s were delivered to the RAF for communication duties as the Devon C.Mk.1; thirteen similar aircraft went to the Royal Navy as the Sea Devon C.Mk.20.

De Havilland Canada

DHC-1 Chipmunk. The Chipmunk won the contract for a basic training aircraft for the Royal Air Force to replace the Tiger Moth. The prototype CF-DIO-X flew for the first time in May 1946. Some 1,000 were built in the UK, with a further 218 in Canada and sixty-six in Portugal. The type was widely exported, serving with at least sixteen air forces. Some aircraft, particularly for Canadian use, were fitted with a more aerodynamically refined one-piece blown cockpit canopy.

1950 De Havilland Canada DHC1 Chipmunk 22 G-APYG takes off from Woburn Abbey, Bedfordshire at the De Havilland Moth Club Rally in August 2014.

A DHC-2 Beaver takes off from Lake Hood, Anchorage, Alaska in May 1983 – floatplane workhorse of the northern skies.

DHC-2 Beaver. The Beaver is a rugged utility aircraft ideally suited for bush operations from short unprepared airfields. It can be equipped with wheels, skis, floats or amphibious floats to suit conditions. The Beaver flew for the first time in August 1947. 1,631 were built in Canada, together with a single Beaver 2 powered by a 550hp Leonides 502/4 engine. 970 were sold to the U.S. Army. The type was widely exported, and served with around thirty-one other nations' forces in addition to the U.S., UK and Canada. The type remains in widespread use.

DHC-2T Turbo-Beaver. The DHC-2T Turbo Beaver (or DHC-2 Mk.III) is a turboprop-powered variant of the DHC-2 Beaver rugged short take-off and landing utility aircraft. It was first flown in December 1963. A total of sixty new-build aircraft were built, and there have also been a number of after-market conversions of DHC-2 from Wasp to turboprop power. Factory-built aircraft have a twenty-eight-inch plug in the fuselage, a taller slightly swept vertical fin and, like the original Beaver, can operate on wheel, floats, skis and amphibious floats.

DHC-2 Mk III Turbo Beaver N1459T at Lake Hood Airstrip, Anchorage, Alaska, May 1983.

1991 Denney Kitfox G-FOXC 'Foxc Lady' photographed at Henstridge, Somerset in April 2009.

Denney

The Denney Kitfox is a kit-built two-seat high wing STOL aircraft designed to much the same concept as the Avid Flyer. The first Kitfox appeared in November 1984, since when more than 5,000 kits have been delivered to builders in forty-two countries. The type has evolved over time, the latest (2014) variant being the S7 Super Sport. In 2014, ninety-two were registered in the UK with around 1,000 in the U.S.

Deperdussin

Deperdussin 1910 Monoplane. The world's second oldest flying aircraft is an original 1910 Deperdussin monoplane in the Shuttleworth Collection at Old Warden, Bedfordshire. Armand Deperdussin was a French aviation pioneer, whose monoplanes were contemporary to the better-known Blériot machines. His Monocoque Racer of 1912 was one of the first aircraft to use a streamlined stressed skin fuselage. The original Deperdussin company was wound up in 1913 and reformed as SPAD (Société Provisoire des Aéroplanes Deperdussin), famous for its fighter aircraft of the First World War.

The Shuttleworth 1910 Deperdussin Monoplane has been maintained in flying condition for many years, albeit only flying in ideal weather conditions. *Jim Smith*

G-AAPZ is a 1930 Desoutter Mk II preserved in flying condition at The Shuttleworth Trust, Old Warden, Bedfordshire.

Desoutter

The Desoutter Mk.II monoplane was designed by the Dutch designer Frederick Koolhoven and is, in essence, a Koolhoven FK41 built under license in the UK. British aircraft have a low set tailplane and other modifications and were sold as the Desoutter Mk.I and Mk.II. Twenty-eight Desoutter Mk.Is and thirteen Desoutter Mk.IIs were built.

Dewoitine

Émile Dewoitine set up a company to manufacture aircraft in Tolouse in 1920. The company produced a series of all-metal parasol wing fighters, of which the most successful was the Dewoitine D9, more than 150 of which were built, before moving on to build a number of pre-war airliners. The Dewoitine D26 and D27 were operated by Switzerland, the D27 as a fighter and the D26 as a trainer. Twelve D26s were built from 1929, remaining in service until 1948, after which they were used as glider tugs.

The last Dewoitine D26, flying at Old Warden, Bedfordshire. This aircraft now forms part of the Kermit Weeks collection with registration N282DW.

G-EMDM is a 2000 Diamond DA40 Diamond Star photographed at Compton Abbas, Wiltshire.

Diamond

Diamond Aircraft is a successor to Hoffmann Flugzeugebau and builds aircraft in both Austria and Canada. Diamond's main products are the all-composite DA40 Diamond Star, which is an enlarged four-seat aircraft developed from the Hoffmann DV20 Katana and the DA42 Twin Star, which is effectively a twin engine Diamond Star with turbo-diesel engines.

The DA40 first flew in November 1997, and by June 2014, there were 733 listed on the U.S. civil register,

thirty-eight in the UK, eight in Australia and seventy-three in Canada.

The Diamond DA42 Twin Star is an all-composite four-seat twin engine aircraft powered by turbodiesel engines. The type is used as a private aircraft, for commercial flight training, and for special missions for military and government agencies. In June 2014, forty-nine DA42s were registered in the UK, with fourteen in Australia, and 180 listed on the U.S. civil aircraft register.

2005 Diamond DA42 Twin Star G-CTCE on the approach to Bournemouth Airport. *Jim Smith*

N50645 is a full-scale VW-powered replica of the Dormoy Flying Bathtub built by Mike Kimbrell in 1978.

Dormoy

Etienne Dormoy built his "Famous Flying Bathtub" airplane out of materials bought from a hardware store; it was powered by a Henderson motorcycle engine. The plane won 1924 Dayton Daily News Light Airplane Race and the Rickenbacker Trophy.

Dornier

Dornier Flugzeugwerke is a famous and historic name in aviation dating back to 1914. The company is perhaps best known for flying boats in the 1920s and 1930s (Wal, Do X and Do 24) and for its military aircraft of the Second World War, including the Do 17 and Do 217 bombers and the Do 335 fighter. Post-war, aircraft construction was banned in Germany and Claudius Dornier moved to Spain before returning to Germany in 1954. In Spain, he designed a high wing short take-off and landing aircraft the Do 25. Two prototypes led to a production machine, the Do 27. 428 production machines were ordered as communication and observation aircraft for the reformed post-war Luftwaffe. Fifty were built under license in Spain and total production including civil machines was around 625 aircraft.

G-BMIJ is a 1961 Do27A-4, seen at Henstrige. It was previously operated by the Malawi Army Air Wing.

Do 28A-1 D-IBIT was photographed at Denham, Buckinghamshire. This aircraft crashed in Italy in June 1979.

Dornier Do 28. The Do 28 is a twin engine variant of the Do 27, with two engines mounted next to the fuselage nose on a stub wing that also mounts the undercarriage legs. 120 production aircraft were built.

Dan Rihn DR107 One Design

The DR107 One Design is a single-seat aerobatic aircraft that was first flown in 1993. The DR109 is a two-seat variant. More than fifty have been built and in June 2014, there were nine registered in the UK and eleven listed on the U.S. civil register.

DR107 One design G-RIHN taking off from Compton Abbas, Wiltshire in June 2014.

Driggs Dart II N1927 at the Pate Museum of Transportation, near Fort Worth, Texas.

Driggs

The Driggs Dart I was a single-seat high wing monoplane of 1926. Its designer Ivan Driggs developed a two-seat sesquiplane variant, the Driggs Dart II in 1927. Three Dart I and at least four Dart II were built and it is believed that some additional aircraft were built from plans in the 1930s. One airworthy example is displayed at the Historic Aircraft Restoration Museum near St Louis.

Druine

Roger Druine designed a number of successful light aircraft, most notable of which are the Turbulent, Turbi and Condor. The Turbi and Turbulent have been built by home constructors and the Turbulent and Condor were also produced commercially by Rollason Aircraft & Engines. The D.31 Turbulent is a Volkswagen powered single-seat low wing monoplane. In addition to numerous homebuilt examples, Rollason built thirty aircraft in the UK and Starck Flugzeugbau, thirty-five Turbulent Ds.

Plans-built Druine D.31 Turbulent G-ASFX at Henstridge, Somerset in April 2009.

Druine D.5 Turbi G-APFA on the approach to Dunkeswell, Devon.

D.5 Turbi is a two-seat low wing monoplane designed home building. The majority built have open cockpits, although a couple of aircraft have been modified with enclosed cockpits. Typically, the aircraft may be powered by a Continental A-65 engine, although a number of examples use the Walter Mikron. About fifteen examples have been built, mainly in France.

The Druine D.60/D.62 Condor is a low wing monoplane seating two occupants, side-by-side. A small number were built in France, but the type entered series production in the UK as the Rollason Condor, of which forty-eight were built as follows: 90hp D.62A (2), 100hp D.62B (42) and 130hp D.62C (4). Thirty-six Condor aircraft were registered in the UK in June 2014.

1967 Rollason-built Druine D62B Condor G-OPJH (previously G-AVDW, now G-RELL) photographed at Compton Abbas, Wiltshire in April 2007.

Dyke Delta JD-2 N27DF at North Las Vegas, Nevada. The unique wing planform is clearly revealed by the shadow.

Dyke

The Dyke Delta is a plans-built homebuilt aircraft designed by John Dyke and first flown (JD-1) in 1962. The definitive model is the JD-2. The Dyke Delta seats the pilot on the centerline ahead of a bench seat for up to three passengers. The most distinctive feature is the double delta wing planform, with all control services at the wing trailing edge. Some 400 sets of plans have been sold and around fifty are flying.

Delta Stingray. Lowell Borchers built a single-seat aircraft inspired by the Dyke Delta and called the Delta Stingray. The type had an O-200 engine and had an additional tail surface to improve elevator control at low speeds.

The one-off Delta Stingray seen at Oshkosh, Wisconsin.

DynAero

The DynAero MCR-01 Banbi is a two-seat all-composite aircraft that can be purchased as a kit or as a completed aircraft. The Banbi is a Rotax-powered low wing monoplane with a T-tail with the two occupants sat beneath a bubble canopy. The Banbi was first flown in July 1996 and some hundreds have been built. In June 2014, twenty-four were registered in the UK.

2003 DynAero MCR-01 Banbi ULC G-CCMM on the approach to land at Henstridge, Somerset in August 2010.

EAA Biplane G-BBMH at Cranfield, Bedfordshire. This aircraft was built in 1982.

EAA

EAA Biplane: The EAA Biplane is a small single-seat biplane with staggered wings and N-struts designed for home construction. The design was based on that of the 1930s Gere Biplane. The type proved popular, with plans sold for just $20 and it is believed at least eighty-eight were flown in the USA (although some sources claim many more than this). First flown in 1960, the plans remained on sale until 1972. In June 2014, seventy-eight were listed on the U.S. civil register.

EAA Acrosport I. The Acrosport I was designed by Paul Poberezny as a more powerful and fully aerobatic version of the EAA Biplane, from which it is distinguished by its I-strutted wings. The type was first flown in January 1972. Plans are sold by Acro Sport Inc. and parts kits are also available.

EAA Acrosport I OO-80 at Balen-Keiheuvel, Belgium.

EAA Acrosport II G-DAGF lands at Henstridge, Somerset in June 2013.

EAA Acrosport II. The Acrosport II is a lengthened two-seat derivative of the Acrosport I. The type first flew in July 1978 and at least 100 have been built and are flying in several countries, including USA, Canada, UK, France, Australia and New Zealand. The Acrosport II has been built in greater numbers than the Acrosport I.

Edgley Aircraft Co. Ltd. (and successors)

The Edgley Optica prototype first flew at Cranfield in December 1979. The type was of novel design optimized for slow flying and for cockpit field of view. The company ran into financial problems and development continued with a number of different firms (Optica Industries, Brooklands Aerospace and FLS Lovaux). Optica production comprised the initial prototype, fifteen aircraft built by Optica Industries, five built as the Scoutmaster by Brooklands Aerospace, and two OA7-300 constructed by FLS/Lovaux. In June 2014, three remained registered in the UK.

1993 FLS-built Edgley OA7 Optica Srs 301 G-BOPO during a practice display at Henstridge, Somerset at the end of July 2014.

Emigh Trojan N8345H photographed at Sun 'N Fun, Lakeland, Florida in April 1990. *Jim Smith*

Emigh

The Emigh A-2 Trojan is a two-seat side-by-side monoplane, distinguished by having external reinforcing ribs on its tapered metal wing. The Trojan flew for the first time in December 1946 and a total of fifty-eight were built, seventeen of which were listed on U.S. register in December 2013 (although not all may be active).

English Electric Ltd.

Chiefly known for their military jets, the Canberra and the Lightning, the first English Electric design to be completed and flown was the Wren motor glider, an entry in the 1923 Motor Glider Competition. With its 398cc motorcycle engine and empty weight of only 232 pounds, the Wren achieved the quite remarkable performance figures of a maximum speed of 64mph and an economy of 87.5 miles per gallon. Three Wren motor gliders were built, two of which competed in the Lympne trials.

English Electric Wren preserved and flown in calm conditions by The Shuttleworth Trust at Old Warden, Bedfordshire.

The Engineering & Research Corporation (Erco) (and related designs)

Erco 415C Ercoupe. Erco was formed in 1930 and in 1937 flew what was to become the Erco 415 Ercoupe. The Ercoupe was a low wing all-metal monoplane and was unusual for its time in having a tricycle undercarriage. Its twin elliptical fins were also a distinguishing feature. Designed by Fred Weick, the aircraft initially had an unconventional control system with a steering yoke that automatically applied rudder with aileron input. No rudder pedals were fitted. Most aircraft were converted subsequently to conventional controls, due to difficulties when flying in strong crosswinds. Erco built 5,081 Ercoupe pre-war and post-war until 1951. The design was then taken up by a series of other manufacturers. Forney Aircraft (and Air Products Inc.) built 165 Forney F-1 and F-1A Aircoupe between 1955 and 1962. Alon Inc. revised the aircraft as the Alon A-2 and A-2A, with revised cockpit glazing and a rearward-sliding canopy, building a total of 308 aircraft. Finally, after Alon were taken over by Mooney Aircraft, the A-2 was revised again with an upright single 'Mooney-style' tail fin and sold as the M-10 Cadet, a total of sixty-one being built. The grand total of Ercoupe-based designs to be built was 5,551.

1947 Erco 415C EI-CIH at Henstridge, Somerset in August 2007.

1967 Alon A-2A G-BKIN at Finmere, Oxfordshire.

1960 Forney F-1A G-ARHC at Wroughton, Wiltshire.

1970 Mooney M-10 Cadet VH-JXS at Avalon, VIC, Australia. *Jim Smith*

G-PADE is a Jabiru-powered Escapade built in 2004 and photographed in June 2010.

Escapade

The Escapade is a single-seat, or two-seat side-by-side, high wing light aircraft developed jointly in the UK and U.S. by Reality Aircraft Ltd. and Just Aircraft LLC. UK production was carried out by Escapade Aviation Ltd., the rights then passing to TLAC (The Light Aircraft Co. Ltd.).

The type has given rise to a number of variants, as follows: The Escapade is a single-seat aircraft; Escapade Two is a two-seat version; the Highlander is a bushplane derivative that is available as a kit-built aircraft in the U.S.; the Just Superstol is a short takeoff and landing version of the Highlander with full-span leading edge slats and strengthened undercarriage. In July 2014, thirty-nine Escapades were registered in the UK with thirty-six listed on the U.S. register, together with ninety-six Highlander models.

The Europa Aircraft Co.

Europa: The Ivan Shaw-designed Europa single-engine, low wing monoplane offers outstanding performance and is a two-seater of composite construction, featuring a central retractable single main wheel. Its performance figures of 150mph cruise speed on an 80hp Rotax 912 engine, 500nm range, 50mpg, and 620lb. useful load are impressive. Designed for the homebuilt and kit construction market, the Europa first flew in September 1992. The Europa XS was introduced with 115hp Rotax 914T engine and increased wing aspect ratio. On 24 November 2003 the total number of kits sold passed 1,000 in thirty-four countries. In December 2013, there were 225 examples on the British civil aircraft register.

2001 Europa XS G-KIMM taking off from Henstridge, Somerset in July 2011.

1983 Evans VP-1 G-BGLF at Henstridge, Somerset, UK.

Evans

William Evans designed a notable aircraft for home construction, the Evans VP-1 or Volksplane, which first flew in 1968. The VP-1 is a single-seat low wing wooden monoplane with open cockpit, rectangular wing planform, square section fuselage and open cockpit. Power is normally provided by a converted Volkswagen engine. The emphasis of the design was for ease of construction and the type proved to be exceptionally popular, with thousands of sets of plans sold. In June 2014, thirty-four were registered in the UK, with seventy-three on the U.S. civil register.

Evans VP-2. The VP-2 is a two-seat version of the Evans VP-1, with a wider cockpit to seat two side-by-side. Some aircraft retain an open cockpit, others have a built up rear fuselage decking that fairs-in an enclosed cockpit. Power is typically provided by a Volkswagen, or a Continental A-65 engine. Eleven were registered in the UK in June 2014, with twenty-four listed on the U.S. civil register.

G-BHUO is an enclosed cockpit version of the Evans VP-2, seen at Cranfield, Bedfordshire. This aircraft was built in 1982 and is powered by a Continental A-65 engine.

2010 Evektor EV-97A Eurostar G-CGOG landing at Henstridge, Somerset, UK in June 2013.

Evektor – Aerotechnik

Evektor is a Czech company building a highly successful range of light aircraft. The range includes the broadly similar EV-97 Eurostar and Sportstar Light Sports Aircraft and the fully certificated Sportstar RTC. The range is being extended and now includes the VUT100 Super Cobra four-seat retractable undercarriage low wing monoplane. The Eurostar and Sportstar have proved popular both for private owners and for flight training organizations. In December 2013, there were eighty-six Eurostars registered in the UK, and around ninety Sportstars registered in the USA.

Extra Flugzeugebau

Extra is best known for its world class aerobatic monoplanes, the single-seat Extra EA230 and the two-seat Extra EA300. The Extra 230 was designed by Walter Extra for unlimited competition aerobatics and first flew in July 1983.

Extra EA230 N230X (c/n 001) flown by Clint McHenry, the then US National Champion. at the 1986 World Aerobatic Championships, South Cerney, August 1986. *Jim Smith*

Extra EA300. The Extra EA300 is a lengthened two-seat derivative of the Extra EA230, suitable both for competition and for advanced aerobatic training. The Extra EA300 first flew in May 1988. The Extra EA300S and EA330S are single-seat versions with shorter wingspan and larger ailerons. The Extra EA300L has a low, rather than a mid-wing, also of reduced span and with more powerful ailerons. Thirty-six EA300s were registered in the UK in December 2013, with more than 250 on the U.S. register.

The Blades display team at the Farnborough Airshow flying four Extra EA300LP aircraft.

2010 Extra EA330SC G-IIIK photographed at Compton Abbas in June 2014.

Extra EA400. The Extra EA400 is a pressurized, carbon fiber, six-seat touring high wing monoplane with a retractable undercarriage. The type first flew in April 1996, and has sold in modest numbers. The EA500 is a turboprop version of the EA400.

Extra EA400 N400YY at Henstridge, Somerset, UK in May 2011. This is one of eleven EA400s on the U.S. register in December 2013.

1933 Fairchild 22 C7D photographed at Oshkosh, Wisconsin.

Fairchild

The Fairchild Aircraft Corporation's association with light aircraft began with its takeover of Kreider-Reisner Aircraft Co. in April 1929, leading to production of the successful KR-21 biplane, some forty-eight of which were built. Fairchild's Canadian subsidiary also built the KR-34 Challenger.

Fairchild 22. Fairchild then produced the Fairchild 22 parasol monoplane, some 127 of which were built in a series of models (C7 to C7G) with different engine types. The characteristic undercarriage strut arrangement was carried over into the successful Fairchild 24 series. In June 2014, twenty-four Fairchild 22s were listed on the U.S. civil register.

Fairchild 24. The Fairchild 24 high wing monoplane initially appeared in 1932 as a two-seat side-by-side design, the F24 C8 and C8A. A total of 25 C8 and C8A were built. After 1934, with the introduction of the C8C, a three-seat cabin was introduced. From

this point on, the aircraft (C8C to C8F) was available either with a Warner Super Scarab radial engine or the Ranger six-cylinder inverted in-line engine.

Some 250 had been built up to the introduction of the three-seat 'deluxe' or four-seat 'standard' Fairchild F24G in 1937. Production continued with Warner and Ranger powered variants up to the U.S. entry into the Second World War. By this stage, the designation settled on F24W for Warner-powered aircraft and F24R for Ranger-engined models. The type was ordered by the USAAC as the UC-61 Forwarder, many being shipped to the UK as the Fairchild Argus, being mainly used as communication aircraft by the Air Transport Auxiliary (ATA). Some 830 Argus were used in this role. A total of 1,310 UC-61, UC-61A and UC-61K saw military service. A grand total of 2,232 Fairchild 24s of all models were built between 1932 and 1946.

1934 Fairchild 24 C8A N957V at Oshkosh Wisconsin.

1938 Fairchild F24G at Merrill Field, Anchorage, Alaska.

Fairchild F24W Argus G-AJPI demonstrating at White Waltham in 1977 (this aircraft was later re-engined with a Ranger engine).

1944 Ranger-powered UC-61K/F24R-9 G-BCBH landing at Badminton House airstrip in April 1988.

Fairchild PT-19, PT-23 and PT-26. The PT-19 low wing monoplane was selected as a basic trainer during the Second World War, serving with the USAAF, and with the RCAF, as the Cornell, in support of the Commonwealth Air Training Scheme. The type first flew in May 1939 and may be seen with either two open cockpits, or with a cockpit enclosure (a feature used in particular on RCAF PT-26 Cornell aircraft). The PT-23 made use of a Continental R-670 radial engine, due to problems with Ranger engine supply. Although it is hard to find consistent production data, the combined total built of these three types is around 6,400.

N46693 is a 1943 Fairchild M62A, photographed at Oshkosh, Wisconsin. This aircraft was built as a PT-19 and subsequently converted to a PT-26.

N69590 is a 1942 Fairchild PT-23 (M62A-4) photographed at Oshkosh, Wisconsin.

Fairchild Husky F-11-2 G-CGYV seen at Vancouver Airport in May 1983; it is now preserved by the Western Canada Aviation Museum. It last flew in 1984.

Fairchild Aircraft Ltd.

This company was the Canadian subsidiary of Fairchild Aircraft Corporation. Post-war, it designed and built the F11 Husky as a utility and bush aircraft to replace aircraft such as the Noorduyn Norseman. The design incorporated a number of features for the role, including large doors and the ability to carry long items of cargo, loaded through a rear cargo door. The type first flew in 1946, but was rather underpowered. Despite the practicality of the design, only twelve were built. War-surplus Norseman were available in numbers and the success of the DHC-2 Beaver inhibited Husky sales. It is not thought that any remain active.

F-CRON is a Fauvel AV.221 (c/n 01) tailless motor glider photographed at Brienne Le Chateau, France.

Fauvel

Fauvel is mainly known for the design of a series of tailless gliders, such as the Fauvel AV.36. The AV.45 is essentially an AV.36 with a Hirth O-280R engine driving a pusher propeller at the wing trailing edge between the two fins and rudders. The AV.221/AV.222 are larger machines, based on the AV.22 glider, seating two side-by-side and typically powered by a converted Volkswagen engine. The AV.221 first flew on 8 April 1965.

FFA (Flug & Fahrzeugwerke AG)

FFA is a Swiss company, chiefly known for the S.202 Bravo training aircraft, which was developed in cooperation with the Italian firm SIAI-Marchetti. The type first flew in March 1969. Two versions have been built in quantity, the AS202/15 and the AS202/18A with respectively 150/180hp engines. The type was sold to several air forces, in addition to its civil use. Approximately 215 were built, together with a couple of experimental prototypes – the AS202/26A and AS202/32T with additional engine options.

HB-HEX is an AS202/18A demonstrator aircraft, seen at the Farnborough Airshow.

Fiat G46-3B trainer G-BBII on the runway at Badminton House airstrip. This is currently the only aircraft of its type flying in the UK. N46FM is the sole example on the U.S. register in June 2014.

Fiat Aviazione

The Italian company Fiat, in addition to their motor industry interests, is well known as a manufacturer of fighters, bombers, transport and training aircraft.

The Fiat G46 is a low wing, retractable undercarriage monoplane seating two in tandem and designed as a military trainer. First flown in June 1947, some 220 were built and used by the Italian, Argentinian, Austrian and Syrian Air Forces.

Fieseler Fi 156 Storch and Morane 500 Criquet

The short take-off and landing Fieseler Storch was the primary German Army liaison and communication aircraft of the Second World War. At least 2,900 were built, both in Germany and in occupied France, Czechoslovakia and Romania. Most aircraft currently flying were built by Morane Saulnier in France post-war as the MS500 Criquet, fitted with the Argus As410c inverted-V engine. Other engines were also used, including the Renault 6Q (MS501), Salmson 9AB (MS502) and Jacobs R-755 (MS504 and MS505). Two aircraft (MS506L) were also modified with a Lycoming horizontally opposed engine. The MS500 is externally identical to the Fieseler Fi 156 and all variants have the gangling insect-like appearance of the original design.

Morane Saulnier MS500 Criquet G-AZMH at Henstridge.

Morane Saulnier MS500 Criquet G-AZMH at Yeovil.

Jacobs powered Morane Saulnier MS505 OO-STO at Balen Keiheuvel, Belgium.

F-BDXM is one of two Lycoming powered MS506L seen here at Middle Wallop, Hampshire showing the full span flaps, drooping ailerons and leading edge slats that confer the type's STOL performance.

Fleet Aircraft

Fleet began its existence as part of the Consolidated Aircraft Corporation (founded by Reuben Fleet in 1923). The intention was to enter the civil market with the Consolidated 14 Husky Junior. Shortly before the prototype flew, Consolidated decided not to enter the sector and Reuben Fleet purchased the rights and set up Fleet Aircraft in 1928, the type becoming the Fleet Model 1. The design was a success and some 300 Fleet Model 1 and Model 2 were sold. Consolidated reacted to Fleet's success by buying the company back to become its subsidiary, with production in both the U.S. and Canada. Development continued through the Fleet Models 3 to 11, 16 and 21. The most important models (with numbers built) were the Model 1 (about 90); Model 2 (203); Model 7 Fawn (64); Model 10 (at least 70); Model 14 (300 licence-built in Romania); the Model 16 Finch (447 built mainly for RCAF use); and Model 21 (forty plus as PT-11 and twelve for the USAAC). All were single-engine biplanes, the different models being fitted with a variety of in-line and radial engines. Some ninety-five aircraft of this family are listed on the December 2013 U.S. Civil Register, although a significant proportion of these will not be currently active.

Fleet Model 2. This type was powered by the Kinner K-5 engine and some 203 were built.

NC413K is representative of the early Fleet biplane and is a Model 2, at Oshkosh, Wisconsin.

Fleet 2 NC618M at Pearson Field, Vancouver, Washington in September 2005. *Jeff Jacobs*

N162V (RCAF 264) is a 1936 Fleet 16B Finch II, photographed at Oshkosh, Wisconsin.

Fleet Model 16B. This type, as the Fleet Finch, was a standard primary trainer for the RCAF. 606 were built, many being fitted in service with a sliding cockpit canopy, similar to that used on Canadian-built DH82C Tiger Moths. Twenty-seven were listed on the U.S. civil aircraft register in June 2014.

Fleet 80 Canuck. The Canuck is a two-seat high wing monoplane that was produced for the private aircraft market. The type had its origin in the Noury N-75, whose production rights were sold to Fleet Aircraft. The Canuck was first flown in September 1945 and series production took place between 1946 and 1948, a total of 225 being built (including the Noury prototype). Seventy-seven examples were listed on the Canadian register in 2010.

C-FDEG is a 1946 Fleet Model 80 Canuck.

Flight Design

The Flight Design CT family is a series of light and ultralight aircraft of German origin. The CT is a Rotax-powered high wing composite design seating two side-by-side. The CT was first flown in March 1996 and more than 900 have been built. The type's clean lines confer excellent performance. The type is extremely popular with 361 listed on the U.S. register, seventy-six registered in the UK and eighteen in Canada in June 2014.

G-OASA is a 2009 Flight Design CTSW photographed at Compton Abbas, Wiltshire in August 2013.

Focke Wulf

Undoubtedly best known for the superlative Fw 190 of the Second World War, Focke Wulf built a number of other notable types, including the Fw 44 Steiglitz training aircraft. First flown in 1932, the main production model was the Fw 44J. In addition to several thousand built in Germany, fifty-seven were built in Sweden, forty in Brazil and some 190 in Argentina.

Focke Wulf FW44J Steiglitz D-ENAY taxies at Woburn Abbey in August 2014.

Fokker S-11 E-1/OO-PCH on the approach to Cranfield, Bedfordshire in July 1984.

Fokker

A true pioneer firm, Anthony Fokker began building aircraft in 1912 and produced many notable aircraft, including the DR1 Triplane, D7 and EIII fighters of the First World War, the Fokker F.VII3m inter-war airliner and the Fokker F.27 Friendship turboprop airliner. The Fokker S-11 Instructor primary trainer was produced to replace the Tiger Moth in that role. Two prototypes were followed by thirty-nine for the Netherlands, and forty-one for Israel. 180 were built under license in Italy and a further 100 in Brazil, together with fifty of a nosewheel version, the T-22. A number are still flying in Europe (UK, Netherlands, Belgium) and one aircraft appears on the U.S. register.

Foster-Wikner

The Foster-Wikner Wicko single-engine, high wing light aircraft was initially built in Bow Common, London and first flown in September 1936. A total of ten were built.

G-AFJB, the last surviving Wicko seen at Popham, Hampshire in August 2006 flying again after extensive rebuild in the workshops of Ron Souch.

Found Brothers Aviation

This company designed and developed a high-wing cantilever monoplane for Canadian bush operations. The initial design, the FBA-1 was developed into the all-metal FBA-2, which first flew in August 1960. The FBA-2B had a tricycle undercarriage, whereas the FBA-2C had a tailwheel; both versions could be fitted with floats or skis. In December 2013, a total of thirty-two Found models appeared on the U.S. register and twenty-seven on the Canadian register. Later developments under Found Aircraft included the FBA-2C1 Bush Hawk, FBA-2C2 Bush Hawk-XP and the FBA-2C3 Expedition 350, which became the production model from 2007.

Found FBA-2C CF-RXD of BC Air Lines. *Charles Ford Collection*

2003 Found FBA-2C1 Bush Hawk C-FKAC of Bamaji Air, Ontario. *Jan Koppen www.oldjets.net*

C-GEXY is a Found FBA-2C3 Expedition 350 owned by Steve Halls. *Steve Halls*

Fournier

René Fournier originated a family of motor gliders and light aircraft that were manufactured in France (Alpavia), Germany (Sportavia-Putzer) and the UK (Slingsby), the German and British companies continuing development to produce further related types. In the light of this, the main discussion of the RF4 and RF5 and their derivatives is presented under Sportavia. Similarly, the Fournier RF6-derived Slingsby T.67 is presented under Slingsby.

RF1, RF2 and RF3. Fournier's first motor glider, the RF1 F-PJGX was flown in May 1960, powered by a 25hp Volkswagen. It was a clean, low wing, high aspect ratio monoplane with single-seat and retractable undercarriage. Two examples of the RF2 were built, the first flying in May 1962. The production version was the RF3, built by Alpavia who produced ninety-five aircraft, the first flying in March 1963.

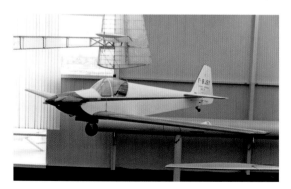

The second Fournier RF2 displayed in the Musée de L'Air et Aérospace at Le Bourget, Paris, France.

G-BCWK is a production Fournier RF3 built in 1964 and photographed at Cranfield, Bedfordshire.

G-BOLC is the prototype RF6B (previously F-WPXV) landing at Dunkeswell, Devon.

G-BLWH is a Fournier RF6B-100 c/n7 also seen at Dunkeswell, Devon.

Fournier RF4. The RF4 is a fully aerobatic version of the RF3, externally distinguished by the rounded lower edge to the fuselage. Two aircraft were built in France before manufacture was transferred to Sportavia-Putzer at Dahlemer-Binz in Germany, who built 155 as the RF4D.

Fournier RF5. The RF5 was a two-seat development of the RF4 powered by a 68hp Limbach SL1700E engine. A single prototype was followed by production of 126 by Sportavia-Putzer, who carried out further development. At least two have been homebuilt in France. Twelve additional aircraft were built in Spain as the AeroJaén RF5-AJ1 Serrania, between 1992 and 1999.

Fournier RF6B. The RF6B is a fully aerobatic wooden, two-seat, side-by-side, low wing monoplane that was first flown in March 1974 powered by a Continental C-90. The main production versions were the RF6B-100, and the RF6B-120 with 115hp Lycoming O-235, around forty-five being built. Slingsby in the UK took over the production rights to the Fournier RF6B completing ten aircraft from French-built components, these being completed as the wooden T67A. Further development as the all-composite Slingsby Firefly is presented under the entry for Slingsby (also see Sportavia for the RS6-180 four-seater).

Fournier RF7. The RF7 is essentially a Fournier RF4 with reduced wingspan fitted with the more powerful engine of the two-seat RF5. The prototype F-WPXV was built in France, subsequently being registered D-EHAP, G-EHAP and G-LRTF in Germany. One example has been homebuilt in France.

Fournier RF7 D-EHAP at Sportavia-Putzer, Dahlemer Binz awaiting application of its registration. This aircraft was later G-EHAP and G-LTRF.

The prototype Fournier RF9 F-CARF (previously F-WARF) at Wroughton, Wiltshire.

Fournier RF8. A single prototype F-WSOY, similar to an all-metal RF5 with a 115hp engine.

Fournier RF9. This two-seat wooden motor glider with side-by-side seating was first flown in January 1977. Twelve were built, with further development as the Fournier RF10.

Fournier RF10. The RF10 is a composite derivative of the Fournier RF9. Initially flown with a low-set tailplane, a T-tail was introduced with the third aircraft and about twenty-one were built. Further development took place in Brazil as the Aeromot AMT100 Ximango and AMT 200 Super Ximango, which have built in some numbers.

Fournier RF10 c/n 4 at the Paris Air Show, Le Bourget, France.

F-WNDF is the prototype RF47 as the Paris Air Show, Le Bourget, France.

Fournier RF47. The last Fournier model is the RF47, first flown in April 1993. A two-seat low wing monoplane with a tricycle undercarriage, the RF47 has not yet entered production although a number have been built, with five appearing on the French register in December 2013.

Fuji

Fuji LM-1, KM-2. Japanese manufacturer Fuji built Beech T-34 Mentors under licence and developed from this type a four-seat derivative, the Fuji LM 1 Nikko. Twenty-seven LM-1s were built for the JGSDF, together with sixty-one of the similar KM-2, which was used as a two-seat trainer by the JMSDF. Nine LM-1s appeared on the U.S. register in December 2013.

1960 Fuji LM-1 Nikko N2105N at Oshkosh, Wisconsin.

G-BBRC is a 1973 FA-200-180 photographed at Compton Abbas, Wiltshire.

Fuji FA-200 Subaru. The Subaru is a four-seat touring aircraft, which was first flown in August 1965. A total of 274 were built with either 160hp or 180hp engines. Twelve Fuji-200s were registered in the UK in December 2013.

Funk Aircraft

The Funk Model B first flew in 1933. A range of models was available, the most important being the B75L (75hp Lycoming) and B85C (85hp Continental). 151 were built pre-war and a further 229 post-war. In June 2014, just over 120 Funk Model B were listed on the U.S. civil aircraft register.

N1606N is a 1946 Funk B85C photographed at Oshkosh, Wisconsin

The prototype Gatard Statoplan AG03 Poussin F-PHUO at the RSA Rally, Brienne-le-Chateau, France.

Gatard Statoplan

Gatard Statoplan AG02 Poussin. The Poussin is a small single-seat low wing monoplane. Designed for home construction, it has an unusual longitudinal control system. A combination of all-moving tailplane and wing flaps are used to enable the aircraft to climb with minimal changes in fuselage attitude. First flown in 1957, there were nine examples on the French register in January 2014.

Gazuit-Valledeau

The Gazuit-Valledeau GV1020/GV1031 Gazelle is a two to four-seat low wing monoplane that was first flown in May 1969. A range of variants was proposed with different engines. At least seven were built and there were plans for license production in Canada that did not come to fruition.

F-BSQE is a Gazuit-Valledeau GV1031 c/n 03, photographed in Canada in the Vancouver, BC area. This and one other aircraft remained on the French register in January 2014, but may not be active.

The third F.20 Pegaso, photographed near Milan, Italy.

General Avia

General Avia was set up by Stelio Frati, the Italian designer, for prototype construction and product development. The F.20 Pegaso is a light cabin twin, similar to a Cessna 310 with two 300hp IO-520 engines. First flown in October 1971, three were built, together with the prototype of a turboprop powered military version, the F.20TP Condor, flown in May 1983.

F.22 Pinguino. The F.22A is an all-metal low wing two-seat light aircraft which first flew in 1989 powered by a 115hp Lycoming O-235. The F.22B is similar, with a 160hp engine. The higher-performance F.22C Sprint features either a fixed or retractable undercarriage and is powered by a 180hp Lycoming IO-360. The F.22R has a retractable undercarriage and 160hp O-320 engine. More than twenty-five F.22s have been built.

General Avia F.22C Sprint I-GEAH at the Paris Air Show with F.22B Pinguino I-GEAG in background.

VH-RSD is a Gere Sport powered by a Rotec radial engine and photographed at Avalon, VIC, Australia in 2007. *Jim Smith*

Gere

The Gere Sport single-seat biplane was first flown in 1932 and plans were published in 1933 in *Modern Mechanix and Inventions* magazine for home-building. The design was later to become the starting point for the EAA biplane. A number have been constructed more recently in the United States, Argentina, New Zealand and Australia.

GippsAero

Gippsland GA-8 Airvan. The Airvan is a rugged utility aircraft designed to fit between the Cessna 206 and Cessna Caravan. First flown in March 1995, the type has been extremely successful worldwide with fleets (January 2014) including Australia (56), U.S. (26), South Africa (18), UK (6), France (5) as well as sales to many other countries. A ten-seat turboprop development, the GA-10 is under development.

VH-BPL is a Gippsland GA-8 Airvan c/n 117, photographed at Avalon, VIC, Australia. *Jim Smith*

VH-BYB is a 1946 Globe GC-1B Swift seen landing at Echuca, VIC, Australia in April 2013.

Globe (Temco)

Globe Swift and Temco Swift. The Swift is a high performance, two-seat, low wing, retractable undercarriage monoplane that was first flown in 1942. It was mass produced post-war as the GC-1A (85hp) or GC-1B (125hp). Production comprised three prototypes and 408 GC-1As and 1,094 GC-1Bs. Production was sub-contracted to Temco, who took over the type certificate in 1947. The aircraft remains popular, with large numbers flying worldwide; sixty-two GC-1As and 666 GC-1Bs were listed on the U.S. register in January 2014.

GlosAir

Victa Airtourer aircraft assembled in the UK by GlosAir are covered under the Victa Airtourer entry.

Granger

The Granger Archaeopteryx is a tailless ultralight single-seat aircraft with a parasol wing. The sole example was first flown in October 1930 and is preserved at The Shuttleworth Trust, Old Warden, UK.

The unique and rarely flown Granger Archaeopteryx at The Shuttleworth Trust, Old Warden, Bedfordshire. *Jim Smith*

NR718L is a 1984 Gee Bee Model Y replica (the second of two Gee Bee Y was registered NR718Y)

Granville Brothers

Gee Bee racers. The Granville Brothers of Springfield, Massachusetts, produced a series of racing aircraft in the 1930s. The most extreme was the 'flying barrel,' the Pratt & Whitney Wasp-powered Gee Bee R1/R2 Super Sportster. In view of their outstanding performance and extraordinary design, the Gee Bee series has been kept alive in the form of some superb full-size flying replicas.

Gee Bee Model Y Senior Sportster. Two built in 1931, both of which were destroyed in accidents.

Only one Gee Bee Model Z Super Sportster was built, winning the Thompson Trophy in 1931, before being destroyed in a fatal accident.

1996 Gee Bee Model Z flying replica NR77V in Kermit Weeks' collection at Polk City, Florida. This collection also holds a flyable Gee Bee R2 Super Sportster replica NR2101.

G-BUPV is a 1932 Kinner-powered Great Lakes ST-1A, photographed at Cranfield, Bedfordshire.

Great Lakes

Great Lakes ST-1A Sport Trainer. The popular Sport Trainer first flew in 1929 and was originally supplied with an American Cirrus inline engine. Some 260 were built before production stopped in 1933, many aircraft being re-engined with more powerful engines, such as the Jacobs radial.

The Great Lakes Sport Trainer had a resurgence in the 1970s, when it was put back into production in 1973 as the 2T-1A-1 and 2T-1A-2, with revised structures and modern 140hp or 180hp Lycoming engines. Around 150 were built, along with a small number of homebuilt examples. Many remain active.

A new build Great Lakes Sport Trainer at Oshkosh, Wisconsin in 1985.

Grinvalds G.802 Orion F-WZLX photographed at the RSA Rally at Brienne Le Chateau, France.

Grinvalds

Grinvalds Orion. The G.801/G.802 Orion is a four-seat, all-composite touring aircraft. It is a low wing monoplane with a retractable undercarriage and a 'buried' engine installation driving a pusher propeller at the rear of the fuselage. The G.801 prototype flew in June 1981, followed by the G.802 in November 1983 with an enlarged cabin and other revisions. Aerodis America Inc became a distributor in 1983 and the first U.S. aircraft flew in 1984. Jean Grinvalds died in 1985 and this impacted on the further development of the type. Homebuilt aircraft have appeared with a number of names including DG-87 Goeland, Gerfaut, Gypaète, Scorpion and AA200. About twenty have been completed.

Grob

Grob is chiefly known for the production of glass fiber sailplanes. The Grob G109 is a two-seat side-by-side motor glider and touring aircraft, which first flew in March 1980. The G109B featured increased engine power to 90hp. Production comprised 151 G109 and 377 G109B for a total of 528 aircraft.

1985 Grob G109B landing at Popham, Hampshire in July 2014.

G-MERF is a 1989 Grob G115A photographed at Dunkeswell, Devon, UK.

Grob 115. The Grob 115 is a two-seat training and touring aircraft. The G115 first flew in November 1985, powered by a 115hp Lycoming O-235 engine. A number of higher-powered variants include the G115B, C, D, and E, 117 of the latter being ordered to replace the Scottish Aviation Bulldog in RAF service. The Egyptian Air Force operates a fleet of seventy-four aircraft. The type remains in production.

Groppo

The Groppo Trail is an Italian all metal high wing kit built aircraft seating two in tandem and designed by Nando Groppo. A tricycle undercarriage variant is known as the Groppo XL. Styling is somewhat angular with a flat-sided fuselage and a large swept fin. Quick-folding wings are also incorporated in the design. The type was first announced in 2009, the first UK-built aircraft flying in 2011. In June 2014, twelve were registered in the UK and around fifty were believed to be flying in total.

Groppo Trail G-CHZT taxying after a flight from its home base of Henstridge, Somerset in May 2014.

Grumman

Grumman is a famous name in aviation, the producer of many notable naval aircraft. The company was founded in 1930 and its roll-call of famous products includes the Grumman F3F biplane, the Wildcat, Hellcat, Bearcat, Tigercat, F9F Panther and Cougar, F-11 Tiger and F-14 Tomcat carrier-borne fighters. Other notable naval aircraft include the TBF/TBM Avenger torpedo bomber, the A-6 Intruder and EA-6 Prowler and a series of twin-prop carrier cargo, ASW, electronic intelligence and AEW aircraft, the Trader, Tracker, Tracer, Greyhound and Hawkeye. 380 OV-1 Mohawk were built for the U.S. Army for observation and counter-insurgency operations.

The company has been less active in the civil field, producing the twin turboprop Grumman Gulfstream I and the twin engine executive jet, the Gulfstream II, which has been subject to continuous development into a large family of aircraft by Gulfstream American and remains in production and development in various forms as this is written in 2014. One other notable civilian type is the Grumman Ag Cat agricultural biplane, nearly 2,500 of which have been built.

Grumman bought an interest in light aircraft with the acquisition of American Aviation, forming the Grumman American subsidiary. These types were also later taken over by Gulfstream American, but are described in this work under American Aviation.

The company's final design class is a series of amphibious aircraft, including the Duck, Goose, Widgeon, Mallard and Albatross. These remaining types are now mostly flown under private ownership and are discussed below.

Grumman Duck. The Grumman Duck is a single-engine biplane, whose lower fuselage is adapted as a single float hull or pontoon, fitted with a retractable undercarriage to provide amphibious capability. The undercarriage installation is reminiscent of that used by Grumman's pre-war carrier fighter biplanes such as the F3F. The JF Duck first flew in 1933, but the main production model was the J2F, which was built from 1936. Production comprised forty-eight Grumman JFs and 584 Grumman J2Fs. Six aircraft were listed on the U.S. register in January 2014.

Grumman J2F-6 Duck on display as part of Kermit Weeks' collection at Polk City, Florida.

N4575C is a 1945 Grumman G-21A seen at an event called Sea Wings 2000 at Southampton, Hampshire.

Grumman G-21 (JRF) Goose. The Grumman Goose is a twin engine amphibious flying boat, originally designed as an eight seat civilian commuter aircraft. The type was widely used as the JRF Goose during the Second World War, including by the RAF and RCAF as well as the U.S. Navy and Coastguard. Power was provided by two 450hp Pratt & Whitney Wasp engines and the type's performance and capacity made it of enduring use for small airline and utility work post-war.

Turbo-Goose. A number of Grumman Goose have been modified to accept twin turboprop engines, particularly by McKinnon Enterprises. Their first modification was to fit four piston engines as the G-21C, but this was not proceeded with. Most McKinnon aircraft have twin PT-6A engines, but one aircraft, N221AG, was fitted with Garrett TP331 turboprops in Alaska.

Garrett-powered G-21G Turbo-Goose N221AG on display at the Farnborough Air Show in 2010. This aircraft was originally converted by the Alaska Fish and Wildlife Service. This aircraft was originally registered N780 and was previously photographed by the author in that guise at Merrill Field, Alaska.

N444M is a re-engined Grumman G-44A photographed on the airstrip at Badminton House.

Grumman G-44 Widgeon. The Widgeon five-seat light twin amphibian first flew in 1940 and was originally fitted with Ranger in-line engines; many of those still operating have been re-engined. 317 were built, including forty-one built under license in France. Many of the upgrades were done by McKinnon Enterprises, who styled the type as the McKinnon Super Widgeon.

Grumman HU-16 Albatross. The Albatross is a large twin engine amphibious flying boat first flown in 1947 and used by the U.S. Navy, Air Force and Coastguard, primarily for search and rescue operations. A total of 466 were built, with a number of retired ex-service aircraft now operating with private owners. Some fifty-two examples were listed on the U.S. register in January 2013.

Grumman HU-16D Albatross N693S parked outside the EAA Museum at Lakeland, Florida.

Gyroflug

Gyroflug Speed Canard. The SC01 Speed Canard is a German tandem two-seat canard light aircraft with a pusher propeller, whose design is inspired by the designs of Bert Rutan, but was developed independently. The cockpit is based on that of the Grob Twin Astir two-seat sailplane. The type was first flown in 1980 and sixty-two were built.

G-FLUG is a 1989 Gyroflug SCO1B-160 Speed Canard, photographed at Cranfield, Bedfordshire. *Jim Smith*

1940 Harlow PJC-2 N3947B at Oshkosh, Wisconsin.

Harlow

The Harlow PJC-2 is an all-metal four-seat low wing monoplane. The PJC-2 is the production version of the PJC-1, which flew for the first time in September 1947. Eleven PJC-2s were built, some six of which remain on the U.S. register. Power is provided by a 145hp Warner Super Scarab radial engine.

Hatz

The Hatz CB-1 biplane is a very conventional two-seat open cockpit biplane with a steel tube fuselage and wooden wings, designed for home construction. First flown in April 1968, the type has proved popular, particularly in the U.S., where more than 100 appeared on the register in January 2014.

2012 Hatz CB-1 N225 at San Clemente, California in October 2013. *Peter Davison*

G-CAMM is a full-size replica of the diminutive Hawker Cygnet built by Don Cashmore. It was photographed at The Shuttleworth Trust, Old Warden, Bedfordshire.

Hawker Aircraft Ltd.

The Hawker Company was formed from Sopwith Aviation and Engineering Co. Ltd. after the First World War and is famous for the design of RAF fighter aircraft from the Demon and Fury through to the Hurricane, Hunter and Harrier.

Hawker Cygnet. The Cygnet is notable as Sidney Camm's first design. Two were built (G-EBJH and G-EBMB) powered by the 32hp Bristol Cherub engine and entered in the 1924 and 1926 Two-seat Light Aeroplane Trials, being the clear winners of the 1926 competition. G-EBMB is displayed in the RAF Museum at Cosford, Shropshire.

Hawker Tomtit. The Tomtit was a trainer for the RAF and for civil use – production comprised the prototype, five civil machines, twenty-four RAF aircraft, two for the RCAF, and four for the RNZAF – a total of thirty-six aircraft

K1786/G-AFTA is the last flying Hawker Tomtit, built in 1931 and seen at Old Warden, Bedfordshire.

N752Y is a 1930 Heath LNB-4 photographed at Oshkosh, Wisconsin.

Heath

The Heath Parasol is a homebuilt parasol monoplane dating from 1926. Many were built in the 1930s from kits and from plans published in *Modern Mechanix* magazine, together with some factory built aircraft. Relatively few of these early machines survive. The type has also been built more recently by homebuilders to plans published by the Experimental Airplane Association.

Helio Aircraft

The chief product of the Helio Aircraft Corporation (and its successors) is the Helio Courier short take-off and landing aircraft. This aircraft, with its full span automatic slots, effective flap system and excellent low speed handling was derived following tests of the Koppen-Bollinger Helioplane, which was based on a highly modified Piper PA-15 Vagabond.

The Helioplane (or Helio-1) N9390H forms part of the National Air and Space Museum collection and was photographed at Oshkosh, Wisconsin.

N242B is the sole Helio 391 Courier (c/n 001) 'Ole No 1' seen at Oshkosh, Wisconsin.

Helio Courier and Super Courier. The Courier was the production aircraft that built on experimentation with the Helioplane. A range of variants were built with different engine power and designations. Following a single H391, the first production models were the H391B and H395 Super Courier. The H392 Strato Courier had a 340hp engine and was intended for high altitude use. The H250 and H295 variants had a longer rear fuselage, with the HT295 being fitted with a tricycle undercarriage. Different production numbers can be found, the combined total for these models is around 483 aircraft, plus eighteen examples of the later H-700/H800 models.

There have been a number of derivatives of the Helio Courier airframe, including the twin engine H500 Helio Twin and a ten seat turboprop STOL model using the same high lift technology, the H550/550A Stallion.

N88726 is a non-standard Helio H-395 Super Courier turboprop conversion (Allison 250 powered) seen at Oshkosh, Wisconsin, in 1985. This aircraft was subsequently sold to Brazil as PP-ZVJ.

G-LARK is a Helton Lark 95 photographed at Cranfield, Bedfordshire.

Helton

Helton Lark. The Helton Lark 95 is, in effect, a revised version of the PQ-8 a target drone version of the Culver Cadet. The Lark is a two-seat side-by-side low wing monoplane with a fixed tricycle undercarriage and sliding cockpit canopy. Designed by Al Mooney, the Lark has the same elliptical wing planform as its Culver predecessors. A prototype and sixteen production aircraft were built. Six remained on the U.S. register in June 2014.

Hindustan Aeronautics Ltd. (HAL)

Hindustan Aeronautics of Bangalore has designed and manufactured a wide range of aircraft of its own design in addition to the licensed manufacture of aircraft such as the Hawker Siddeley 748, Sepecat Jaguar and BAE Systems Hawk. The Hindustan HT2 was a primary trainer fulfilling the same role as the De Havilland Canada Chipmunk and was first flown in August 1951. More than 150 were built.

Hindustan HT-2 IX737 of the IAF Historic Flight in the Indian Air Force Museum, Palam, New Delhi.

G-AVPO is a 1967 Hindustan HAL 26 Pushpak, photographed at Cranfield, Bedfordshire. This aircraft was imported into the UK in 1983.

The HAL 26 Pushpak is a license-built version of the Aeronca 11 Chief. Some 160 were built for use by civilian flying clubs. Fifty remained on the Indian civil register in January 2014.

Hindustan HAOP-27 Krishak. The Krishak started life as a four-seat civilian development of the Pushpak, broadly similar in concept to the Aeronca 15 Sedan. Two civil prototypes were followed by seventy aircraft modified for Army observation use as the HAOP-27.

HAOP-27 Krishak N949 at the Indian Air Force Museum. This aircraft may fly with the IAF Historic Flight.

Hirth

Wolf Hirth Gmbh built a competition aerobatic aircraft, the Hirth Acrostar, to the design of the Swiss aerobatic champion Arnold Wagner. The Acrostar Mk.II first flew in April 1970. The aircraft, with its zero dihedral, symmetrical wing section and control system linking the ailerons and flaps to the elevator system, is designed to have the same handling characteristics upright or inverted. The aircraft performed well at both European and World Championships. Nine Acrostar Mk.II were built followed by a single, lighter, Acrostar Mk.III.

Hirth Acrostar II EC-CBS at Cuatro Vientos, Madrid, September 2006. *Robert Hodgson 2006*

Hoffmann

Hoffmann Dimona. The H-36 Dimona motor glider seats two side-by-side and has been extremely popular, with more than 900 being built. The Dimona was first flown in October 1980. Although originating under Hoffmann, the company has evolved via HOAS into Diamond Aircraft, who have continued development with different engine options. A tricycle undercarriage version is also available.

G-BLCV is a 1984 Hoffmann H36 Dimona on the airstrip at Badminton House Estate.

G-KATA is a 1993 HOAC DV20 Katana photographed at Shobdon, Herefordshire.

Hoffmann (Diamond Aircraft) Katana. The DV20 Katana was developed by HOAS initially as the LF2000. This was a clipped wing version of the Super Dimona with a tricycle undercarriage for private ownership and flight training. Development continued after the change of company name to Diamond Aircraft and a number of variants are available with different engine choices. More than 600 have been built. A four-seat derivative is the DA40 Diamond Star. Diamond also produces the twin engine diesel-powered DA42 Twin Star. In June 2014, ten Katana were registered in the UK.

Holste

Holste MH1521 Broussard. The Broussard is perhaps the best-known design by Max Holste. Designed to meet a very similar requirement to that of the De Havilland Canada DHC2 Beaver, the Broussard is powered by a 450hp Pratt & Whitney Wasp Junior. Developed from the lower-powered MH152, the Broussard flew in November 1952. Including prototypes and pre-production aircraft, a total of 396 Broussard were built.

G-BKPU is a 1960 Holste MH1521 Broussard photographed at Henstridge, Somerset.

1988 Hovey Whing Ding II G-MBAB photographed at Cranfield, Bedfordshire.

Hovey

Bob Hovey has designed a number of minimalist light aircraft for home construction. These include the Whing Ding II, Delta Bird, Delta Hawk and Beta Bird.

The Whing Ding is a diminutive pusher biplane, the Whing Ding II first flying in January 1971. Unusually, the type uses wing warping rather than ailerons for lateral control. The structure consists of a plywood box fuselage keel and interwing structure, with a tubular tail cone to support the tail surfaces. At least

13,000 sets of plans were sold, but it is not clear how many projects were completed and remain active.

The Whing Ding was followed by the Delta Bird and Delta Hawk tractor biplanes. These were followed by the Beta Bird, which is a high wing pusher monoplane, with a fuselage structure that is essentially a scaled-up version of that of the Whing Ding. The Beta Bird first flew in April 1979; 350 sets of plans were sold and at least six are believed to have been flown.

G-BKRV is a 1988 Hovey Beta Bird photographed at Cranfield, Bedfordshire.

1944 Howard DGA-15P N3347G at San Clemente in October 2013. *Peter Davison*

Howard

Howard DGA-15. The Howard high-wing monoplanes were aimed at the high performance quality market sector addressed by other well-known types such as the Beech 17 Staggerwing and the WACO series of biplanes. The type has its origin in Benny Howard's DGA-6 racing monoplane 'Mister Mulligan.' DGA is said to have stood for 'Damn Good Airplanes' and the five-seat DGA-15 remains in demand as a high performance classic. In wartime, the type served as a fast transport and instrument trainer, particularly with the U.S. Navy as the GH-1 or NH-1 Nightingale. More than 500 were built.

Hummell

The Hummel Bird is a small single-seat low wing monoplane. It is a derivative of the Parker Teenie via the Watson Windwagon, and is typically powered by one half of a VW engine. Related types are the Hummel Ultracruiser and the H5, all of which a small LSA-compliant light aircraft.

N213TD is a Hummel Bird photographed at San Clemente in October 2013. *Peter Davison*

Hunting

The Hunting Percival P.56 Provost prototype flew for the first time on 23 February 1950. In addition to 391 aircraft for the RAF, the Provost was widely exported with total production being 461 aircraft. Eighteen have appeared on the British civil register, five of these being current in January 2014.

P.56 Provost XF836/G-AWRY photographed at the hilltop airfield of Compton Abbas, Wiltshire.

IAR (Romanian Aeronautical Industry)

IAR has a long history of building a very wide range of military and civil aircraft since 1925, including piston and jet engine fighters, gliders, agricultural aircraft, light aircraft, and latterly helicopters. Production has included the company's own designs and aircraft built under license. Notable products include the IAR 80 Second World War fighter, and the IAR 823 four-seat light aircraft.

IAR IS-28 motor gliders. The IAR or ICA Brasov IS-28M is a motorglider derivative of the IS-28 sailplane. The aircraft seats two side-by-side and has a narrow track retractable undercarriage, the wheels retracting rearwards into the wing roots. The type has been produced in a number of models in both long span and short span versions. The main production variant

IAR 823 N823PB at Lakeland, Florida in April 2008. *Peter Davison*

IAR IS-28M2A G-BMMX at Cranfield, Bedfordshire.

IAR 831 Pelican prototype YR-IGA at the Paris Air Show, Le Bourget, France.

YR-1026 is the first IS-28MA photographed at the Paris Air Show, Le Bourget, France.

IAR 823. This four-seat retractable undercarriage low wing monoplane was first flown in June 1973. It was mainly used as a trainer by the Romanian Air Force and some seventy-eight were built. Thirty-seven IAR 823s appeared on the U.S. civil register in January 2014.

IAR 831 Pelican. The Pelican was a derivative of the IAR 823, seating two in tandem. The prototype was flown in 1983 and displayed at the Parish Air Show, but did not enter production. This aircraft is, in effect, a piston engine version of the IAR 825TP Triumf.

has been the seventeen- meter span IS-28M2 that first flew in July 1976. The IS-28 MA is a reduced-span version. The IS-28M2 is powered by a Limbach SL1700E converted Volkswagen engine, the IS-28MA having a Limbach 2000E engine. Production of all variants is believed to be around eighty-five aircraft.

The prototype IAR-46 YR-1037 photographed at the Paris Air Show, Le Bourget, France.

IAR 46. The IAR 46 is a Rotax-powered derivative of the IS-28 series designed for certification against JAR VLA (very light aircraft) requirements. At least two prototypes have been built, but the type has not entered production. The type first flew in 1993 and certification was achieved in November 1999.

Ikarus

Ikarus C42. The Ikarus C42 is a highly successful German light training aircraft that first flew in 1996. It is Rotax-powered and seats two side-by-side, one notable feature being the somewhat stalky tricycle undercarriage. The type has become very popular with flying clubs and flight training schools due to its low operating costs and 172 appeared on the UK register in January 2014. More than 1,000 have been built.

2008 Ikarus C42 G-CFIT taking off from Henstridge, Somerset in July 2013.

Ilyushin Il-103 RA-10300 on display at the Paris Air Show, Le Bourget, France.

Ilyushin

The Ilyushin design bureau is associated with the famous Il-2 Shturmovik ground attack aircraft of the Second World War, the Il-28 'Beagle' light bomber and a series of civil and military transport aircraft including the Il-14, Il-18. Il-62, Il-76 and Il-86 types.

Ilyushin Il-103. The Il-103 is Ilyushin's only light aircraft product. This four/five-seat low wing monoplane first flew in May 1994. The type has mainly won orders with military air arms, including those of Laos, South Korea and Peru. At the time of writing, some sixty-six had been built.

Iniziative Industriali Italiane '3I' Sky Arrow

The Sky Arrow is a tandem seat all-composite light aircraft with a high wing pusher layout. It was first flown in July 1992. After the failure of 3I, the design was taken over by Magnaghi Aeronautica. The aircraft has been produced in a number of variants meeting different certification requirements with engines ranging from 80hp to 115hp. In April 2014, thirty-eight appeared on the U.S. civil register, with thirteen in the UK, three in Canada and two in Australia.

1999 Sky Arrow 650TC G-ROME photographed at Old Sarum, Wiltshire.

N49066 is a 1943 Interstate S-1B1 Cadet, photographed in May 1983 at Lake Hood Airstrip, Anchorage, Alaska.

Interstate

The Interstate S-1B1 Cadet was operated during the Second World War as the L-6A Grasshopper and some 321 were built. The type was subsequently developed into the S-1B2 Arctic Tern. More than 100 remain listed on the U.S. civil register, although it is not clear how many of these are active.

Isaacs

After the Second World War, the Hampshire Aero Club revived the pre-war Currie Wot single-seat biplane. One of the club members, John Isaacs, then further re-worked the design introducing wing stagger and a rounded fin shape reminiscent of the inter-War series of Hawker biplane fighters. The result was the Isaacs Fury. The prototype G-ASCM was flown in August 1963 and the type has proved popular with homebuilders, particularly in the UK, where sixteen were registered in June 2004.

Ron Martin's award-winning 1984 Isaacs Fury II G-BIYK flies past at Dunkeswell, Devon.

1975 Isaacs Spitfire G-BBJI photographed at Cranfield, Bedfordshire.

Isaacs Spitfire. John Isaacs designed and built a wooden sixth tenths scale replica Spitfire G-BBJI. This aircraft first flew in May 1975, the author being part of the team that moved the incomplete aircraft to Thruxton for final assembly prior to its first flight. A second aircraft G-BOXM has subsequently been built and flown in the UK.

G-OZZI is a 1998 two-seat Jabiru SK, kit-built to meet Class A requirements, photographed at Henstridge, Somerset.

Jabiru Aircraft

Jabiru manufactures and sells kits of a highly successful two-seat and four-seat single-engine light aircraft.

The two-seat design is certificated in different categories including as an ultralight and a Light Sport Aircraft (LSA) and as a fully certificated light aircraft. The two-seat version is also available in either nosewheel or tailwheel configuration. Model designations distinguish between factory and kit-built aircraft, certification standard and engine power. Examples of the two-seat and four-seat configuration are shown below. In January 2014, there were 157 Jabiru aircraft on the UK civil register. Jabiru sales data, kindly supplied at the end of January 2014, indicated the following total sales (kit and factory-built): 852 J230; 358 J160/J170; 68 J120; 669 UL/SP/SK/LSA giving a grand total of 1,947 aircraft and kits.

G-PHYZ is a 2008 four-seat Jabiru 430 seen at Dunkeswell, Devon in January 2014.

Janowski J-5 photographed at Cranfield, Bedfordshire.

Janowski

The Janowski J-5 (also known as the Marco J-5 or Alpha Marco J-5) is a diminutive all-composite single-seater with a mid-wing, a pusher 25hp KFM engine immediately behind the cockpit pod and a butterfly tail. Designed in Poland, kits were made available to homebuilders. The J-5 first flew in October 1983 and at least twenty have been built with aircraft flying in France, UK, Germany and the USA.

Javelin

The Javelin Wichawk is a conventional biplane, seating two occupants side-by-side. Designed for kit building, the type was first flown in May 1971. Eighteen aircraft have appeared on the U.S. civil register, with nine being listed in January 2014.

The first Javelin Wichawk N71DB, built by Dave Blanton in 1971 and photographed at Oshkosh, Wisconsin.

N78WB is a 1981 Jeffair Barracuda powered by a Lycoming IO-540 engine and seen at Oshkosh, Wisconsin in 1985.

Jeffair

The Jeffair Barracuda is a high performance wooden two-seat homebuilt low wing monoplane. The type first flew in June 1975. Fitted with a retractable undercarriage and typically provided with a 220hp engine, a high climb rate and 200 mph cruising speed are available. A significant number of plans have been sold and in January 2014, twenty-five were listed on the U.S. civil register.

Jodel

The inspired and characteristic cranked wing design of the Jodel was first seen in the air in January 1948 with the first flight of the single-seat Jodel D9 Bébé designed by Edouard Joly and Jean Delemontez whose abbreviated surnames led to the name Jodel. This was the start of a huge family of aircraft spanning the years and including numerous factory- and amateur-built aircraft. Three main groups are dealt with separately in this work the 'Jodels' (this entry), Centre Est designs (the DR200 to DR360) and Avions Pierre Robin designs (the DR400 and subsequent designs).

Aircraft discussed in this Jodel entry include the D9 single-seat aircraft; the two-seat D11 and its derivatives including the D112, D117, D119, D120 and others; the three-seat (or 2+2) DR100 and related types (DR105, DR1050, DR1051, DR1050M, DR1051M); the five-seat 180hp D140 Mousquetaire; the two-seat long range D150 Mascaret; and the homebuilt two-seat D18 and D19. These types are grouped under 'Jodel' irrespective of their actual individual manufacture. Manufacturers involved in production of this group of machines include the following companies: Avions Jodel, Aerodifusion, Aero Jodel, Alpavia, Denize, SAN, Centre Est Aeronautique, Wassmer. Jodel types have also been built by numerous individuals and to plans created by Falconar in Canada and Frank Rogers in Australia, among others.

Jodel D9 OO-45 photographed at the RSA Rally at Brienne le Chateau in France.

Jodel D9. The diminutive single-seat D9 is often powered by a VW engine; a range of designations (D91 to D98) relate to alternative powerplants. From its first flight in 1948, the type became extremely popular and more than 500 have been built. Commercial production was undertaken by Denize and Wassmer, but the majority were homebuilt from plans or kits.

Two-seat Jodels D11, D112, D117, D119, D120 etc. The numerically most important group of Jodels are the two-seat versions, generically known as the D11, all of which are externally similar in appearance. The main models are D11 (mostly homebuilt), the 65hp

D112, 90hp D117, D119 (homebuilt D117), and the D120, 337 of which were commercially built by Wassmer. A suffix to the designation is used as follows: 'A' airbrakes,' 'R' Remorqueur glider tow hook, 'T' nosewheel. Additional designations including D113 to D116, D118, and D121 to D126 indicate different engine choices. Commercial production included D112 by Wassmer (350), SAN, Valledau, Denize, Aerodifusion (Spain); D117 by SAN and Alpavia; D119 by Aerodifusion (D119OS Compostella). The Wassmer-built D120 offered an electrical system, and a rear 120-liter fuel tank (for five hours endurance) instead of a fuel tank between the panel and bulkhead.

1976 homebuilt Jodel D11 G-BAPR at Sywell, Northamptonshire.

1963 Wassmer-built Jodel D112 G-BHNL taking off from Henstridge, Somerset in May 2009.

1957 SAN-built Jodel D117 G-AXCG at Dunkeswell, Devon in July 2013.

1957 homebuilt D119 G-BATJ (ex F-PIIQ) at Sywell, Northamptonshire.

F-PYQY is 1983 Jodel D119 TK at Brienne le Chateau in July 1983.

1961 Wassmer Jodel D120A G-ASXU (note airbrakes) landing at Henstridge, Somerset in June 2013.

Jodel three-seat variants (DR100, DR105, DR1050, DR1051) Ambassadeur and Sicile. The development of a three-seat Jodel was down to Pierre Robin. After Robin built a single experimental Jodel-Robin using the wing of the incomplete Jodel D10, M Delemontez joined with M Robin to produce a production three-seat aircraft, the Jodel DR100. Pierre Robin then set up Centre Est Aeronautique to build the type. The DR100 had a Continental C90, the DR105 with hydraulic brakes and the DR105A Ambassadeur with a 100hp Continental engine. Further development led to the DR1050 Ambassadeur and DR1051 Sicile (with 105hp Potez 4E20).

1959 SAN-built Jodel DR100A G-ATHX.

1959 SAN-built Jodel DR105A G-AXLS at Cranfield, Bedfordshire.

1964 CEA-built Jodel DR1050 Ambassadeur G-AWWO at Eggesford, Devon.

1963 CEA-built Jodel DR1051 Sicile G-IOSI at Comptonn Abbas, Wiltshire.

Jodel DR1050-M Excellence and DR1051-M1 Sicile Record. Both SAN and CEA produced improved versions of the DR1050 and DR1051 as the SAN DR1050M Excellence and the CEA DR1050M1 and 1051M1 Sicile Record. The difference in type number 1050 or 1051 related to Continental or Potez power. The Excellence has an empennage like that of the D150 Mascaret, with all-moving tailplane and swept fin with a small, straight dorsal fin. The CEA aircraft have the all-moving tailplane but a curved dorsal fin fillet, like that of later Robin types.

SAN Jodel D140 Mousquetaire. The D140 Mousquetaire, which first flew in July 1958, is a five-seat 180hp growth version of the Jodel (known by some as the 'Big Jodel') that offers an unmatched combination of payload and range. The D140A and B have triangular tail fins. The D140C Mousquetaire III has a taller swept fin, while the D140E Mousquetaire IV introduced an all-flying tailplane, like that used on the D1050M and D150. The final version is the D140R Abiele, equipped for glider towing. A total of 243 Mousquetaire aircraft were built, all by SAN.

1959 G-ATLB SAN-built DR1050M Excellence at Redhill, Surrey.

1961 SAN Jodel D140B G-ARRY at Cranfield, Bedfordshire.

1964 F-BMPH CEA-built DR1051 M1 Sicile Record at Cranfield, Bedfordshire.

SAN Jodel D10E Mousquetaire IV with all-moving tailplane and larger fin and rudder.

The author takes off in his 1963 Jodel D150 Mascaret G-BHVF from Henstridge, Somerset in October 2010. *Neil Wilson*

Jodel D150 Mascaret. Developed by SAN, the D150 Mascaret is a long range two-seat aircraft powered by a 100hp Continental O-200 (D150), or 105hp Potez 4E20 (D150A). Two forty- liter wing root tanks and a 117-liter rear tank provide an endurance of nine hours and a range of around 1,000 miles. The absence of a front tank and an increase of four inches in fuselage width make for a roomy cockpit, while the all-moving tailplane ensures a wide CG range. Sixty-two were built by SAN and more than twenty plans built-aircraft have been constructed in the UK, France, Australia (Sky Prince) and Spain.

Jodel D18 and D19. The Jodel D18 is a homebuilt two-seater designed to be flown with Volkswagen or similar lightweight engines such as the Rotax or Jabiru. The D18 was first flown in the spring of 1984. The D19 is a version with a tricycle undercarriage. In January 2014, there were 111 D18 and forty D19 on the French civil register, with aircraft operating in many other countries.

G-OLEM is a 2005 Jabiru 2200-powered Jodel D18, seen here landing at Henstridge, Somerset.

The sole 1942 Johnson Rocket 125 NX41674 under restoration at Zelwood, Florida.

Johnson

R.S. "Pop" Johnson built the first Globe GC-1 Swift NX17688 in 1941. Although reported "scrapped" by Globe in 1942, the airframe is rumored to have been reclaimed from Globe and modified to create the prototype Johnson Rocket 125 NX41674. The Rocket was subsequently substantially redesigned with a 185hp Lycoming O-435 engine and retractable tricycle undercarriage and put into production as the Johnson Rocket 185. Eighteen were built and six were still listed on the U.S. register in January 2014.

Jurca

Marcel Jurca has designed a number of fighter-like homebuilt aircraft, notably the single-seat MJ-2 Tempête and the two-seat MJ-5 Scirroco. He also produced designs for scale replica warbirds, including the MJ-7/-77 Gnatsum (Scale Mustang), MJ-10/-100 Spitfire, MJ-8/-80 FW190; plans also exist for the MJ-12 Curtis P-40 replica. Data from the marcel-jurca.com website lists the following aircraft built as of January 2014: forty-nine Tempêtes, seventy-eight Sciroccos, around fifteen MJ-7/-77 Gnatsums, four Fw 190s, and five Spitfires.

MJ-2 Tempête. The MJ-2 first flew in June 1956 and can be built from plans (kits are not available for Jurca designs). The aircraft has a low wing with no dihedral and the pilot is sat under a bubble canopy. Construction is of wood throughout. Different engine types are available, although the Continental C-90 is commonly used.

1973 Jurca MJ-2D F-PTER c/n 34 at Brienne le Chateau, France in July 1983.

F-PYLQ is a 1982 MJ-5 Scirocco with retractable undercarriage and 150hp Lycoming O-320 at Brienne le Chateau, France in July 1983.

The MJ-5 Scirocco seats two in tandem and can be built with either a fixed or retractable undercarriage.

The MJ-7 or MJ-77 Gnatsum (Mustang spelt backward) are scale replicas of the P-51D Mustang. The MJ-7 is two-third scale and the MJ-77 is three-quarter scale.

F-PYPG is a 1980 Jurca MJ77 photographed at the RSA Rally, Brienne le Chateau, France in July 1983.

1978 Kaminskas Jungster I C-GPLB seen at Oshkosh, Wisconsin.

Kaminskas

The Kaminskas RK1 Jungster I is a diminutive homebuilt aerobatic wooden biplane that is an 80% scale replica of the Bucker Bu133 Jungmeister. A parasol winged variant is known as the Jungster II. The type was first flown in 1962. A number are flying, particularly in the USA, but also in Canada, France, Sweden and Norway. The FAA site indicates that seven Jungster I and four Jungster II aircraft were registered in the U.S. in January 2014.

K & S Cavalier

The K & S Cavalier (or Squarecraft Cavalier) is a Canadian two-seat wooden homebuilt aircraft derived from the Bearn GY20 Minicab. It can be built with tailwheel or tricycle undercarriage and many aircraft are fitted with wingtip fuel tanks. The aircraft has been popular in Canada, the U.S. and the UK. In January 2014, twenty-seven were registered in Canada; five in the UK, (with a further fifteen listed as deregistered); and more than twenty in the U.S.

N10VM is a 1975 Cavalier SA102.5 photographed at Oshkosh, Wisconsin.

24-4038 is a Kappa KP2U on the Australian Recreational Aircraft register, seen at Temora, NSW, Australia in April 2010. *Jim Smith*

Kappa

The Czech Kappa KP2U Sova or Jilhavan Skyleader is an all-metal two-seat monoplane and is marketed as a kit plane. It first flew in May 1996 and although ownership has passed through a number of hands, well over 200 have been completed with around 150 operating in Europe. Power is normally provided by a Rotax engine.

Kelly

The Kelly-D biplane is a homebuilt biplane based on a larger simplified version of the Hatz CB1 biplane eliminating the separate center section, and with squared-off wingtips. Around twenty have been built and thirteen appeared on the U.S. civil register in January 2014.

Kelly-D N5172S at Lakeland, Florida in April 1990. *Jim Smith*

Salmson-powered 1929 Klemm L-25 1A G-AAUP flies past at Cranfield, Bedfordshire.

Klemm Leichtflugzeugbau GmbH

Klemm L-25. The Klemm L-25 is a long-winged low wing monoplane seating two in tandem in open cockpits. First flown in 1926, a number of variants were built with different engines. More than 600 were manufactured, with license production in the UK (as the British Klemm/British Aircraft Swallow, and the United States (by Aeromarine-Klemm).

Klemm 35. The Klemm 35 is a clean inverted gill-wing monoplane seating two in tandem in open cockpits. The type was adopted as a basic trainer by the Luftwaffe and some 2,000 were built, with license production in Sweden and Czechoslovakia.

The clean lines of 1940 Klemm 35D HB-UBK at Cranfield, Bedfordshire in July 1983.

Kreider Reisner

The Kreider Reisner Aircraft Company was founded in 1926 and became part of the Fairchild Aircraft in 1929. The first series production aircraft of Kreider Reisner was the three-seat C-2A Challenger of 1927, powered by a 90hp Curtiss OX-5 (later re-designated KR31).

A Kinner-powered version was designated C-6B Challenger, being subsequently re-designated KR21A, of which forty-three were built. Twelve KR21s and eleven KR31s were listed on the U.S. civil register in January 2014.

1930 Kreider Reisner (Fairchild) KR21A NC207V photographed at Brodhead, Wisconsin in September 2009. *Gilles Auilard*

1930 Kreider Reisner (Fairchild) KR31 NC10290 flies past at Blakesburg, Iowa in September 2009. *Gilles Auliard*

N66370 is a 1964 L-13 Inc. L-13 conversion photographed at Lake Hood Airstrip, Anchorage, Alaska in May 1983.

L-13 Inc.

300 L-13 liaison and observation aircraft were built by Consolidated Vultee, the first flying in 1945. Several civil conversions were developed once the type left active service, including the L-13 Inc. L-13, the Caribbean Traders Husky and the Centaur 101. Most of these conversions use the 300hp Lycoming R-680 radial in place of the Franklin O-425 engine of the original L-13. Seven L-13 Inc. conversions were completed from 1964.

Laird

After building some forty-five Swallow biplanes and selling the rights to the Swallow Airplane Co, EM Laird set up the EM Laird Airplane Co. in Chicago and built a series of racing biplanes. Most notable were the Solution and Super Solution. The 300hp Solution competed in the 1930 and 1931 Thompson Trophy, while the 535hp Super Solution was flown to victory in the 1931 Bendix Trophy race by Jimmy Doolittle. Flying and non-flying replicas have been built of the Super Solution. Kermit Weeks has a flying replica in his Polk City, FL collection. At least one other replica is believed to be under construction.

Laird Super Solution replica NR12048 at Oshkosh, Wisconsin in 1980 with wheel fairings yet to be fitted.

VH-DQN is a 1984 Lake LA4-200. *Jim Smith*

Lake

The Lake LA4 Buccaneer has its origins in the similarly-configured Colonial Skimmer (C1 two-seat, C2 four-seat), of which some forty-two were built. The company was purchased and renamed Lake Aircraft, who produced the four-seat Lake LA4 in 180hp and 200hp variants. Production of all LA4 variants totaled 834 aircraft.

The Lake LA250 Renegade is a five/six-seat 250hp development of the LA4 with a taller fin of increased sweep. The type was first flown in 1982 and more than 150 have been built. Military versions (Seawolf) have also been marketed.

N84219 is a Lake LA270 Turbo Renegade demonstrator at the 1990 Farnborough Air Show.

1994 Lancair 360 VH-TMR, Temora, NSW, Australia. *Jim Smith*

Lancair

Lancair, founded by Lance Neibauer, produces very high performance all-composite light aircraft designs for kit-building. The first design was the Lancer 200 (100hp O-200), followed by higher power variants, the main model becoming the Lancair 360 with a 180hp Lycoming O-360 engine. With two-seats and a retractable undercarriage, the Lancair 360 offers effortless cruise speeds around 200kt TAS. More than 2,100 Lancair kits have been sold and new products continue to be developed, such as the turboprop Lancair Evolution.

Lancair IV. The Lancair IV is a four-seat development that is also available (IV-P) with a pressurized cabin. A 350hp TSIO-550 engine is normally fitted, offering a cruise speed around 285kt. The Propjet variant uses either a Walter or a Pratt & Whitney PT6 engine and achieves a 300kt cruise speed.

2002 Lancair IV-P Propjet, Avalon, VIC, Australia. *Jim Smith*

OM-CYL Lancair ES at Henstridge, Somerset in July 2011.

G-ARTV is an ex-military Prospector (subsequently N747JC), photographed at Elstree, near London. *Jim Smith*

Lancashire Aircraft

Lancashire Prospector and Edgar Percival EP9. The first EP9 Prospector flew on 21 December 1955. Used for utility and agricultural work, the Prospector enjoyed only modest success. The company was sold in 1958 and the name was changed to Lancashire Aircraft Co. Ltd., the type becoming known as the Lancashire Prospector. When production ceased, a total of twenty-seven Prospector aircraft had been built. Two or three aircraft remain airworthy, together with a similar number displayed in museums.

Laser Akro Z VH-AUZ at a British Aerobatics Association competition at Dunkeswell, Devon. This was the first Laser Aerobatics Akro Z, flown in 1981.

Laser Akro Z (also Laser Z230)

The Laser Z200 and Z230 are competition aerobatic aircraft derived from the Stephens Akro. The Extra 230 and 300 series also trace their design inspiration from these types, with the Stephens Akro, Laser Z230/Akro Z and Extra 230 all being somewhat similar in appearance.

Laverda

The F8L Falco is one of the best-known designs of the Italian aircraft designer Stelio Frati. First flown in 1955, it was initially produced by Aviamilano and Aeromere, the type then passed to Laverda. Plans were subsequently made available for homebuilding (kit or plans), despite the types complex wooden structure, and these were distributed by Sequoia Aircraft. The type is renowned for its performance and excellent handling. Fourteen appeared on the UK register and forty on the U.S. register in February 2014. Approximately 100 have been built overall.

Amateur-built 2003 Falco F8L G-BVDP photographed at Dunkeswell, Devon in January 2014.

1938 Leopoldoff L7 G-AYKS at Cranfield, Bedfordshire.

Leopoldoff

The Leopoldoff Colibri is a French light sporting biplane that first flew in 1933. Pre-war production included thirty-three L3 Colibris; post-war production included six built in Morocco and designated CAM-1 and a number of homebuilt L7 Colibri powered by the Continental A-65 engine, and L55 with the Continental C-90. The total number built is believed to be around 125. One aircraft remains registered in the UK in February 2014, with one L3 and nine L55s registered in France.

LET (Omnipol)

The LET 200 Morava is a twin engine five-seat light aircraft designed and built in Czechoslovakia and distributed by the national marketing organization Omnipol. The type was first flown in April 1957 and remained in production until 1966, 367 being built. The main production model was the LET 200D, many of which were used by Russia's Aeroflot airline for air taxi operations.

1965 LET L200D Morava SE-LAG at Cranfield, Bedfordshire in July 1997.

Levier

The Levier Cosmic Wind is a diminutive Continental C-85 powered racing aircraft designed in 1947 by Lockheed chief test pilot Tony LeVier and his colleagues. A total of six have been built, four by Lockheed. The type competed in U.S. and UK air races achieving speeds up 185mph, and winning the 1948 Goodyear Trophy race at Cleveland and the prestigious King's Cup Air Race in Britain in 1964. With excellent handling, the Cosmic Wind was flown by Neil Williams in the 1964 World Aerobatic Championships, although the lack of a full inverted fuel system meant that the fuel had to be turned on and off sixteen times during the Free sequence.

Cosmic Wind G-ARUL "Ballerina" on display in October 2014.

LightWing

The Australian LightWing company produces a family of high wing monoplanes (PR – Power Rocket single-seat, GR-582 and 912 two-seat); and low wing monoplanes (SP2000 two-seat and SP4000 four-seat). The Power Rocket is also available as a biplane or as an open cockpit monoplane (Breeze). In February 2004, the numbers built (LightWing data) were GR-582 about fifty; GR-912 about 100; amphibious GR-912 about ten; GR-912-T (100hp) about ten; SP-2000 about fifteen. A re-vamped GR-912 LSA 100hp is being produced. One SP4000 kit has been sold. The Sport 2000 is a nosewheel version of the GR-912.

LightWing GR912 photographed at Temora, NSW, Australia in April 2010. *Jim Smith*

LightWing SP2000S 24-5183 at Temora, NSW, Australia in April 2010. *Jim Smith*

1930 Lincoln PT-K N275N photographed at Oshkosh, Wisconsin.

Lincoln

Lincoln PT. Around thirty examples of this two-seat training biplane were built, the first flying in 1929. In June 2014, four aircraft were listed on the U.S. civil register. The type was produced as the Lincoln PT (OX-5), PT-K (Kinner), PT-W (Warner) and PT-T (Brownback 'Tiger'), of which the PT-K was the most successful model.

Lockheed

It is hard to imagine a company that has built as many different classes of aircraft as the Lockheed company (originally Loughead Aircraft Manufacturing Co. and now Lockheed Martin). The roll call of notable types include fighters (P-38 Lightning, F-80 Shooting Star, F-16 (ex-General Dynamics), F-104 Starfighter, F-117 Nighthawk, F-22 and F-35); tactical and strategic military transport aircraft (C-130 Hercules, C-5 Galaxy, C-141 Starlifter); reconnaissance aircraft (Lockheed U-2, SR-71 Blackbird), commercial transports (Constellation, L-188 Electra, L-1011 Tri-Star), trainers (T-33), business jets (Jetstar), naval aircraft (S-3 Viking) and maritime patrol aircraft (Hudson, Ventura, P-2 Neptune, P-3 Orion). Smaller commercial types that are considered to fall within the scope of this work are the Lockheed Vega, Model 10 Electra and Model 12 Electra Junior.

Lockheed Vega. The Lockheed Vega was a fast, innovative five or six-seat commercial monoplane featuring a monocoque plywood fuselage of circular cross-section and a high cantilever plywood-skinned wing. The Vega was first flown in July 1927 and was subsequently used for major long distance record-breaking flights by famous pilots including Amelia Earhart and Wiley Post. Between June 23 and July 1 1931, Wiley Post and his navigator set a record for a flight around the world flying Vega 5 *Winnie Mae* completing the circumnavigation in eight days, fifteen hours and fifty-one minutes. If that were not enough, he repeated the feat, flying solo, in 1933, shaving twenty-one hours off his previous record time. About 130 Vega were built. Two have been restored to flying condition and a number of aircraft, including the original *Winnie Mae*, are held in museum collections.

This original Lockheed Vega 5C (originally NC898E) is painted in the colors of Wiley Post's *Winnie Mae* NC105W and forms part of Kermit Weeks' collection at Polk City, Florida.

1935 Lockheed 10E Electra N72GT (ex-NC14900) carrying the registration NR16020 of Amelia Earhart's lost aircraft. Photographed at Denton, Texas, this aircraft was flown round the world after restoration by Linda Finch and is now exhibited at the Seattle Museum of Flight.

Lockheed 10 Electra. Developed as a fast airliner, the Lockheed 10 Electra was first flown in February 1934. The aircraft was sold to many major airlines, both in the U.S. and worldwide, and is perhaps best known for its use by Amelia Earhart when she disappeared while attempting a round-the-world flight in July 1937. The twin engine, twin fin configuration later featured on many other Lockheed models. A total of 148 were built.

1937 Lockheed 12A VH-HID at Illawarra Regional Airport, NSW, Australia. *Jim Smith*

Lockheed 12. The Lockheed 12 is smaller than the similar Lockheed 10 Electra, from which it can be distinguished by its longer and more pointed nose, less rounded fins, and different cockpit and cabin glazing. The type was known as the Electra Junior and seats six passengers, compared with the eight of the Electra. The Lockheed 12 was first flown in June 1936. 130 were built, but the type was not used in airline operation to the same extent as the Lockheed 10, being more likely to be used as a company or executive aircraft.

Luscombe

Don Luscombe was a key designer for Monocoupe and left there to set up his own business. His first design was the high performance Luscombe Phantom, which featured a metal monocoque fuselage and was powered by a 145hp Warner radial. The Phantom was first flown in May 1934 and a total of twenty-five were built.

NC272Y is wearing the registration of the prototype Phantom, although this is actually the last to be constructed, built up from parts to hand in 1941 and originally registered as NC28799. *Jim Smith*

G-KENM is a 1946 Luscombe 8E seen landing at Henstridge, Somerset in June 2013.

Luscombe 8 Silvaire. The two-seat Luscombe Model 8 was initially powered by a Continental A-50 engine and first flew in December 1937. The aircraft again featured all-metal construction, and a full monocoque fuselage. The main production models were the 8A (Continental A-65) and the 8E and 8F (C-85 or C-90). Early aircraft had fabric-covered wings and twin vee struts. Later, a metal skinned wing was used with only one strut. The later aircraft had a revised more angular fin and rudder shape and twin wing tanks, allowing additional cockpit rear windows to be added.

5,635 were built, of which 3,695 were Luscombe 8A (data from *The Luscombe Story*).

Luscombe T-8F Observer. The T-8F was designed to meet a U.S. Army observation aircraft requirement. It is a tandem seat version of the Model 8E, with extended cabin glazing and a raised rear cockpit area to provide headroom for the rear occupant. Although unsuccessful in terms of military orders, it received civil certification and a total of 108 were built, thirty-five of these as the T8F Sprayer for agricultural use.

N1824B is a 1948 Luscombe T-8F, photographed at Oshkosh, Wisconsin.

1949 Luscombe 11A Sedan (later registered as N1962B) at Oshkosh, Wisconsin.

Luscombe 11 Sedan. Also known as the Silvaire Sedan, the Model 11 was designed as a four-seat private and utility aircraft, reflecting requirements of the Flying Farmers of America organization. The prototype flew in September 1946. The Model 11A was the production variant, with modifications following the loss of a prototype in spin testing, which delayed production until 1948. A total of 198 were built.

Luton Aircraft

Luton LA.4 Minor. The LA4 Minor is a small parasol monoplane which is popular for home construction. It was built by Luton Aircraft Ltd. The first LA.4 G-AFBP was flown in 1937 and a small number were built prior to the Second World War. After the War, the type was refined as the Luton LA.4A, which has been built in significant numbers. Plans for the Luton LA.4A were distributed by Phoenix Aircraft Ltd, and the type is also known as the Phoenix Luton Minor. Around forty-five have been registered in the UK, of which twenty-five remained on the register in January 2014. Others are registered in Australia, Canada and South Africa.

1990 JAP-powered Luton LA4A Minor G-BRWU photographed at Eggesford, Devon.

Luton Major. Luton Aircraft also built an enlarged design, the LA.5 Major, the Walter Mikron powered prototype G-AFMU being flown in March 1939. Despite the attractions of an enclosed cabin and two-seats, only a limited number of the LA.5A Major have been built, and the type considerably less common than the Luton Minor.

Luton LA5 Major HB-YAH at Cranfield, Bedfordshire in July 1994.

MFI-9B SE-FID photographed at Cranfield, Bedfordshire in July 1990.

Malmo MFI
The Malmo MFI-9 was the production version of the Andreasson BA7. It was later produced in Germany under licence by Bölkow as the Bö208. The main external recognition feature is the bulged fuselage side at shoulder height that is characteristic of the MFI-9. The MFI-9 first flew in October 1958 and a total of seventy MFI-9 and MFI9B were built.

Marquart
The Marquart MA-5 Charger is a two-seat aerobatic homebuilt biplane, developed from the single-seat MA-4 and first flown in October 1970. In February 2014, forty-nine appeared on the FAA U.S. civil aircraft register.

N55GT is a 1979 Marquart MA-5 Charger at Oshkosh, Wisconsin.

F-PBHQ is a 1946 Mauboussin 123 photographed at Brienne le Chateau, France.

Mauboussin

The Mauboussin Corsaire was first flown as the MB.120 in 1932. It is a two-seat low wing monoplane, the occupants being seated in tandem in either open cockpits, or under a cockpit canopy. The rights were acquired by Fouga in 1936, who produced the MB.123 version for the French Air Force, with production continuing post-war for flying club use. The type was produced with a variety of engines, resulting in type designations from MB.120 to MB.129, with the most numerous being the MB.123 with Salmson 9 (65 built) and MB.129 with Minié DA48 (23 built). Total production was 116 aircraft. In June 2014, eleven aircraft of this series remained on the French register.

Maule

Maule has carved out a very successful niche with a series of high wing single-engine short take-off and landing (STOL) aircraft with high power and a low stalling speed. They can be operated on floats or skis, and have been popular for backcountry and bush flying. First in the family was the Maule M-4, which was first flown in February 1957. The main M-4 models had either 180hp or 220hp engines; 474 were built before being replaced by the M-5. The M-5, M-6 and M-7 have an angular swept fin and increased flap area. The M-5 was offered with engine powers from 180hp to 235hp. The M-7 has increased cabin volume and is available with a tricycle undercarriage as the MXT-7. The M-9 is available with 230hp diesel engine power. Around 2,200 Maule M-4 to M-9 aircraft have been sold.

HB-ETR is a Maule M-4 210C, photographed at Cranfield, Bedfordshire in July 1983.

N56643 is a Maule M-5 180C photographed at Henstridge, Somerset in June 2010.

G-BZDT is a 2000 Maule MXT-7 180 photographed at Eggesford, Devon.

N34376 is a 1954 Meyers MAC-145 photographed at Oshkosh, Wisconsin.

Meyers 145

Al Meyers designed an attractive two-seat low wing cabin monoplane, the Meyers MAC 125, which first flew in 1947. Two were built, before switching to a production model, the more powerful MAC 145.

Twenty were built to order and the type was subsequently evolved into the four-seat Meyers 200, with a tricycle undercarriage. This design subsequently became the Aero Commander 200.

Meyers OTW

The Meyers OTW (Out-to-Win) two-seat biplane was first flown in May 1936 and was aimed at the U.S. Civilian Pilot Training Program. The type was of mixed construction with a stressed skin metal fuselage and wooden wings. Certification was delayed until February 1941, restricting total sales to 102 aircraft. Available with 125hp Scarab OTW-125, 145hp Super Scarab (OTW-145) or 160hp Kinner R5 (OTW-160), the most numerous version was the OTW-145.

Mignet and related types

M. Henri Mignet published his book *Le Sport de l'Air* at the end of 1933, describing his novel single-seat tandem wing aircraft for the masses, the Pou de Ciel, or Flying Flea. The HM14 had only two means of control: a variable incidence front wing for pitch control and a rudder for directional control. Once plans were published there was a wave of enthusiastic construction, both in France and in Britain.

A number of aircraft flew successfully before problems were encountered with uncontrolled dives leading to fatal accidents. It emerged following wind tunnel tests that if the aircraft exceeded a certain negative incidence (due to entering a downdraft, or following a sharp control movement), there was insufficient

N34324 is a 1942 Kinner-powered Meyers OTW-160. *Jeff Jacobs*

nose up control available to recover from the resultant dive. This brought an end to the 1930s Flea craze. The basic design concept (when modified) was sound however and a range of new Mignet types (and Mignet-inspired designs) were developed and flown in France, where they remain popular to the present day. A number of Mignet (and Mignet-inspired) types are illustrated below. See also the entry for Croses for a number of similar types. The photographs below were taken at the fiftieth Anniversary event at Brienne le Chateau, unless otherwise noted.

Turmeau HT-01 (VW powered HM14) at the Brienne le Chateau Flea 50th Anniversary, July 1984

F-PLUZ Mignet HM 360

OO-96 HM293, Cranfield, Bedfordshire, July 1998.

HB-SPG Mignet HM19C

OO-32 HM293, Balen Keiheuvel, Belgium

G-MYDZ Mignet HM1000 Balerit, Henstridge

F-PSYT Roy Mignet GR01.

Landray GL4 Visa Pou;

F-PYOJ Briffaut GB10 Pou Push.

Miles M.2L Hawk Speed Six G-ADGP photographed at Old Warden, Bedfordshire at the Royal Aeronautical Society Centenary of Aviation Garden Party in June 2003.

Miles Aircraft

F.G. Miles began aircraft construction with Southern Aircraft Ltd, designed the Miles Satyr and then the Miles Hawk. The Miles M.2 Hawk first flew in March 1933 and proved to be a pivotal design, with an alphabetically challenging series of variants running (with almost no gaps) from the M.2A to the M.2Z. The company went on to develop a range of cabin touring aircraft and training aircraft. Wartime saw large-scale production of the Magister and Master (3,250 built) RAF trainers, the Martinet target tug and a series of often unconventional experimental prototypes.

The company's main post-war products were the Messenger and Gemini (in effect a twin engine Messenger). A range of other types including the Aerovan reached production (fifty-six built), although none survive today. The Miles Marathon was intended to be a four engine regional airliner, but its development was protracted, leading to the take-over of the business by Handley Page Ltd. A sample of the company's successful light aircraft designs are presented below.

Miles M.2L Hawk Speed Six. A Gipsy Six powered racing variant of the Miles Hawk, built in a number of versions including M.2E (one), M.2L (two) and M.2U (one). The Miles M.2L Hawk Speed Six G-ADGP first flew at Woodley in June 1935, and was raced extensively from the late 1940s until the 1960s. Its most notable success came in 1950 with the establishment of a world 100km closed circuit record in Class C1b of 192.83mph.

Miles Hawk Trainer I and II. A number of trainer derivatives of the Miles Hawk were built, including the four M.2Rs, twelve M.2Ws, eight M.2Ys and ten M.2Zs for Romania. The later Hawk Trainer III was adopted as the Magister as a basic trainer for the RAF (see below). The first Hawk Trainer was flown in July 1935.

1935 Miles M.2W Hawk Trainer G-ADWT photographed at Abingdon, Oxfordshire in May 2004. This aircraft was previously based in Canada as CF-NXT.

1936 Miles M.3A Falcon G-AEEG photographed at Old Warden, Bedfordshire at the Royal Aeronautical Society Centenary of Aviation Garden Party in June 2003.

Miles M.3 Falcon. The Miles Falcon was a fast cabin derivative of the M.2 Hawk. The prototype flew in September 1934, followed by thirty-six production aircraft built in five versions. The most important versions were the M.3A (nineteen built) and the M.3B Falcon Six.

Beautifully restored 1936 Miles Witney Straight G-AERV photographed in October 2014, at which time it was the only aircraft of the type still flying.

M.11A Whitney Straight. The two-seat M.11 first flew in May 1936, the production variant being the M.11A. The type was designed to the requirements of the racing driver Mr Whitney Straight for a long range touring aircraft. Some fifty were laid down for production, but not all were completed.

Miles M.14 Hawk Trainer III/Magister. The M.14, first flown in March 1937, was the definitive trainer variant of the Hawk, which led to Miles (Phillips & Powis) achieving major production success with its adoption as the standard RAF basic trainer. A total of 1,281 aircraft were built of all M.14 variants.

1941 Miles M.14 Hawk Trainer III/Magister V1075/G-AKPF photographed at Old Warden, Bedfordshire at the Royal Aeronautical Society Centenary of Aviation Garden Party in June 2003.

1938 Miles M.17 Monarch G-AFLW photographed at a Vintage Aircraft Club fly-in at Blackbushe Aerodrome, Hampshire.

Miles M.17 Monarch. Three-seat development of the M.11A Whitney Straight; first flown in February 1938, eleven built.

The Miles M.28 Mercury. The Miles M.28 Mk.1 was a cabin two-seat light aircraft with twin fins and a retractable undercarriage that had a strong influence on the design of the later Messenger and Gemini aircraft. Also known as the Miles Mercury, the M28 was first flown in July 1941. It was followed by five further M.28s in three and four-seat versions.

Miles M.28 Mercury 6 OY-ALW photographed at White Waltham airfield, Berkshire, May 1998.

1945 Miles Messenger 4B G-AKVZ landing at Woburn Abbey, Bedfordshire during the De Havilland Moth Club Rally in August 2014.

The Miles M.28 Messenger. The development prototype for the M.38 Messenger was first flown in September 1943. The first true prototype did not fly until February 1944, and only twenty-one of the 250 military aircraft ordered were delivered by the end of the war. The Messenger continued in production post-war. A total of 113 Messenger aircraft were built in several variants.

The Miles M.65 Gemini. The M.65 Gemini was first flown in October 1945. A total of 150 were laid down for production. Of these, Miles Aircraft Ltd. completed a total of 139. After the closure of Miles Aircraft, two further examples were completed by Handley Page (Reading) Ltd. as Gemini 1A. Six additional airframes were completed by Ron Paine as Gemini 3A. Three further aircraft were completed by F.G. Miles Ltd, as a single Gemini 1A and two Miles M.75 Aries.

1947 Miles M.65 Gemini 1A G-AKKB landing on the airstrip at Badminton House.

1972 Mong MS-1 Sport N5544 photographed at Oshkosh, Wisconsin.

Mong

The Mong MS-1 Sport is a small homebuilt biplane, similar to a Pitts S-1 Special. The type was first flown in May 1953 and more than 400 sets of plans were sold. At least fifty have been successfully completed and around half that number appeared on the U.S. register in February 2014.

Monnett and Sonex

John Monnett has been a prolific designer of light sporting aircraft sold both under his name and that of Sonex Aircraft, a company that he founded to sell a range of plans-built and kit-built models. A number of the most important models are illustrated below, others including the one-off Monex and the Monerai sailplane and its Monerai P powered version.

The VW-powered Sonerai was originally built as a single-seat Formula-V racer. Nineteen Sonerai Is were registered in the United States in February 2014, with three appearing on the UK register.

Sonerai I N84TW takes off from the Texas Northwest Regional Airport at Roanoke.

Monnett Sonerai II. The Sonerai II is a two-seat development of the Sonerai I and has become a very popular homebuilt aircraft. Initially flown, like the Sonerai I, with a mid-wing, a low wing version is available and designated Sonerai IIL. The Sonerai IILT is a nosewheel-equipped variant. The VW-powered Sonerai II was designed in 1973. In February 2014, there were 171 Sonerai IIs on the U.S. register and nine on the UK register.

G-CCOZ is a 1982 mid-wing Sonerai II seen taxying after its landing at Cranfield, Bedfordshire.

19-3973 is a Sonerai IIL operating on the Australian Recreational Aircraft Register and photographed at Temora, NSW in April 2010. *Jim Smith*

N19CE is a Monnett Moni photographed at Oshkosh, Wisconsin in 1985.

Monnett Moni. The Moni is a low wing motor glider with a butterfly tail. The influence of the Moni and the one-off Monnett Monex can be seen in the design of the later Sonex Xenos (see below). The Moni first flew in July 1981 and some 380 kits were sold. In February 2014, sixty-one were registered in the U.S. and four in the UK.

Sonex Aircraft Sonex. Sonex Aircraft was set up by John Monnett, based at Oshkosh, Wisconsin. The Sonex, which draws on a number of Monnett's earlier designs, meets Light Sport Aircraft (LSA) requirements and has proven to be very popular. In February 2014, no less than 386 Sonex registrations were listed on the U.S. civil register, although it is not clear how many of these are fully completed and flying.

G-SONX is a 2003 Sonex Aircraft Sonex photographed at Popham, Hampshire in July 2014.

19-7411 is a Sonex Waiex operating on the Australian recreational Aircraft register and photographed at Temora, NSW. *Jim Smith*

Sonex Waiex. The Waiex is, in effect, a Sonex with a butterfly tail unit. In February 2014, sixty-eight Waiex registrations were listed on the U.S. civil register, although it is not clear how many of these are fully completed and flying.

Sonex Xenos. The Xenos is a motorglider variant of the Waiex, and is similar in concept to the earlier Monnett Moni and Monex. Like the Waiex, it has a butterfly tail, but its wingspan is approximately twice as great. In February 2014, sixteen Xenos appeared on the UC civil aircraft register.

19-7235 is a Sonex Xenos operating on the Australian recreational Aircraft register and photographed at Temora, NSW. *Jim Smith*

G-AFEL is a Lambert-powered Monocoupe D-90A photographed at Cranfield, Bedfordshire.

Monocoupe

Clayton Folkerts and Don Luscombe designed a series of high wing two-seat high performance light aircraft sold under the type name Monocoupe. The first Monocoupe flew in April 1927 powered by the 60hp Viele, some 350 being built. Subsequent models, with differing engine types included the Monocoupe 90 (about 100 built), 90A (more than 150 built), 90AF (44), 90AL (eleven post-war), 110 (about fifty) and 125 (five built). The type was a successful racer, with the Monocoupe 110 Special featuring clipped wings and 145hp Warner engine. One aircraft was modified to this standard, followed by six factory-built examples.

The Monocoupe D-145 featured a wider cabin an 145hp Warner Super Scarab engine. Around thirty were built, notable owners including Charles A Lindbergh.

NR211 is Charles Lindbergh's personal 1934 Monocoupe D-145 proudly displayed at St Louis Lambert Airport.

1954 Mooney M-18C N4142. *Johan Visschedijk*

Mooney

The designer Al Mooney, who had previously been responsible for the Dart Model G and the Culver Cadet, set up Mooney aircraft, its first product being the single-seat M-18 Mite of 1948. 283 Mooney Mite were built between 1948 and 1955 powered by 65hp Continental or Lycoming engines. 127 were listed on the U.S. civil register in February 2014, although these will not necessarily all be active.

Mooney M20 family. the Mooney M20 is a retractable undercarriage four-seat low wing monoplane that was first flown in 1953. Initially of mixed construction

with wooden wings (M20, M20A), from the M20B onward, the type was produced with all-metal construction. Enormously successful, with well over 10,000 aircraft sold, The M20 family has been the subject of progressive development with increases in installed power, fuselage length, and take-off weight over the type's well over fifty year production run. The most important production models are the M20E (1,475), M20F (1251), M20J (1,700+) and M20K (1100+). A representative sample of Mooney M20 models is presented below.

G-ARWY is a 1958 Mooney M20A photographed at Sywell, Northamptonshire; note the early cabin glazing and short fuselage length.

D-EFFS 1968 Mooney M20F Executive at Cranfield, Bedfordshire.

VH-NFP 1982 Mooney 201 (M20J), at Echuca, Victoria April 2013.

G-OONE 1987 Mooney 206 (M20J). Blackbushe, Hampshire; note revised window shape.

VH-JEU 2008 Mooney M20TN at Avalon, Victoria; note the further fuselage stretch. *Jim Smith*

1949 MS 230 G-AVEB photographed at Wroughton, Wiltshire. This aircraft is now registered N230ET.

Morane-Saulnier

The pioneer firm of Morane-Saulnier dates back to 1911 and is noted for a number of monoplane fighters used with distinction during the First World War, and the MS406 fighter of the Second World War. The company's most notable light aircraft family was the family of Rallye light aircraft. These are discussed under the entry for SOCATA (Société de Construction d'Avions de Tourisme et d'Affaires). Morane-Saulnier was renamed SOCATA in 1966, production of the Rallye being mainly undertaken under the SOCATA brand.

Morane-Saulnier MS230: The MS230 was one of a number of general purpose and training parasol monoplanes produced by Morane-Saulnier during the 1930s. The MS230 was first flown in February 1929 and became the standard trainer for the French Air force. Some 1,080 were built, including a number completed post-war.

Morane-Saulnier MS315 series. The 1932 MS315 was a lighter, lower-powered variant of the MS230 for civilian and flying school use. The type had a longer fuselage and was powered by a 135hp Salmson 9Nc; a number of aircraft were re-engined with the 220hp Continental W-670 and designated MS317. 354 were built.

1953 MS317 F-BGKX photographed at Brienne le Chateau in France.

N5440 is a 1954 Morane-Saulnier MS733 Alcyon, one of two registered in the United States and was photographed at Oshkosh, Wisconsin.

Morane-Saulnier MS733 Alcyon. The MS730 was first flown in August 1949 as a two or three-seat trainer aircraft. The production aircraft was the 1951 MS733 Alcyon with a 240hp Potez 6D engine. An armed version, the MS733A was used for counter-insurgency operations. 208 MS733 were built and a number of privately owned examples continue to operate (mainly in France).

Morgan Aeroworks

Garry Morgan set up Morgan Aeroworks in 2002 to produce kitplanes in Australia. The first product was the Rand KR2-based Joey, but this was not particularly successful, being followed by the successful two-seat Morgan Cheetah. The Cheetah (with metal fuselage and fabric covered wing) has been developed into the all-metal Cheetah Sierra. Power is provided by Rotax and Jabiru engines of between 80hp and 125hp. Other products are the single-seat Super Diamond and aerobatic Super Diamond Twister, two-seat Joey Mk.II, and the four-seat Morgan Cougar. Around fifty-one Cheetah/Sierra kits have been sold, with about half having flown.

19-7367 is a Morgan Aeroworks Cheetah Sierra 100 photographed at Echuca, VIC, Australia in April 2013.

1990 Murphy Renegade Spirit G-MWMW *Spirit of Cornwall* photographed at Land's End St Just, Cornwall.

Murphy Aircraft

Murphy is a Canadian kitplane manufacturer, offering a range of designs. Two highly successful examples are the Murphy Renegade two-seat light biplane and the Murphy Rebel high wing two or three-seat aircraft. The Murphy Elite is a nosewheel version of the Rebel, with additional structural refinements. Other products include the Maverick, which is a scaled down Rebel and the Moose, which is a four to six-seat utility aircraft or bush plane with a radial engine of up to 360hp.

Murphy Renegade. Initially flown as a single-seat biplane, the type was modified to a two-seat configuration as the Renegade II. A version with a radial-style helmeted cowling is known as the Renegade Spirit, power being normally provided by a Rotax 582 engine. In February 2014, forty-seven Renegades were registered in Canada, twenty-four in the UK and thirty-seven in the USA.

Murphy Rebel. The two or three-seat Murphy Rebel STOL aircraft was first flown in 1990 and has proved to be very popular. In February 2014, 125 were registered in Canada, fourteen in the UK and fifty-three in the USA.

1999 Murphy Rebel VH-REB *The Cheese Grater* taxying at Illawarra, NSW, Australia.

1988 Nanchang CJ6A G-CGHB painted in Chinese Air Force colours landing at Popham, Hampshire in July 2014.

Nanchang

The Nanchang CJ-6 is a fully aerobatic trainer designed in China as an improvement over the Yak 18 using a fully flush riveted structure and a fully retractable undercarriage. In these respects, it is regarded as superior to its nearest equivalent, the Yak-52. In February 2014, there were 191 on the U.S. register, forty-four in Australia, and five in the UK. Between 2,000 and 3,000 were built.

Nardi

The Nardi FN-333 Riviera is an Italian-designed four-seat amphibious flying boat. It was first flown in December 1952. Prototypes were built by Nardi, with series production by SIAI-Marchetti. A total of twenty-nine were built, the majority being sold in the USA, where three aircraft remained on the civil register in February 2014.

An unidentified Nardi FN-333 Riviera at Merrill Field, Anchorage, Alaska.

N45084 is a 1941 Naval Aircraft Factory N3N-3 modified for fire-bombing use and seen at Pima County Air Museum, Tucson, Arizona.

Naval Aircraft Factory

997 Naval Aircraft Factory N3N training biplanes were built (most of these being N3N-3). The type was first flown in August 1935 and was the last biplane to be retired from U.S. military service in 1961. No less than 183 were listed on U.S. register in February 2014, although relatively few of these are likely to be active.

Neiva

Some 749 CAP-4 Paulistinha aircraft were built in Brazil by Companhia Aeronautica Paulista. This aircraft was very similar to the Piper Cub, albeit powered by a 65hp Franklin engine and having slightly less rounded wingtips than the Cub. Neiva built 240 examples of a higher power version, with either 100hp or 90hp as the Paulistinha 56B and 56C.

CP-684 is a Neiva P56C Paulistinha operated by Alas Orientales at Santa Cruz, Bolivia. *Peter Davison*

1969 Nesmith Cougar 1 N89300 photographed at Oshkosh, Wisconsin.

Nesmith

The Nesmith Cougar is a two-seat high wing homebuilt aircraft, which is very similar in appearance and configuration to the Wittman Tailwind. The type was first flown in March 1957 and some ninety examples are believed to have flown in the USA.

New Standard

New Standard built a series of biplanes, the most notable being the five-seat joyriding D-25 (around forty-five built) and the two-seat trainer D-29 series (D-29, -31, -33), around thirty of which were built. 12 D-25 were listed on the U.S. civil register in February 2014, although not all are active.

1930 New Standard D-25 N930V at Casa Grande, Arizona in October 2013. *Peter Davison*

Two HN433 Menestrel (F-PYJZ and F-PYKA) photographed at Brienne-le-Chateau, France.

Nicollier

The Nicollier HN433 and HN434 Menestrel are attractive wooden single-seat low wing monoplanes designed for homebuilding. With its elliptical wing planform the type resembles a smaller Volkswagen-powered Piel Emeraude. A two-seat variant, the HN700 Menestrel II has also been flown. More than ninety Menestrels have been built, with eleven Menestrel IIs on the UK register in February 2014. At the same time, the French register listed twenty-seven single-seat Menestrels and fifty-four two-seat Menestrel IIs.

Noorduyn

The Noorduyn Norseman is a Canadian utility aircraft for bush operations that first flew in November 1935. The later DHC-3 Otter is, in many ways, a Norseman replacement. 904 Norseman were built, mainly due to the type serving during wartime as the C-64A (later UC-64A), with 749 being ordered for U.S. service. In February 2014, four were listed on the U.S. register, with more than forty remaining on the Canadian register.

N55555 is a 1943 Noorduyn Norseman, photographed at Merrill Field, Anchorage, Alaska.

1945 Nord N.1002 Pingouin G-ATBG photographed at Wroughton, Wiltshire.

SNCAN and Nord Aviation

The Nord Pingouin was a Messerschmitt Bf 108 re-engined with the Renault 6Q engine. Nord built 170 Argus-powered Bf 108 during the Second World War, followed by 286 Pingouin, built post-war in two variants, the Nord N.1001 and Nord N.1002, dependent on which version of the Renault 6Q engine was fitted. The type was used for military communications and is often seen in spurious Luftwaffe colours. In February 2014, three were registered in the UK and seven in the USA.

Nord N.1101 Noralpha. Nord built two prototypes of a tricycle undercarriage version of the Bf 108 in 1943 as the Messerschmitt Me 208. One was destroyed and the other became the prototype Nord Noralpha, built post-war and powered by the Renault 6Q engine. 205 were built. In February 2014, one example was registered in the UK, with eight others being no longer registered; six were registered in the USA.

Nord N.1101 Noralpha G-ATIX in a spurious Luftwaffe color scheme at Duxford, Cambridgeshire. *Jim Smith*

F-BHTF is a 1956 Nord N.1203 Norécrin VI photographed at Sywell, Northamptonshire.

Nord N.1200 series Norécrin. The Norécrin was a two to three-seat cabin low wing monoplane, derived from the N.1101, with which it shares a marked wing dihedral. The prototype flew in December 1945 and the type was powered by a Renault 4P engine, although other powerplants were fitted to some marks. A total of 378 Norécrin were built. In February 2014, nineteen Norécrin of different variants were registered in France.

Nord NC850 series. The Nord NC850 series has its origins in the 1947 Aérocentre NC853 two-seat light aircraft for club use. Twenty-nine were built before the design was taken over by Nord as the NC853S. The type is characterised by its relatively flat ground attitude, twin tail fins, shoulder mounted wing and bubble canopy. Nord continued the type's development, producing ninety-five NC853Ss, and 112 NC856A Norvigies, an army cooperation model. Continental A-65 conversions are designated NC854; C-90 conversions are designated NC858. The type remains in service both in France and in the UK.

G-BJEL is a 1951 Nord NC854S photographed at Henstridge, Somerset.

G-BIZK is a 1962 Nord 3202-B1 photographed at Cranfield, Bedfordshire in spurious Luftwaffe colors.

Nord NC3202. The Nord NC3202 is a two-seat military trainer first flown in April 1957 as a replacement for the Stampe SV4. A total of 101 were built. In February 2014, there were three registered in the UK, fourteen in the USA and sixteen in France.

North American Aviation

North American Aviation is one of the greatest names in aviation, noted for a range of almost unmatched military aircraft. The company's list of products includes:

T-6 Texan (or Harvard in UK and Canadian service) trainer;
B-25 Mitchell medium bomber;
P-51 Mustang, the superlative escort fighter;
F-86 Sabre of Korean War fame;
F-100 Super Sabre, America's first supersonic fighter;
T-28 Trojan advanced trainer/strike aircraft;
T-2 Buckeye naval training aircraft;
T-39 Sabreliner, first of the business jets;
A-5 Vigilante supersonic carrier based strike aircraft;
XB-70 Valkyrie, dramatic six engine supersonic bomber prototypes;
X-15, the research aircraft that probed the
    boundaries of speed and space;
OV-10 Bronco, twin tailed forward air control
    and counter-insurgency aircraft
B-1/B-1B Lancer supersonic, swing wing, four engine bomber

North American Aviation became part of Rockwell International, which has subsequently been taken over by the Boeing Company.

G-TXAN flies at an airshow at Henstridge, Somerset in June 2013. This is a 1943 AT-6D Harvard III, painted in the colors of a U.S. Navy SNJ-5 51970.

T-6 Texan and Harvard. The T-6 was the most important U.S. trainer of the Second World War and was widely exported to many nations. The RAF and RCAF were important allied users of the type, which was also built in Canada by Noorduyn Aviation and Canadian Car and Foundries. The NA-16 prototype flew in April 1935 and production continued into the 1950s, with a grand total of 15,495 of all variants being built. Many aircraft are still flying in the hands of private owners worldwide.

T-28 Trojan: The Trojan was used as a trainer by both the U.S. Navy and U.S. Air Force and was also used for counter-insurgency operations during the Vietnam War. First flown in September 1949, a total of 1,948 were built. Many are operated as warbirds by private owners in a number of countries. Some 300 remain on the U.S. civil register.

371 is a 1957 T-28C Trojan N28CQ Bu146254 at Kissimmee, Florida.

D-EEAG is an Oberlerchner Job 15-150 at Balen Keiheuvel in Belgium.

Oberlerchner

The Oberlerchner Job 15 is a three-seat low wing monoplane of Austrian design, developed from the two-seat Job 5. The Job 15 flew in 1960, three variants being produced, the Job 15-135, Job-150 and Job-150/2 with either 135hp or 150hp. A total of twenty-four aircraft were built.

Oldfield

The Oldfield Baby Great Lakes is a diminutive single-seat biplane designed to capture the spirit of the Great Lakes Sport Trainer. With a wingspan of less than 17 ft, the Baby Great Lakes is significantly smaller than a Pitts S-1 Special. In February 2014, there were around fifty registered in the U.S., with six in the UK.

Baby Great Lakes G-BKHD photographed at Sleap, Shropshire in June 1985. The aircraft to its left is G-BKGJ, another Baby Great Lakes.

Orlican

The Orlican L-40 Meta Sokol is a Czech four-seat low wing monoplane with a retractable tricycle undercarriage. Unusually, the undercarriage in in a 'reverse tricycle' arrangement, which offers a reduced ground angle compared with a conventional tailwheel undercarriage. The L-40 first flew in March 1956 and a total of 106 were built. Eight examples were registered in the UK, of which two remained on the register in February 2014.

1959 Orlican L-40 Meta Sokol G-APUE taxying at Wroughton airfield, Wiltshire.

19-5145 is a Parker Teenie Two operating on the Australian Recreational Aircraft Register and photographed at Goulburn, NSW in April 2013.

Parker

The Parker Jeanie's Teenie is a diminutive all-metal single-seat homebuilt aircraft that first flew in 1967. In March 2014, more than sixty appeared on the U.S. civil aircraft register, with others flying in Europe and Australia. The Teenie Two is a lengthened updated version of the same design, using a conventional tailplane and elevator, rather that the all-moving stabilator of the original design.

Partenavia

The Italian manufacturer Partenavia is known for its high wing single-engine Partenavia Fachiro and Oscar light aircraft and the P68 Victor light twin and its derivatives. The P.64/P.66 Oscar is a two or four-seat aircraft developed from the P.57 Fachiro. A total of 312 Oscar aircraft were built in a number of versions with engines of between 100hp and 200hp. The type was first flown in April 1965.

Partenavia P.64B Oscar 200 HB-EPQ (later G-MBDP) photographed at Cranfield, Bedfordshire.

2004 Partenavia P68C Victor VH-VMV on the approach to Canberra Airport, ACT, Australia. *Jim Smith*

The twin engine P68 Victor is characterized by its fine fuselage lines and high, untapered wing. This six-seat aircraft was first flown in 1970. The type remains in production with Vulcanair with more than 350 built. A number of derivatives have been flown (with retractable undercarriage – P.68R, turboprop engines – P.68T and AP.68TP). Variants that have achieved production status are the P.68

Observer and the AP.68TP-300 Spartacus, which are both described below.

The P.68 Observer is a variant of the P.68B with extensive cockpit glazing. A number were converted from existing aircraft, but the type is also available as a new-build design.

G-SVEY is a 2003 Partenavia (Vulcanair) P68TC Observer patrol and observation aircraft, photographed at Farnborough, Hampshire.

Prototype P.69TP-300 Spartacus I-RAIK photographed at the Paris Air Show, Le Bourget, France. This aircraft is now registered as N75CY.

The Partenavia P.68TC-300 Spartacus is a lengthened, turboprop-powered version of the P.68. Unlike the P.68T, it has a fixed undercarriage. A retractable undercarriage version of the Spartacus is designated P.600 Viator. Around fifteen Spartacus aircraft have been built.

Pazmany

A number of homebuilt aircraft designs have been produced by the Pazmany Aircraft Corporation, including the PL-1, PL-2, PL-4 and PL-9.

Pazmany PL-1. The PL-1 is a is a two-seat low wing all-metal monoplane, the wing being fitted with tip tanks. The first aircraft flew in March 1962 and some 375 sets of plans were sold before the company switched to the PL-2. 58 PL-1B were built in Taiwan for the Republic of China Air Force. Some twelve were registered on the U.S. civil register in March 2014.

1976 Pazmany PL-1 G-BDHJ photographed at Finmere, Buckinghamshire.

Pazmany PL-2 HK-3966-Z photographed at Guaymaral just north of Bogota in March 2008. *Peter Davison*

Pazmany PL-2. The Pazmany PL-2 is similar to the PL-1, but has a wider cockpit, increased wing dihedral and other structural changes. The first PL-2 flew in April 1969. A large number have been homebuilt, and fifty aircraft were built in Indonesia as the LT-200. Around fifteen were registered in the U.S. in March 2014.

Pazmany PL-4A. The Pazmany is a single-seat low wing all metal monoplane with a T-tail. The type first flew in July 1972. Some 700 sets of plans have been sold. In March 2014 some fifteen were registered in the USA and five in the UK.

1986 Pazmany PL-4A G-BMMI photographed at Wroughton, Wiltshire.

1937 P.10 Vega Gull G-AEZJ photographed at Eggesford, Devon.

Percival

Percival Aircraft was established in 1934, its first product being the three-seat P.3 Gull long range touring aircraft. Forty-six were built. Note: Percival (and Hunting Percival) went on to build other types, including the Q.6 twin and the Proctor, Prentice, Prince, Pembroke and Provost. The Proctor is described below, with the Provost being included under Hunting Percival; the Prentice is presented under Aviation Traders, who were responsible for civil conversions of the type.

P.10 Vega Gull. the Vega Gull was a four-seat development of the Gull and first flew in November 1935. Ninety Vega Gulls were built.

Percival E2 Mew Gull. The Mew Gull racing aircraft first flew in March 1934. Five examples were built pre-war, with a new example G-HEKL being completed by David Beale in 2013. The most famous aircraft is G-AEXF, used by Alex Henshaw to complete a record-breaking out-and-return trip from London to Cape Town in 1938, the entire trip being completed in four days and ten hours. G-AEXF has been the subject of several extensive rebuilds, but continues to fly in 2014.

The newly-built Percival Mew Gull G-HEKL displays vigorously at Woburn Abbey, Bedfordshire during the De Havilland Moth Club Rally in August 2014.

LZ766 (G-ALCK) is a P.34A Proctor 3 photographed at Duxford, Cambridgeshire.

Percival Proctor. The Proctor was a development of the Vega Gull. First flown in October 1939, 1,142 were built for use as military communications aircraft. 154 were built post-war specifically for civil use. Total production was of 1,296 aircraft. Six were registered in the UK in June 2014.

Pereira

Pereira Osprey II. The Osprey is a two-seat amphibian designed as a homebuilt. The type has a mid-set wing and a high-mounted engine driving a pusher propeller. First flown in April 1973, the Osprey has proved popular and aircraft are flying in Europe, the U.S. and Canada. In March 2014, four Ospreys were registered in the UK, nineteen in Canada and more than fifty in the U.S.

1986 Pereira Osprey G-BEPB (now G-PREY) at Cranfield, Bedfordshire in July 1994

N40025 is a 1956 Piaggio P.136L-1 photographed at Meacham Airport, Texas.

Piaggio

Piaggio is a noted Italian aircraft manufacturer which has been building aircraft since the 1920s. Notable products include the Piaggio 108 four engine bomber of the Second World War, the Avanti twin pusher turboprop business aircraft and the PD-808 executive jet, in addition to the types described below.

Piaggio P.136. The P.136 is a five-seat gull-wing amphibian powered by twin engines driving pusher propellers. The type first flew in August 1948 and a total of sixty-three were built, twenty-four of these being assembled in the United States where the type was known as the Royal Gull, or the Trecker Gull. Nine P.136s remained on the U.S. register in March 2014.

Piaggio P.149 (and FWP.149D). The Piaggio P.149 is a high performance four-seat touring aircraft that was adopted as a trainer and communications aircraft by the German Air Force. The type first flew in 1953 and eighty-eight were built by Piaggio, with a further 150 built under license by Focke Wulf in Germany as FWP.149D. Thirty-two P.149s appeared on the U.S. register in March 2014 and a number of ex-German Air Force aircraft are also operating in Europe.

OO-VMH is a Focke Wulf-built Piaggio P.149D at Balen Keiheuvel, Belgium.

1959 Piaggio P166 G-APWY forms part of the Science Museum Reserve Collection at Wroughton, Wiltshire.

Piaggio P.166. The Piaggio P.166 is a ten seat landplane derivative of the P.136, marrying the earlier aircraft's wing to a new streamlined fuselage. The type first flew in November 1957 and was produced in a number of variants for civil and military operators. A total of 113 piston engine models were built, followed by the turboprop-powered P.166DL3 (see below). A small number of aircraft remain registered in the United States.

Piaggio 166DL3. This is a revised version of the P.166, fitted with LTP-101 engines. This model was first flown in July 1976. The type was sold mainly in Italy and served with the Alitalia flying school and with a number of Italian government agencies.

I-PIAE is a Piaggio P.166DL3 photographed at Farnborough, Hampshire.

Piel

Claude Piel was a prolific French designer of light aircraft, including the enormously successful Pile CP-301 Emeraude, of which more than 550 have been built. A selection of the most significant Piel designs are discussed below.

Piel CP.301 Emeraude. The Emeraude is a two-seat low wing monoplane with a fixed tail wheel undercarriage and an elliptical wing shape. It has been manufactured by several companies and examples have also been homebuilt. The CP.30 first flew in June 1954; the initial production model was the CP.301A powered by a Continental C-90 and with forward-hinged doors for entry to the cockpit. The type was produced and developed further by a number of companies, with outline differences given in the captions below. 118 CP.301A were built, the majority by Coopavia.

G-ARUV is a CP.301-1 Emeraude, amateur-built in the UK in 1963 and seen at Henstridge, Somerset in April 2009.

G-APNS is a 1958 Garland-Bianchi Linnet (licensed CP.301A) built at White Waltham and photographed at Sywell, Northamptonshire.

Three aircraft were manufactured in the UK as the Fairtravel Linnet. G-ASMT, built in 1964, has the sliding canopy of later production Emeraude aircraft and was photographed at Cranfield, Bedfordshire.

G-AZYS is a 1961 Scintex CP.301C1. This aircraft has a Continental O-200 and an enlarged sliding canopy and is one of 84 CP-301C to be built. It was photographed at Dunkeswell, Devon.

PH-MOT is a Scintex CP.1315-C3 Super Emeraude. The Super Emeraude was strengthened for aerobatics and this example was photographed at Lydd, Kent. 23 Scintex CP.1310-C3 were built with O-200 power and 17 CP.1315 with the Potez 4E-20 engine. 43 further CP.1310-C3 were built by CAARP.

G-BSVE is a 1961 German-built Binder CP.301S Smaragd (Emerald). 21 were built, distinguished by their use of an extended dorsal fin. G-BSVE was photographed at Henstridge, Somerset in August 2014.

PH-RVH is a CP.328A Super Emeraude with a swept tail fin, photographed at Cranfield, Bedfordshire.

F-PKXX is a 1963 CP.601 Diamant photographed at Guyancourt, France.

Piel CP.60 and derivatives. The CP.60 Diamant is essentially a three-seat version of the Emeraude, powered (CP.601) by a 100hp Continental O-200 and being very similar in external appearance to a late model Scintex Super Emeraude. As with the Emeraude, a range of variants was produced (see below).

Piel Super Diamant. The Piel Super Diamant (CP.604 to CP.608 and CP.615) is a development of the Diamant designed to accommodate more powerful engines in the 145hp to 180hp range. The Super Diamant has a swept fin and may be fitted with a tailwheel undercarriage, or fixed (or retractable) tricycle undercarriage.

F-PNUN is a 1965 CP.605B Super Diamant with a retractable tricycle undercarriage at Brienne le Chateau, France..

F-PHPC is a 160hp 1995 Piel CP.615A Super Diamant photographed at Cranfield, Bedfordshire.

F-PYLJ is a CP.80 Zef, built in 1982 and photographed at Brienne-le-Chateau, France.

Piel CP.80 Zef:. The Piel CP.80 is a single-seat sporting and racing aircraft. The aircraft features an enclosed cockpit, sharply swept tail fin, sprung cantilever undercarriage and streamlined engine installation. The CP.80 was first flown in August 1973. At least twenty have been built in France with a number of different engine types and associated designations; in March 2014, nineteen appeared on the French civil aircraft register.

F-PYHM is a 1980 Piel CP.751 photographed at Brienne-le-Chateau.

Piel CP.750 Beryl. The CP.750 is a derivative of the Emeraude seating two in tandem. The first prototype (CP.70) had a nosewheel undercarriage, but the type was redesigned as an aerobatic aircraft with reduced span, significantly increased power and a tailwheel undercarriage. The two main variants are the CP.750 and the more powerful CP.751. Around seven examples were flying in France in March 2014, with three on the U.S. register.

Piel CP.1320. The Piel CP.1320 Saphir is a three-seat low wing monoplane produced with fixed or retractable tricycle, or tailwheel, undercarriage. The occupants sit under a large bubble canopy. The type was first flown in August 1980. Seven CP.1320 were registered in France in March 2014.

F-WYIE was the first CP.1320 Saphir to fly. It was converted to operate on liquefied petroleum gas (LPG) and undertook a demonstration tour of France in 1981; it is seen here at the Paris Air Show.

2000 Pietenpol Air Camper G-BYZY landing at Popham, Hampshire in July 2014.

Pietenpol

Pietenpol Air Camper. The Air Camper is a single-engine homebuilt parasol monoplane, whose design dates back to 1928. The type was immediately successful and continues to be built to this day. Its popularity is evidenced by the numbers registered in March 2014, including 283 in the U.S., sixty-two in Canada and thirty-seven in the UK.

Pilatus

The Swiss company Pilatus is best known for its military trainers the PC-7 and PC-9 as well as the short take off and landing PC-6 Porter and Turbo-Porter.

Pilatus PC-2. The PC-2 is a military trainer, which was first flown in April 1945; several now operate in the hands of private owners. A total of fifty-five were built. Six aircraft have appeared on the UK register and others fly in Switzerland, Germany and the USA. Examples of the later Pilatus P-3 trainer are also operated by private owners.

U-110 (G-PTWO) is a 1946 Pilatus P-2 seen at Wroughton, Wiltshire following its retirement from Swiss service.

N812FS is a 2008 Pilatus PC-12 operated by FLIR Systems and seen landing at Farnborough, Hampshire in July 2010.

Pilatus PC-12. The PC-12 is a single-engine pressurized turboprop that is used in the executive role, as well as with private owners, the Australian Royal Flying Doctor Service and the USAF (as the U-28A). The type first flew in May 1991 and has been very successful, with more than 1,300 built by March 2014.

Piper

Piper Aircraft, with Cessna and Beechcraft, is one of the pre-eminent manufacturers of private aircraft. A brief history of the company is given below (summarized from the author's *Piper Cherokee, A Family History*, Amberley Publishing). William T. Piper of Bradford, Pennsylvania became involved in aircraft construction when he took control of the Taylor Aircraft Co. in 1931. C.G. Taylor became President of the company with Piper being its Treasurer.

The first product of the new company was the Taylor E-2 Cub, a high wing light aircraft, seating its pilot and passenger in tandem. The E-2 Cub had rather angular tail surfaces and wing tips, and no cockpit side glazing. A modified version, the J-2, was produced and featured revised tail surfaces, rounded wing tips and full cockpit glazing. CG Taylor did not approve of these changes and Piper bought out Taylor's interest in the company in 1935. The company moved to Lock Haven, Pennsylvania, a site it was to occupy for many years, and was renamed as the Piper Aircraft Corporation.

J-2 production continued, some 1,200 being built before the type was supplanted by the Piper J-3 Cub. The most successful version, the J-3C-65, was powered by the Continental A-65 engine of 65hp; this was to become Piper's most famous product, the vast majority of American pilots who learned to fly prior to the entry of the U.S. into the Second World War making their first flights in Mr Piper's Cub.

After the War, Piper continued evolving its high wing line to include side-by-side seating, and three and four-seat aircraft (more of which later). The product line was expanded with the high performance Comanche; the Cherokee family; and a range of twin engine 'Indian/native American' designs including the Apache; Aztec; Twin Comanche; Seneca; and Seminole. New single-engine types included the Tomahawk basic trainer and the pressurized Malibu and its variants. This section presents those designs intended for the private owner and excludes the Pawnee and Pawnee Brave agricultural aircraft and the twin engine Navajo and Cheyenne aircraft.

N12607 is a 1931 Taylor E-2 Cub photographed at Oshkosh, Wisconsin.

Taylor E-2 Cub. Although introduced by Taylor Aircraft, the E-2 Cub is the true progenitor of the Piper series of light aircraft and is therefore included in this section. The E-2 was first flown in September 1930 and 353 were built. In March 2014, seven Taylor E-2 Cubs were listed on the U.S. civil aircraft register.

Taylor/Piper J-2 Cub. The J-2 was an improved E-2 with revised fin and rudder, rounded wingtips and full cockpit glazing. Appearing in October 1935, 1207 were built, production continuing as the Piper J-2 after CG Taylor had left the company. Eighty-seven Taylor/Piper J-2s were listed on the U.S. civil register in March 2014.

1936 Piper J-2 NC15965 at Oshkosh, Wisconsin. *Rod Simpson*

1940 Piper J-3C-65 NC35054 basks in the Florida sunshine in March 1998 after being flown by the author from Bob White Field, Apopka, Florida.

Piper J-3 Cub and PA-11. The J-3 flew in 1938 and was, in essence an improved J-2. Various engines were available; the most successful version, the J-3C-65, being powered by the Continental A-65 engine. More than 19,000 Piper J-3 were built. In addition to pre-war civilian training, large numbers were used as observation/liaison aircraft with the designation O-39 or L-4. The 1947 PA-11 Cub Special differed primarily in having a fully enclosed engine cowling; 1,500 were built.

Piper J-4A Cub Coupé. The J-4 Cub Coupé provided Piper with a two-seat side-by-side aircraft with which to compete with erstwhile partner CG Taylor's Taylorcraft models. The J-4 was first flown in May 1938. 1,251 J-4 were built production ceasing after U.S. entry into the Second World War. In March 2014 some 300 were listed on the U.S. civil aircraft register.

1940 Piper J-4A G-AFWH is one of five that appeared on the UK register in March 2014. It was photographed at Cranfield, Bedfordshire.

1941 Piper J-5A N38038 photographed in 1991 at Culpepper, Virginia. *Jim Smith*

Piper J-5 Cub Cruiser. The J-5 is in essence a three-seat J-3 Cub with a widened center fuselage to accommodate a rear bench seat. The Cub Cruiser was powered by a Continental A-75 and was first flown in July 1939. An ambulance variant, the AE-1, was used by the U.S. Navy during the Second World War. 1,507 J-5 were built, with production continuing until 1946. More than 360 remained on the U.S. civil register in March 2014.

PA-12 Super Cruiser and PA-14 Family Cruiser. The PA-12 Super Cruiser was an improved J-5C powered by a 108hp or 115hp Lycoming O-235. 3,760 were built and large numbers remain active. The PA-14 Family Cruiser had a widened forward cabin and could accommodate four occupants. The type first flew in March 1947 and a total of 238 were built. 110 were listed on the U.S. register in March 2014, well over half of these operating in Alaska.

1947 Piper PA-12 Super Cruiser N3506M photographed at Winter Haven, Florida.

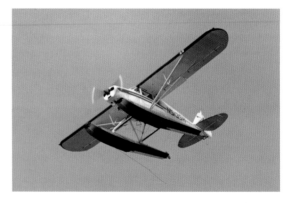

1948 Piper PA-14 Family Cruiser N5315H photographed at Oshkosh.

1949 Piper PA-16 Clipper G-BBUG photographed at Bembridge, Isle of Wight.

Piper PA-16 Clipper. The 1948 PA-16 Clipper was a four-seat aircraft powered by a 108hp Lycoming O-235 using the same wing as the PA-15 Vagabond, but with a longer fuselage. Although somewhat underpowered as a four-seat aircraft, 736 were built, 355 remaining on the U.S. register in March 2014.

Piper PA-15 and PA-17 Vagabond. The two-seat side-by-side PA-15 Vagabond (and its dual control variant the PA-17) married a reduced-span J-3 Cub wing with a new fuselage. Power was provided by a 65hp Lycoming (PA-15), or Continental (PA-17) engine. The PA-15 first flew in 1948. 387 PA-15 and 214 PA-17 were built, giving a combined total of 601 aircraft.

Piper PA-17 Vagabond G-ALEH taking off from Popham, Hampshire in July 2011.

Piper PA-18 Super Cub. The PA-18 Super Cub first flew in 1949 and was a modernized version of the PA-11, offering increased power and electrical system and, on later models, flaps. The initial production model had the 95hp Continental C-90-8F and is sometimes known as the PA-18-95. Its military version was the L-18C (which is sometimes erroneously referred to as the PA-19). It was followed by the PA-18-105, which introduced flaps, and the PA-18-125 and PA-18-135. The most popular version is the PA-18-150 with a 150hp Lycoming O-320. The Super Cub is popular for backcountry flying, performing well from short strips and on floats. It is also widely used for utility roles such as glider towing. More than 10,000 PA-18 Super Cubs have been built. The Super Cub remains in operation worldwide, with several thousand active in the U.S.

G-ATRG is a modified 1962 PA-18-150 used for glider towing at Lasham, Hampshire and photographed in May 2009.

The photos above show two Super Cub variants. On the left, N5127Y is a 1962 Piper PA-18-150 operating on 'tundra tires' in Alaska.

Right, G-BLMI is a Piper PA-18-95 (previously an L-18C) with no flaps and a C-90 engine; it was photographed at Bembridge, Isle of Wight.

1954 Piper PA-20 Pacer VH-TPH photographed at Echuca, VIC, Australia in April 2012.

Piper PA-20 Pacer. The PA-20 Pacer is a more powerful development of the PA-16. Initially available with a 115hp Lycoming O-235, later production aircraft offered 125hp or 135hp. First flown in July 1949, a total of 1,120 PA-20s were built.

Piper PA-22 Tri Pacer and Colt. The Tri Pacer as its name suggests is basically a tricycle undercarriage version of the PA-20. Initially produced with a 125hp engine, power was progressively increased to 135hp, 150hp (Caribbean) and 160hp. The Tri Pacer was followed in 1961 by the two-seat PA-22-108 Colt, which came about because Piper had no product with which to compete with the Cessna 150. The Colt is basically a Piper Clipper with a Tri Pacer undercarriage and no rear windows. The total production of the PA-22 was 9,490, of which 7,642 were Tri Pacer and 1,848 Colt. In March 2014, 778 Colts and 3,247 Tri Pacers appeared on the U.S. civil register with fifty-two in the UK, 390 in Canada, and seventy-one in Australia (plus a few on the RAA register). With aircraft operating in other nations, at least half of the PA-22 aircraft ever built still appear on the world's civil aircraft registers.

In recent years, there has been a fashion to convert both Tri Pacer and the Colt to tailwheel configuration, in which guise they are very difficult to distinguish from the PA-20 Pacer. Some owners even choose to paint the name Pacer on the aircraft, irrespective of its actual origin.

Piper PA-22-160 Tri Pacer D-EHRE was photographed in 1971 at Dahlemer Binz, Germany

PA-22 variants: Above Left, 1961 Piper PA-22-108 Colt photographed at Dunkeswell, Devon in July 2013.

Above Right: Tailwheel conversion of 1953 PA-22-135 G-BUDE climbs out from Henstridge, Somerset.

PA-23 variants: Above Left, 1958 PA-23-160 Apache G-APMY at Doncaster in October 2013.

Above Right, 1963 PA-23-235 Apache 235 G-ASEP.

Piper PA-23 Apache and Apache 235. The PA-23 Apache was Piper's first twin engine aircraft, flying in March 1952. It was developed from the one-off Twin Stinson with a single fin and retractable undercarriage replacing the twin fins and fixed undercarriage of the Twin Stinson. Initial capacity was four-seats, increased to five from 1955. Initially powered by two 150hp O-320 engines, power was increased to 160hp in later models. 2,047 Apache were built, followed by 118 Apache 235 with swept fin and 235hp O-540 engines.

1971 Piper PA-23-250 Aztec E G-AZMK at Dunkeswell, Devon.

Piper PA-23 Aztec. The Aztec is a 250hp development from the Apache G. The Aztec was the subject of progressive development with an increase in capacity to six persons, lengthened nose, and revised engine cowlings. The final model, the Aztec G featured a modified wing tip shape and rectangular tailplane. A total of 4,811 Aztec were built between 1960 and 1981.

Piper PA-24 Comanche. The Piper Comanche is a high performance single-engine low wing monoplane with retractable undercarriage. First flown in May 1956, it was initially powered by a 180hp O-360 engine. A 250hp model was introduced in 1960, changing to 260hp in 1965 until production ceased in 1972, 4,716 having been completed. 148 examples of a 400hp variant, the Comanche 400, were built in 1964-65.

VH-OIB is a 1965 PA-24-260 Comanche photographed at Echuca, VIC, Australia in April 2013.

Above Left: G-BBKX is a 1973 Piper PA-28-180 Challenger taking off from Farnborough, Hampshire.

Above Right: G-BTKX is a 1978 Piper PA-28-181 Archer II landing at Bicester, Oxfordshire in May 2010.

Piper PA-28 Cherokee. The Piper Cherokee is far and away Piper's most successful aircraft. First flown in January 1960, the aircraft remains in production in 2014. There are two main families of Cherokee; those with rectangular wings, comprising the -140, -150, -160, -180 and -235 and those with semi-tapered wings, these being the -151, -161, -181, 201T, and -236. The suffix corresponds to the installed power in horsepower, the suffix being increased by one in the taper wing designations. More than 30,000 Cherokee aircraft have been built. For additional detail concerning variants, see the author's book *Piper Cherokee: A Family History.*

Piper PA-28R Cherokee Arrow. The Cherokee Arrow is a retractable undercarriage version of the Cherokee and was first flown in 1967. The first variants had the rectangular wing planform and either 180hp or 200hp. The 200hp Cherokee Arrow II featured an increase in wingspan and fuselage length, and a larger dorsal fin. The taper-wing variants are the Arrow III and Arrow IV, the latter having a T-tail. The Arrow III and IV are available in normally aspirated or turbocharged variants

G-AYPU is a 1970 PA-28R-200 Cherokee Arrow, photographed at Elstree in July 2013.

Piper PA-28R Arrow variants: Left – 1976 Piper PA-28R-200 Arrow II VH-JWO at Canberra, ACT in July 2008.

Centre: G-JESS is a 1978 Piper PA-28R-201T Turbo Arrow III at Henstridge, Somerset in March 2012.

Right: G-RATV is a 1983 Piper PA-28RT-201T Turbo Arrow IV at Compton Abbas, Wiltshire in April 2012.

Piper PA-30 and PA-39: Above Left, VH-DHC is a 1965 PA-30-160 Twin Comanche at Echuca, VIC in April 2013.

Above Right, VH-EFS is a Twin Comanche C/R at Camden, NSW, Australia.

PA-30 Twin Comanche and PA-39 Twin Comanche C/R. As its name suggests, the Twin Comanche is a twin engine version of the Piper Comanche. First flown in May 1963, 2,001 were built, production ending in 1969. The PA-39 Twin Comanche C/R is a version with counter-rotating propellers; 155 were built between 1970 and 1972. External recognition requires scrutiny of the propellers.

Piper PA-32 Cherokee Six, Saratoga and 6X. The Cherokee Six is a stretched six-/seven-seat version of the Cherokee. The type was first flown in December 1963 and produced in 260hp or 300hp versions. A tapered-wing version was produced as the PA-32-301 Saratoga; an updated version being sold as the Piper 6X (PA-32-301FT). Turbocharged variants of the Saratoga and 6X were also produced. More than 4,400 Cherokee Six and Saratoga aircraft were produced.

G-EDYO is a 1966 Cherokee Six 260 photographed at Compton Abbas in June 2011.

Piper PA-32R Cherokee Lance, Lance II and Saratoga II. As with the Cherokee Arrow, the Cherokee Six spawned a family of retractable undercarriage derivatives. The PA-32R-300 Cherokee Lance first flew in August 1974 and dropped the 'Cherokee' name after 1977. After 1978, the type was produced with a T-tail as the PA-32RT-Lance II. The introduction of the semi-tapered wing was accompanied with a return to a low-set stabilator and a change of name and designation to PA-32R-301 Saratoga II. The Lance II and Saratoga II are both available in turbocharged variants. More than 3,000 aircraft have been produced in this family. License production of the Lance and Saratoga II was undertaken by Embraer in Brazil; the Lance was also produced by Chincul in Argentina. For more details see, *Piper Cherokee: A Family History*.

OO-RAV is a 1976 Cherokee Lance 300 seen at Balen Keiheuvel, Belgium in May 1989.

Piper PA-32R variants: Above Left, G-OJCW is a PA-32RT-300 Lance II at Blackbushe, Hampshire in 1977. *Jim Smith*

Above Right, G-PURL is a 1994 PA-32R-301 Saratoga II HP at Compton Abbas in February 2011.

G-GFCD is a 1981 Piper PA-34-220T Seneca III photographed at Blackbushe, Hampshire in August 2011.

Piper PA-34 Seneca. The Seneca is, in essence, a twin engine Cherokee Six. The type was first flown in October 1969, initially with a pair of 200hp Lycoming IO-360 engines. Development has seen cleaning up of the engine installation and a change of engine to the turbocharged 220hp Continental L/TSIO-360. Piper produced nearly 5,000 aircraft, with additional license production in Argentina, Brazil, Colombia and Poland. The Seneca remains in production in March 2014.

Piper PA-38 Tomahawk. The Tomahawk is a two-seat basic trainer, with a low wing and T-tail. The type was first flown in July 1973. Some 2,500 PA-38 were built by Piper, production coming to an end in 1982. The type remains in service worldwide; more than 250 were registered in the UK, with ninety-four remaining on the register in March 2014.

G-BPHI is a 1979 Piper PA-38-112 photographed at Blackbushe, Hampshire in April 2007.

N3048R is a 1979 Piper PA-44-18 Seminole photographed at North Las Vegas, Nevada.

Piper PA-44 Seminole. The Seminole light twin first flew in May 1976. Smaller than the Seneca, the Seminole seats four and is based on the Arrow IV. Like the somewhat similar Beech Duchess, it has proven to be a popular training aircraft for pilots seeking a twin rating. The Seminole remains in production in 2014.

Piper PA-46 Malibu, Malibu Mirage, Malibu Meridian and Matrix. The Piper Malibu is a high performance pressurized single-engine aircraft offered with either piston engine (Malibu, Mirage and Matrix) or with a 500hp PT6A turboprop engine (PA-46-500TP Malibu Meridian).

The Malibu first flew in November 1979. The first production aircraft, the PA-46-310P, used a 310hp Continental TSIO-520 engine; subsequently, the 350hp Lycoming TIO-540 was fitted, the type then being known as the PA-46-350P Malibu Mirage. The PA-46-350T Matrix is an unpressurized version of the Mirage. The turboprop Malibu Meridian first flew in August 1998. The Meridian, Mirage and Matrix remain in production in 2014. Piper built 404 of the initial PA-46-310P Malibu.

Piper PA-46 variants: Left, G-JCAR is a 1999 Piper PA-46-350P Malibu Mirage photographed at Dunkeswell, Devon.

Right, D-ESSS is a 2008 PA-46-500TP Malibu Meridian photographed at Blackbushe, Hampshire in August 2011.

NC13158 is a 1930 Pitcairn PA-7S Super Sport Mailwing photographed at Oshkosh, Wisconsin.

Pitcairn

The Pitcairn Aircraft Company is notable as a pioneer of the autogyro in the United States, having been the U.S. Licensee of the Cierva Autogiro Co. Ltd. Those aircraft fall outside the scope of this work although some 120 autogyros were built, the most significant being the Pitcairn PA-18 and the PCA-2.

The company's other main product was the series of Pitcairn Mailwing and Super Mailwing biplanes originally developed for the U.S. Postal Service. The Pitcairn PA-5 Mailwing first flew in 1927 and 106 were built. Other notable models (and numbers built) were the 1926 PA-3 Orowing (35 built); 1927 PA-4 Fleetwing II (10 built); 1929 PA-7 Super Mailwing (28 built); and the 1930 PA-8 Super Mailwing.

Pitts

The immensely successful Pitts Special aerobatic aircraft was designed by Curtis Pitts and first flew in September 1944. The type has been built in a number of guises since, with progressive enhancements to maintain its competitive relevance in the sport of aerobatics. Advanced competition aircraft typically have a 180hp engine with full inverted fuel and oil systems. The single-seat version is the Pitts S1. Ailerons on all four wings were introduced on the S1-D, with the S1-S having symmetric wing sections. A number of even more specialist developments include the 300hp S1-11B Super Stinker, the S1 Falcon Special, S1-SS Ultimate, and S1-T.

1988 Pitts S1T N11N displaying at Henstridge, Somerset in August 2014.

G-STUB is a 1989 Pitts S2-B photographed at Old Sarum, Wiltshire in April 2007.

Pitts S2. The S2 is the two-seat version of the Pitts Special, suitable both for aerobatic training and competition. A series of variants include the S2-A, S2-B, S2-C, and S2-S with up to 260hp available and performance to suit. The S-2 was introduced in 1967.

Pitts Model 12. The Pitts 12 (variously known as Monster, or Macho Stinker), was designed specifically around the Russian Vedeneyev M-14P/PF 360-400hp radial engine. Jim Kimball Enterprises of Zelwood, Florida owns the rights to the Pitts Model 12.

N450CT is a 2009 Pitts Model 12 'Monster,' photographed at Casa Grande, California in October 2013. *Peter Davison*

OO-93 is a Belgian Pober P-9 Pixie, photographed at Brienne-le-Chateau, France.

Pober

The Pober Pixie was designed by Paul Poberezny of the EAA to provide an economic homebuilt aircraft. The Pixie is a single-seat parasol monoplane designed for Volkswagen or Continental A-65 power. The type was first flown in July 1974. In March 2014, there were thirty-one registered in the USA and six in Canada.

Porterfield

Porterfield 35 Flyabout. The Flyabout has its origins in an aircraft was designed by Noel Hockaday, known as the Pup. Porterfield bought the design rights to the aircraft and put it into production as the 1935 Porterfield Flyabout. The Flyabout was a two-seat high-wing-monoplane powered by a LeBlond radial engine. The most important version was the LeBlond-powered 35-70, 150 of which were built. Total production ran to around 185 aircraft. Fifteen were listed on the U.S. civil aircraft register in March 2014.

NC17037 is a 1937 Porterfield 35-70 photographed at Oshkosh, Wisconsin.

G-AFZL is a 1939 Porterfield CP-50 photographed at Cranfield, Bedfordshire.

Porterfield CP-40 to CP-65 Collegiate. The Collegiate was a trainer development of the Flyabout. It was first flown in 1936, models being variously designated -40, -50, -55, FP-65, LP-65, or CP-65, dependent on installed power and engine manufacturer. Production totaled 476 aircraft, with ninety-two listed on the U.S. civil register in March 2014.

Potez

Potez was an important French aircraft manufacturer, which was active from 1919 until around 1967, when it became part of Sud Aviation. Important designs included the Potez XV reconnaissance aircraft (more than 600 built); Potez 25 general purpose civil and military biplane (4,000 built); Potez 36 lightplane (more than 300); Potez 63.11 twin engine reconnaissance of the Second World War (more than 700); and the Potez Air-Fouga Magister jet trainer (929 built).

Potez 60. The Potez 60 is a two-seat parasol monoplane that first flew in August 1935. 155 were built, the production variant being the Potez 600 Sauterelle (Grasshopper).

Potez 600 HB-SPM photographed at Abingdon, Oxfordshire.

Pottier

Jean Pottier has designed a varied series of homebuilt aircraft in France, including aircraft of biplane, and low-, mid- and high-wing monoplanes including single, two, three and four-seat aircraft. In March 2014, 146 aircraft of Pottier design appeared on the French register.

Most numerous by some margin were the single-seat P80 (22 aircraft) and its two-seat side-by-side derivative, the P180S (53 examples). There were also eleven examples of the two-seat P220 and twenty examples of its three-seat derivative, the P230. Examples of selected Pottier designs are illustrated below.

1977 Pottier P70S F-PYEF at Cranfield, Bedfordshire.

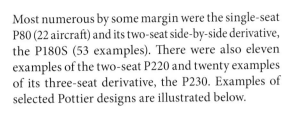

1982 two-seat Pottier P170B F-PYLG at Brienne-le-Chateau, France.

Pottier P80S OO-54 at Balen Keiheuvel, Belgium in May 1989.

1983 two-seat Pottier P180S Pottier P180S at Brienne-le-Chateau, France in July 1983.

F-BULT is a 1961 Procaer F.15A Picchio at Balen Keiheuvel, Belgium in May 1989.

Procaer

Procaer F15 Picchio. The F.15 Picchio is another classic design from the pen of the Italian designer Stelio Frati. The prototype Picchio flew in a three-seat configuration (F.15) in May 1959. The production aircraft F.15A and F.15B accommodated four, a grand total of thirty-eight Picchios being built.

Pützer

Pützer Elster. Alfons Pützer built a motor-glider called the Motoraab in 1955 and developed this into the Pützer Elster, which was used by flying clubs (Elster B) and for glider towing (Elster C). The type had two-seats, a rounded plywood-skinned fuselage and a tricycle undercarriage. A total of forty-five were built.

1959 Pützer Elster B G-APVF/97+04 at Cranfield, Bedfordshire in July 1989.

PZL

PZL (or Pezetel) is a famous Polish manufacturer noted for its series of pre-war high wing gull-wing monoplane fighters such as the PZL P.24. More recently, the company has been a major helicopter manufacturer, PZL- Świdnik building the Mil Mi2 and the PZL Sokol designs at Lublin, Poland.

Fixed wing aircraft are produced by PZL-Mielic and have included the Antonov An-2, MiG-15 and MiG-17, TS-11 Iskra military trainer, agricultural aircraft (Kruk and Dromader), gliders and licensed production of Western designs such as the SOCATA Rallye and the Piper Seneca.

PZL-104 Wilga. The Wilga is a single-engine high wing STOL aircraft for civilian and military use built at the PZL Warszawa-Okęcie factory. More than 1,000 Wilga have been built, the type first flying in 1962. Many civilian Wilgas are used for glider towing. The latest model is the Wilga 2000, which was first flown in 1998. 17 Wilga have been registered in the UK; three of these remaining on the register in March 2014. Forty-six were registered in the USA at the same date.

PZL-104 variants: Left, G-BTNS is a 1990 PZL-104 Wilga 80 photographed at Wroughton, Wiltshire in July 1993.

Right: G-RTRT is a 2006 PZL-104MA Wilga 2000 photographed at Popham, Hampshire in August 2006.

N336RM is a Quickie photographed at Oshkosh, Wisconsin.

Quickie

Quickie. The Quickie is an all-composite tandem wing single-seat homebuilt aircraft designed around the 18hp Onan engine. The front wing has marked anhedral with the two mainwheels integrated into the wingtips. The Quickie was first flown in November 1977 and many kits were sold, although it is not certain how many were completed and flown. In March 2014, sixty-five Quickie aircraft appeared on the U.S. civil register.

Quickie Q2 or Q200. The Q2, first flown in July 1980, is a two-seat homebuilt aircraft of the same general configuration as the Quickie, powered by a 64hp Volkswagen engine. The Q200 offers higher performance and is typically fitted with a 100hp Continental O-200 engine, although other engines in the same power class are also used. Some 2,000 kits have been sold although the number flown is not certain. Thirty-one Quickie Q2s and nine Q200s appeared on the U.S. register in March 2014; five Q2s and four Q200s appeared on the UK register at the same date.

VH-LOQ is a 1991 Quickie Q200 photographed at Temora, NSW, Australia in April 2010. *Jim Smith*

Tri-Q. the Quickie Q2 and Q200 can be completed with a tricycle undercarriage, this version being known as the Quickie Tri-Q. The Tri-Q features a front wing without dihedral or anhedral.

N13QT is a Quickie Tri-Q photographed at Oshkosh, Wisconsin.

N49RW is a Rand Robinson KR-1 photographed at Oshkosh, Wisconsin.

Rand

Kenneth Rand designed the single-seat Rand KR-1 and two-seat KR-2 homebuilt aircraft. Plans were marketed by Rand Robinson Engineering.

KR-1. The Rand Robinson KR-1 first flew in February 1972. The KR-1 is a low wing monoplane powered by a converted Volkswagen engine. A short retractable undercarriage is fitted retracting directly back into the wing and giving a very low ground angle. In April 2014 there were some fifty KR-1s on the U.S. civil register.

The KR-2 is a two-seat side-by-side development of the KR-1. It was first flown in July 1974 and proved highly popular. In April 2014, there were more than 250 on the U.S. civil aircraft register and some twenty-one in the UK. Normally fitted with a retractable undercarriage, some aircraft have been complete with fixed tricycle landing gear. The KR-2S has a fuselage lengthened by sixteen inches compared with the standard KR-2.

G-BLDN is a 1985 Rand KR-2 photographed at Cranfield, Bedfordshire.

C-GQKW is a 1982 Rand Robinson KR-2T photographed at Oshkosh, Wisconsin in July 1985.

Rand KR-2T. This version of the Rand KR-2 seats two occupants in tandem and normally has a fixed tailwheel undercarriage.

Rans

Rans Designs have produced a family of light aircraft that straddle the boundary between microlights (outside the scope of this work) and conventional light aircraft. These designs are mainly intended for homebuilding, but certain types are also factory-built. A selection of types is illustrated below.

Rans S-6 Coyote II. The S-6 is a two-seat version of the earlier single-seat S3 to S5 Coyote microlight. The Coyote II has been extremely successful as evidenced by 167 Rans S6 appearing on the British civil aircraft register in April 2014. The S6 may be built with either a tricycle or a tailwheel undercarriage.

G-BZEW is a 2000 Rans S6-ES landing at Henstridge, Somerset in June 2013.

G-BWKJ is a 1997 Rans S7 Courier photographed at Cranfield, Bedfordshire.

Rans S7 Courier. The S7 seats two in tandem and may be kit-built, or factory-built. Dependent on model, engines of between 50hp and 100hp may be installed. In April 2014, 210 Rans S7 appeared on the U.S. civil aircraft register, with eight registered in the UK.

Rans S9 Chaos and S10 Sakota. The S9 is a single-seat mid-wing aerobatic ultralight aircraft. The S10 Sakota is a two-seat aerobatic development of the Rans S9.

Left: Rans S9 Chaos 28-1836 at Illawarra Regional Airport, NSW, Australia.

Right: Rans S10 Sakota G-BSWB photographed at Dunkeswell, Devon.

19-7443 is a Rans S19 Venterra photographed at Temora, NSW, Australia in April 2013. *Jim Smith*

Rans S19 Venterra. The S19 is a low wing monoplane in the light sport aircraft category that seats two side-by-side. The S19 was first flown in June 2007 and is powered by the 100hp Rotax 912ULS engine.

Rearwin

Rearwin Airplanes built a series of high wing light aircraft from 1931 through to the early 1940s, including the Junior, Speedster, Sportster, Cloudster and Skyranger. Production of the Skyranger continued post-war by Commonwealth.

Rearwin Junior. the Rearwin Junior first flew in 1931 and was a small single-seat high wing monoplane. Around thirty were built, most as Rearwin 3000 with a Szekely SR-3 radial engine.

Rearwin Junior fuselage frame at Albury, NSW, Australia in April 2013.

G-AEOF is a 1936 Rearwin 8500 Sportster with an 85hp Le Blond 5DF engine.

Rearwin Sportster. The Sportster, which first flew in 1935, was among the most successful Rearwin designs with around 330 being built in versions ranging from the Rearwin 7000 (70hp Le Blond) to the Rearwin 9000 (90hp Warner, Le Blond or Ken Royce). 261 were built by Rearwin with a further twelve in Sweden as the Götaverken GV-38.

Rearwin Cloudster. The Cloudster was a more powerful development of the Sportster with side-by-side rather than tandem seating. The Cloudster was first flown in 1939 and produced with various engines ranging from 90hp to 135hp; a total of 125 were built. The Rearwin 8135 was a three-seat version.

G-EVLE is a 1939 Rearwin 8125 Cloudster photographed at Old Sarum, Wiltshire in January 2007.

F8010 G-BDWJ is a 1978 Replica Plans SE5A Replica photographed at Henstridge, Somerset in April 2009.

Replica Plans

Replica Plans SE5A Replica. This is a Canadian-designed 7/8ths scale replica of the Royal Aircraft Factory SE5A, for homebuilt construction using modern materials and is typically powered by engines in the 65hp to 100hp range. The prototype flew in 1970 and more than 100 are known to be flying. Other SE5A replicas and a few original Royal Aircraft Factory SE5A or SE5E aircraft are still flying.

Republic

Republic Aviation is a company best known for its series of fighter and attack aircraft, the P-47 Thunderbolt, F-84 Thunderjet and Thunderstreak and the F-105 Thunderchief. The Republic Seabee is a single-engine four-seat flying boat with a pusher propeller. The Seabee first flew in November 1944, the production model being the RC-3. 1,050 RC-3 were built in a short production run in 1946-47. Many are still operating; in April 2014, 225 were listed on the U.S. civil register, with a further fifty-eight on the Canadian register.

Republic RC-3 Seabee believed to be N6525K at Merrill Field, Alaska in 1983.

D-EIFF is an RW3-P75 Multoplan photographed at Brienne le Chateau, France.

RFB (Rhein Flugzeugebau)

RFB RW3 Multoplan. The RW3 was designed by Rhein-West Flug Fischer where two examples were built before license production began at RFB. The production RW3-P75 is unusually configured, with a buried Porsche engine driving a propeller mounted at the fuselage sternpost and rotating between the fin and rudder. The first production aircraft flew in February 1958; twenty-two were built, together with one amateur-built example and two RW3-90s with increased power.

Riley

Riley are noted for cleaned-up and re-engined versions of twin engine aircraft such as the Cessna series of light twins and the de Havilland DH104 Dove.

Riley Twin Navion. Riley completed nineteen conversions of the Navion (see Ryan below) to twin-engine configuration as the Riley D-16 Twin Navion. Riley built 19, followed by construction by Temco of forty-six D-16s and forty-five D-16As with increased power. The Camair 480 is a separate twin-engine version of the Navion, of which thirty-five were built.

C-FDEC is a Temco-built D-16A Twin Navion, photographed at Oshkosh, Wisconsin.

RLU

RLU-1 Breezy. The Breezy was designed by Charles Roloff, Robert Liposky and Carl Unger, their combined surname initials providing the RLU designation. The type combines an open steel tube fuselage with an existing wing (the prototype using that of a Piper PA-12) and tail feathers, together with a pusher engine and propeller. More than 1,000 plans have been sold and numbers are flying in the U.S., Canada and Europe. Forty were listed on the U.S. civil register in June 2014.

Breezy by name and Breezy by nature, N3184 is an RLU-1 Breezy built using Aeronca aerodynamic surfaces. It is seen at North Las Vegas Airport, Nevada, shortly before the author had a flight on this unusual machine.

Robin (Avions Pierre Robin)

Avions Pierre Robin was the successor to Centre Est Aéronautique and developed the wooden Centre Est 200 series into the DR300 and DR400 series, before producing the all-metal HR- and R- series and the Robin ATL (Avion Très Légère).

DR300 series. The visually very similar DR300 series are, in effect, nosewheel developments of the CEA DR200 series. Their designations have suffices that reflect installed power (in horsepower). A representative selection of Robin DR300 models is presented below.

F-BSLE 1971 DR300-108 2+2 at Compton Abbas, improved DR315.

F-BTBJ DR300-120 Petit Prince in France, four-seats and 120hp O-235-L2A engine.

G-KIMB 1970 DR300-140 at Wroughton, 140hp O-320-E2A engine.

F-BRDY 1965 DR315 Petit Prince in France nosewheel variant of DR221.

G-DRZF 1960 DR360 Chevalier at Eggesford, 160hp O-320-D2A engine.

F-BSJA 1970 DR380 Prince at Toussus-le-Noble, DR300 with 180hp O-360-A3A.

D-EDUY 1971 DR300-180R at Dahlemer-Binz, 180hp O-360-A3A with glider tow hook.

Robin DR400 Series. The DR400 series followed on from the DR300, the main change being adoption of a forward-sliding cockpit canopy replacing the hinged doors of the DR300 series. As with the DR300 series, designations reflect the aircraft's installed power. A representative selection of DR400 models is shown below.

G-GAOH 1977 DR400 2+2, at Henstridge, (DR300-108 with forward-sliding canopy).

G-BAJZ 1972 DR400-120 Petit Prince, Bembridge, (DR300-120 with forward-sliding canopy).

G-BBAY 1973 DR400-140 Earl, Sibson, (DR300-140 with forward-sliding canopy).

G-GCUF 1981 DR400-160, Henstridge, (DR360 with forward-sliding canopy).

G-CONB 1992 DR400-180 Regent, Leicester, (DR300-180 with forward-sliding canopy).

G-BJUD 1981 DR400-180R, Lasham, (DR300-180R with forward-sliding canopy).

G-GMIB 1998 DR400-500 President, Henstridge; (this is a wider fuselage DR400 derivative marketed as the DR500-200i President with 200hp IO-360 200CV engine).

Robin HR Series. Designed by Chris Heintz (who went on to form Zenith), the all-metal HR100 series feature a rectangular planform wing of constant dihedral. The type was first flown in April 1969. The main production variants were the HR100-200B Royal and the HR100-210 Safari, of which a combined total of 113 were built. The 1974 HR100-250 Tiara had a retractable undercarriage and a 250hp Continental Tiara IO-540 engine; twenty-four examples were built, followed by thirty-seven HR100-285 with a 285hp Tiara 6-285 engine.

The HR200 Club is a two-seat trainer smaller development with a large bubble canopy. The main production versions are the HR200-100 with 108hp; HR100-120B with 120hp; or HR200-125 Acrobin with 125hp, all variants using appropriate models of the Lycoming O-235 engine. 107 of these HR200 models were built. For further development of both the HR100 and 200, see the Robin R-series, below.

G-BBAW is a 1973 HR100-210 Safari seen at Compton Abbas, Wiltshire.

G-BEUD is a retractable undercarriage 1975 Robin HR100-285 Tiara.

G-GMKE is a 1993 Robin HR200-120B photographed at Henstridge, Somerset in June 2013.

Robin R Series. The Robin R1180T Aiglon is a lighter weight version of the HR100 with a revised fin and rudder and 180hp Lycoming IO-360 engine. Sixty-six were built, including the R1180TD Aiglon II (a refined version with a new instrument panel and other minor changes). The R2100 family comprises aerobatic developments of the HR200 trainer distinguished by having a long rectangular ventral fin. Main production models are the R2100 Super Club (108hp) and the R2160 Alpha Sport (160hp).

G-ROBN is a 1978 Robin R1180T photographed at Compton Abbas, Wiltshire.

G-BICS is a 1977 Robin R2100A, landing at Farnborough, Hampshire in July 2010.

G-BZOL is a 1986 Robin R3000/140 photographed at Compton Abbas, Wiltshire in August 2013.

Robin R3000: The distinctive Robin 3000 is a four-seat (2+2) low wing monoplane with a bubble canopy and T-tail. Production models were offered with a 116hp Lycoming O-235 (R3000/120 or R3120), a 140hp Lycoming O-320 (R3000/140, or R3140); or a 160hp Lycoming O-320 (R3000/160). Around seventy have been built.

Robin ATL. The ATL (Avion Très Légèr) is a two-seat side-by-sight light training monoplane with a composite fuselage and wooden wings. The type has a long slim fuselage and butterfly tail surfaces. The ATL was first flown in June 1983; 135 were built, seventy-four appearing of the French register in April 2014.

1986 Robin ATL F-GFRK photographed at Cranfield, Bedfordshire.

1932 Robinson Redwing G-ABNX taxying at Sywell, Northamptonshire.

Robinson

The Robinson Redwing was a two-seat open cockpit biplane seating two side-by-side and flew in 1930. A total of twelve were built, the sole survivor being G-ABNX that is under restoration at the time that this book was under preparation.

Rollason

Rollason Aircraft & Engines Ltd. converted large numbers of Tiger Moths for civil use after the Second World War, before constructing thirty Druine

Turbulents and forty-eight Druine Condors under license. The company also acted as UK importers for Jodel aircraft.

Luton Beta. The Luton Beta midget racer was designed by a group of BAC technicians based at Luton for an aircraft design competition. Rollason built the prototype G-ATLY, which first flew in April 1967, and three further examples. Plans were made available and a further five aircraft have been homebuilt.

The prototype Rollason Luton Beta G-ATLY *Forerunner* seen in the Tiger Club hangar at Redhill around the time of its first flight. The aircraft behind the Beta is a Rollason-built Druine Condor.

N27Q is registered as a Hanson Parakeet A-4 replica built in 1978 and photographed at Oshkosh, Wisconsin.

Rose

Rose A-1 Parakeet. The Parakeet (some sources Parrakeet) is a single-seat biplane that first flew in 1934, with nine being built with the 40hp Henderson engine. A single diagonal strut replaces the normal flying wires used to brace a biplane structure, a feature also found on the Andreasson BA4 biplane. The type has also been constructed as a homebuilt or replica with around ten on the U.S. register in April 2014, although few are active.

N73LD is a Rutan Vari Viggen built in 1981 and photographed at Oshkosh, Wisconsin in July 1985.

Rutan

Burt Rutan is noted for the originality of his designs and for his espousal of canard configurations and, in his later designs, the use of composite materials.

Vari Viggen. The Vari Viggen has a canard combined with a low aspect ratio delta wing and a rear-mounted engine with pusher propeller. The two occupants are seated in tandem in a wooden fuselage fitted with outer wing panels of metal construction. First flown in 1972, twelve Vari Viggen appeared on the U.S. register in April 2014.

VariEze G-BKVE in the foreground, with a Long EZ to the rear showing the larger fins and rudders of the latter type. Photographed at Henstridge, Somerset.

Rutan VariEze. The VariEze is Rutan's classic design combining urethane foam and glass fiber construction to produce a fast efficient homebuilt design, whose canard layout and sharply swept wings produced a new shape in the sky when it first flew in May 1975. A retractable nosewheel combined with fixed mainwheels gives a characteristic stance when parked and allows access to the cockpit when on the ground. The type was an immediate success worldwide and led on to the enlarged Long EZ described below. Some hundreds appear on the U.S. register, with seven in Canada, nine in Australia, thirty-seven in France and thirteen in the UK in April 2014.

Rutan Long EZ. The Long EZ is a development of the VariEze, with larger wings and tail surfaces and a longer range than the earlier design. The Long EZ follows the same design principles as the VariEze and first flew in June 1979. Several hundred have been built. In April 2014, many appeared on the U.S. register, with seventeen in Canada, forty-one in France, twenty-five in the UK and twenty-one in Australia.

1985 Rutan Long EZ G-RAEM in the evening light at Gamston, Nottinghamshire shortly before being flown by its builder Graham Singleton and the author to its home base at Netherthorpe, South Yorkshire.

1981 Shaw Twin-EZ G-IVAN at Cranfield, Bedfordshire.

Rutan-inspired variants. The tandem wing Quickie was developed with some input from Burt Rutan, as was the three-seat Cozy, which is a Long EZ development. The Shaw Twin-EZ is a twin-engine version of the Long EZ flown in the UK by Ivan Shaw in 1981.

Rutan Defiant. The four-seat twin engine Defiant marries the canard and swept wing configuration of the VariEze and Long EZ with a push-pull engine installation An offset forward-mounted rudder surface is attached to the lower front fuselage. The Defiant first flew in June 1978 and is a relatively complex aircraft for home construction. Twenty-six appeared on the U.S. register in April 2014, with two in Australia.

1986 Rutan Defiant G-OTWO at Cranfield, Bedfordshire in July 1988; this aircraft was subsequently sold in the USA.

N-X-211 is a replica Ryan NYP *Spirit of St Louis* at Lambert Field, St Louis, Missouri.

Ryan

The Ryan name is associated with Lindbergh's *Spirit of St Louis,* the first plane to be flown solo non-stop across the Atlantic. Another famous product was the pioneering Firebee reconnaissance drones used during the Vietnam War.

Ryan high wing monoplanes. Ryan's first design was the Ryan M-1 mail plane and the similar M-2; a total of thirty-six were built. Next came the Ryan B-1 Brougham, 236 of which were built. The custom-built Ryan NYP *Spirit of St Louis* was developed to Lindbergh's requirement, making its Transatlantic crossing on 20-21 May 1927. A number of flying replicas have been made, including at least three based on the B-1 Brougham

Ryan ST, PT-20 and PT-22. The clean Ryan ST (sport trainer) low wing monoplane seats two in tandem open cockpits and was first flown in June 1934. Eighty-nine Ryan ST and ST-A were constructed, followed by the ST-M, which was a military trainer version of the ST-A, and served with the USAAC as the PT-16, PT-20. The PT-21 had a 125hp Kinner, but the definitive development was the ST3-KR (PT-22) with 160hp Kinner. More than 1,500 aircraft of the ST family were built.

1940 Ryan STM-S2 VH-ASD at Illawarra, NSW, Australia in October 2009. *Jim Smith*

1943 Ryan ST3-KR VH-RPT at Echucha, VIC, Australia in April 2013.

NC18915 is a 1938 Ryan SCW photographed at Lakeland,Florida in April 1990. *Jim Smith*

Ryan SCW. The 1937 Ryan SCW was a three-seat low wing monoplane powered by a 145hp Warner radial engine. The aircraft is distinguished by a tapered wing with marked dihedral, together with a small radial engine under a close-fitting helmeted cowling. Like the de Havilland Moth Minor, the SCW is fitted with a speed brake fitted between the undercarriage legs. A total of thirty Ryan SCW were built.

Ryan Navion. The Ryan Navion is a high performance four-seat retractable undercarriage low wing monoplane that was originally designed and built by North American Aviation, that company's initials being used to generate the type name Navion. North American built 1,027 Navion from 1947 before passing production rights to Ryan, which built a further 1,224 aircraft.

In the 1960s, a new variant of the design, the Navion Rangemaster, was introduced by the Navion Aircraft Company and featured an integrated passenger cabin and tip tanks. A total of 180 Navion Rangemaster G and H were built. 1,062 Navions were listed on the U.S. civil register in April 2014.

N4851K is a 1949 Ryan Navion, photographed in Arizona in 1999.

N2503T is a 1967 Navion H Rangemaster, photographed at Oshkosh, Wisconsin.

G-HRLK is a 1959 Saab 91D Safir, photographed at Old Sarum, Wiltshire.

SAAB

The Swedish company SAAB is known for automobiles and, in the aerospace world, innovative fighters such as the J-29, Lansen, Draken, Viggen and Gripen. The Saab 91 Safir first flew in November 1945; 323 aircraft were built in four versions, the most numerous being the Saab 91D of which 134 were built.

SAI (Skandinavisk Aero Industri)

The Danish firm SAI built a number of light aircraft types from 1937 to the early-1950s. A selection of SAI designs is presented below.

SAI KZ-II. the two-seat KZ-II low wing monoplane was built as a side-by-side aircraft with a closed cockpit (KZII Kupé) and with tandem open cockpits (KZ-IIS Sport and KZ-IIT Træner). The type first flew in 1937 and the forty-five aircraft produced were split almost equally between the three variants.

1940 KZ-II Kupé OY-AEA taxying at Stauning, Denmark.

1946 KZ-IIT OY-FAK at Wroughton, Wiltshire.

OY-DGV is a 1946 KZ-IIIU-2 photographed at Cranfield, Bedfordshire.

SAI KZ-III. the KZ-III is a two-seat Cirrus Minor-powered high-wing monoplane that was first flown in September 1944. Sixty-four KZ-IIIs were built.

SAI KZ-IV. The KZ-IV was an elegant twin engine wooden aircraft with twin fins and two Gipsy Major engines in DH89 Rapide-style cowlings. Two were built, one remains flying today and the other is currently displayed at the Danmarks Flyvemuseum

1948 SAI KZ-IV U-1 OY-DZU on the approach to Stauning, Denmark.

OY-STJ is a 1948 KZ-VII U-8 photographed at Cranfield, Bedfordshire.

SAI KZ-VII Lærke. The KZ-VII is a four-seat development of the KZIII, first flown in October 1946. The KZ-VII used either a 125hp or a 145hp Continental engine. A total of fifty-eight were built. The KZ-X development of the KZ-VII was designed for army cooperation duties and sat two in tandem and featured increased cabin glazing; fourteen were built.

SAI KZ-VIII. The single-seat aerobatic KZ-VIII was powered by a Gipsy Major engine and first flew in November 1949; two were built.

1949 KZ-VIII OY-DRR at Stauning, Denmark. The other KZ-VIII flies on the UK register as G-AYKZ.

1959 Scheibe SF-23A Sperling photographed at Sywell, Northamptonshire.

Scheibe

Scheibe Flugzeugebau Gmbh is a well-known glider manufacturer that had also produced a number of powered aircraft and powered gliders, notably the Scheibe Falke series. Scheibe also collaborated with Sportavia on the SFS-31 Milan, with Scheibe SF-27 glider wings and Sportavia RF4D fuselage.

Scheibe SF23 Sperling. the SF-23 is a two-seat high wing monoplane that was first flown in 1955. Twenty-seven were built in three variants with power ranging from 95hp to 115hp.

Scheibe SF-25 Motor Falke/Falke. The SF-23 was followed by the SF-24 Motor-Spatz (a powered version of the L-Spatz glider). Scheibe then focused on the motor glider concept with the more powerful and highly successful SF-25 Motor Falke/Falke. More than 1,200 examples of the SF-25 have been built in a number of variants. Seventy-five were built by Slingsby in the UK as the T.61.

G-CFMW is a 1985 Scheibe SF-25C 2000 photographed at Bicester, Oxfordshire.

D-KOAM is an SF-28A Tandem Falke photographed at Brienne-le-Chateau, France.

Scheibe SF-28 Tandem Falke. The SF-28 is a tandem seat motor glider development of the SF-25. First flown in May 1971, a total of 119 were built.

Schleicher

Schleicher is a famous glider manufacturer that, like Scheibe, has produced a two-seat side-by-side motor glider. The Schleicher ASK 16 first flew in February 1971 and features a retractable undercarriage. Despite being rather cleaner than its Falke competitor, was less successful, with a total of forty-four being built.

G-BCTI is a 1974 Schleicher ASK 16 photographed at Cranfield, Bedfordshire.

1973 Scottish Aviation Bulldog 122 G-GRRR on the approach to Henstridge, Somerset.

Scottish Aviation

The Bulldog was developed by Beagle Aircraft Ltd. as a more powerful military trainer version of the Beagle Pup. The first prototype flew in 19 May 1969. After the failure of Beagle, responsibility for the type was transferred to Scottish Aviation Ltd. Widely exported, a total of 328 were built, 130 of these for the RAF.

SeaRey

The SeaRey is marketed by Progressive Aerodyne of Florida and is a two-seat amphibious flying boat with a single pusher engine. First flown in November 1992, nearly 600 SeaRey kits have been sold. In April 2014, 287 SeaRey were listed on the U.S. civil aircraft register, many of these operating in Florida.

This aircraft is an Aero Adventure Buccaneer II, a type that preceded the SeaRey and is of similar concept and configuration but flies in the ultralight category.

SIAI-Marchetti

SIAI began the manufacture of seaplanes as early as 1915, becoming Savoia Marchetti in 1922 before becoming SIAI-Marchetti. The company produced some notable bombers and transport aircraft during the Second World War, including the Savoia-Marchetti SM79 bomber. Light aircraft production began with the Nardi FN.333 Riviera amphibious flying boat, before moving on to the company's own designs.

SIAI-Marchetti S.205 and S.208. The S.205 was a four-seat light aircraft, similar in concept to the Piper Cherokee. The S.205 first flew in May 1964 and was produced with fixed or retractable undercarriage and 180hp, 200hp or 220hp engines, type designations reflecting this (e.g. S.205/18F, S.205/20R, etc). The S.208 was a five-seat 260hp development of the S.206/20R. The S.205 was very successful and sold well in the United States where the type was assembled by Waco and known as the Sirius or Vela. Some eighty-five S.208s were built, around half for the Italian military as the S.208M. Thirty-seven S.205s appeared on the U.S. register in April 2014.

1968 SIAI-Marchetti S.205/18R G-AYXS at Cranfield, Bedfordshire.

Later S.205s sold in the United States were fitted with five seats and known as the Vela. This is reflected in the registration of G-VELA an S.205/22R photographed at Dunkeswell, Devon.

SIAI-Marchetti S.208 PH-AIL photographed at Hilversum in September 2010. *Johan Visschedijk.*

SIAI-Marchetti SF.260. Designed by Stelio Frati, the attractive and high performance SF.260 sold well for both civil users and as a military trainer. The type was derived from the Falco and Picchio, the prototype being built by Aviamilano and flying in July 1964. Production was by SIAI-Marchetti (later Alenia Aermacchi), with more than 800 being built. The military versions are the SF.260M and SF.260W Warrior (with underwing hardpoints) and these have sold in greater numbers than the purely civil versions. The SF.260TP is a turboprop-powered version, which first flew in July 1980. Forty-three SF260s of all variants appeared on the U.S. register in April 2014.

Belgian Air Force SIAI-Marchetti SF.260MB trainer at Balen Keiheuvel in May 1989.

I-SFTP is the company demonstrator SIAI-Marchetti SF.260TP photographed at Farnborough, Hampshire in July 2004.

VH-PAC is a 1976 SIAI-Marchetti SM.1019. *Jim Smith*

SM.1019. The SM.1019 is in essence a turboprop derivative of the Cessna O-1 Birdog. The type first flew in May 1969 and is powered by a derated Allison 250 engine. A prototype was followed by eighty-five production aircraft for the Italian Army, some of which are now in the hands of private owners. Twenty-four were registered in the U.S. in April 2014.

SIAT

The SIAT-223 Flamingo seats four under a large sliding canopy and flew for the first time in March 1967. Sold to both civil and military customers, twenty-one were built by SIAT in Germany and a further fifty by CASA in Spain and nineteen by Farner Werke AG in Switzerland.

D-EFC is a SIAT 223T-1 Flamingo experimentally fitted with a Porsche engine, photographed in 1995 at Ober-Schleissheim, Germany. *Jim Smith*

2013 Silence Twister G-TWIS photographed at East Pennard airstrip, Somerset in June 2014.

Silence

The Silence Twister is a modern composite single-seat aircraft designed in Germany for home construction. With its elliptical wing planform the type bears a passing resemblance to the Spitfire fighter; its sleek lines and retractable undercarriage contribute to the high performance the Twister offers on its 85hp Jabiru engine. Eleven Twister aircraft appeared on the UK register in April 2014.

SIPA

The SIPA S.90 and its sub-variants were designed for the use of French aero clubs. The S.90 first flew in June 1947 and gained a government contract for 100 aircraft for the production S.901 model. Many aircraft have been re-engined with the Continental C-90, being then designated S.903. 113 S.90 and sub-variants were built. Of sixteen that were registered in the UK, ten remained on the register in April 2014.

G-ASXC is a 1951 SIPA 903 with a non-standard sprung cantilever undercarriage photographed at Henstridge, Somerset.

1995 Sisler SF-2A Cygnet G-BRZD photographed at Henstridge, Somerset.

Sisler

The Sisler SF-2A Cygnet (also known as the HAPI Cygnet or Viking Cygnet) is a two-seat homebuilt aircraft with a forward-swept shoulder-mounted wing, a configuration reminiscent of the Bölkow 208 Junior other than its tailwheel undercarriage. Around twenty were listed on the U.S. civil register in April 2014, with seven in the UK and a further seven in Canada.

Skyfox

Skyfox Aviation is an Australian company that builds a popular family of light aircraft for both private ownership and flight training. The aircraft are of two-seat side-by-side high wing configuration with either tailwheel (CA-25 Impala) or nosewheel undercarriage (CA-25N Gazelle). The CA-25N first flew in 1995 and is a popular light training aircraft.

55-677 is a Skyfox CA-25 Impala at Tumut, NSW, Australia in April 2013.

24-3693 is a Skyfox CA-25N Gazelle photographed at Goulburn, NSW, Australia in April 2013.

1984 Skyote N1060C photographed at Oshkosh, Wisconsin in 1985.

Skyote

The Skyote is a small aerobatic kit-built single-seat biplane. It was designed in the 1970s by O.E. "Pete" Bartoe and marketed by Skyote Aeromarine. The first aircraft flew in April 1976 and in April 2014, thirteen Skyote aircraft appeared on the U.S. civil register.

24-3239 is a Slepcev Storch Mk4 photographed at Temora, NSW, Australia in March 2013. *Jim Smith*

Slepcev

The Slepcev Storch Mk.4 is a three-quarter scale version of the Fieseler Fi 156 Storch observation and liaison aircraft. The Slepcev Storch first flew in 1994 and is available either as a kit-built product, or as a factory-built complete aircraft, having been built in Australia and Serbia. The Storch is Rotax-powered and seats two in tandem and has the same high lift features as the original Fieseler design.

Slingsby

Slingsby was a major UK manufacturer of gliders before building light aircraft under license (Tipsy Nipper and Scheibe Motorfalke) and developing the Fournier RF6 into the Slingsby T.67 trainer.

Sligsby Motor Tutor or Motor Cadet. The Motor Tutor/Motor Cadet is a single-seat powered version of the two-seat Slingsby Tandem Tutor (or Cadet TX.3) glider. Most are Volkswagen-powered. Some eighteen conversions were made in the UK, with eight remaining on the UK register in April 2014.

G-BCYH is a Cadet Mk. III Motor Glider photographed at Netherthorpe, South Yorkshire.

1989 Slingsby T.67M-260 Firefly G-EFSM photographed at Farnborough, Hampshire.

Slingsby took over the production rights to the Fournier RF6B two-seat aerobatic trainer and assembled ten aircraft as the wooden T.67A. The type was then re-engineered for composite construction, and built in several versions with engines ranging from 116hp (T.67B) to 260hp (T.67M Firefly). The type has been sold to civil and military users, with around 250 having been built.

SMAN

The SMAN Pétrel is a two-seat biplane amphibious flying boat with a pusher engine installation. Based on the Tisserand Hydroplum II, the production rights passed from SMAN to Billie Marine and the Brazilian firm EDRA Aeronautica, who produce the type as the 'Super Pétrel.'

G-GULL is a 1995 SMAN Pétrel built by Amphibians UK Ltd and photographed at Dunkeswell, Devon.

Smith Miniplane photographed at Oshkosh, Wisconsin.

Smith

Smith Miniplane. The Smith DSA-1 Miniplane is a small single-seat homebuilt biplane similar to a small Pitts Special. The type was first flown in October 1956 and is normally fitted with engines between 65hp and 100hp. In April 2014, sixty-two Miniplanes appeared on the U.S. civil register.

Smyth

Smyth Sidewinder. The Smyth Sidewinder is a two-seat all-metal homebuilt with a sharply swept fin and low profile canopy. The type first flew in February 1969. Some hundreds of sets of plans have been sold, but it is not clear how many are flying; twenty-nine appeared on the U.S. civil register in April 2014, with one in the UK, one in Canada and one in Australia.

1992 Smyth Sidewinder G-BRVH photographed at Wroughton, Wiltshire in July 1993.

1965 Sud Aviation-built SOCATA GY-80=160 Horizon taking off at Henstridge, Somerset in August 2014.

SOCATA

This company (Société de Construction d'Avions de Tourisme et d'Affaires) was formed in 1966 when Morane Saulnier was taken over by Sud Aviation to become their general aviation manufacturing arm. The company manufactured a wide range of types, notably including extensive development of the Morane Saulnier MS.880 Rallye family.

SOCATA (Gardan GY80) Horizon. The GY80 is a retractable undercarriage, four-seat low wing monoplane distinguished by a raised cabin roofline, marked dihedral and a tricycle undercarriage having a short wheelbase and narrow track. The GY80 was first flown in July 1960 and 267 were built by Sud Aviation, coming under SOCATA on that company's formation.

SOCATA Rallye family. The Rallye was designed by Morane Saulnier as the MS.880 and for many years formed the backbone of the SOCATA product line, being produced in numerous variants, some of which are illustrated below. The type is noted for its excellent short field performance and all-round cockpit field of view. The first production version was the two-seat 100hp MS880B Rallye Club, which first flew in May 1961, some 1,100 being built. The MS.885 Super Rallye flew in April 1961 with a 145hp Continental O-300; 215 were built.

Other models included the Rallye 100S, which was cleared for spinning, the 100ST offering 2+2 seating,

and the 150T and ST with four-seats and 150hp and the similar 180T with a 180hp Lycoming O-360. More than 400 of these variants were built.

The Rallye Commodore (MS.890 series) offered a strengthened airframe, enlarged fin and rudder, four-seats and between 145hp (MS.890A) and 220hp (MS.894 Minerva). The most significant aircraft in terms of production were the MS.892A Rallye Commodore 150 (281 built), MS.893A Rallye Commodore 180 and 180GT (777 built) and the MS.894A and E Minerva (246 built).

The final production variants were the Rallye 235E and 235GT of which 132 were built. A tailwheel variant of the Rallye 235E for agricultural work was marketed as the Gaucho, but only nine were built.

The list above is not fully comprehensive, although it does cover most of the major variants covering some 3,000 of the Rallye aircraft built. License production was also undertaken in Poland as the PZL 110 Koliber, which is also available with a number of engine options.

In April 2014, sixty-five Rallye aircraft were listed on the UK civil aircraft register, with many operating in other European countries.

G-AXGE is a 1969 SOCATA MS.880B Rallye Club photographed at Compton Abbas in September 2013.

G-BLGS is a 1978 SOCATA Rallye 180T Galerien fitted with a four blade propeller and operating as a glider tug. It was photographed at Lasham, Hampshire.

F-GBXF is a 1979 SOCATA Rallye 235 CA-M Gaucho photographed at Farnborough, Hampshire in September 1980.

D-EMPA is a SOCATA MS885 Super Rallye photographed at Braunschweig, Germany.

G-AZVI is a SOCATA MS892A Rallye Commodore 150 at Henstridge, Somerset, in May 2011.

OO-KMZ is a SOCATA MS.893A Rallye Commodore 180 at Balen Keiheuvel in May 1989.

G-BFGS is a 1975 SOCATA MS.893E Rallye 180GT Gaillard photographed at Lands End, St Just, Cornwall.

G-CBGA is a Polish-built 2001 PZL 110 Koliber 160A at Old Sarum, Wiltshire, in April 2007.

A German-registered SOCATA ST-10 Diplomate photographed at Dahlemer-Binz, Germany in 1971.

SOCATA ST-10 Diplomate. Developed from the GY80 and originally known as the Super Horizon, the ST-10 was a more refined design with a 200hp IO-360 engine. The type was first flown in November 1967 and fifty-five were built.

SOCATA TB-series. The TB series are low wing four-seat monoplanes produced in three models, the 160hp TB-9 Tampico, the 180hp TB-10 Tobago, and the retractable undercarriage 250hp TB-20 Trinidad. The first two models were flown in 1977, with the TB-20 following in November 1980. In April 2014, nineteen TB-9s; fifty-six TB-10s and forty-six TB-20s appeared on the UK civil aircraft register.

1981 SOCATA TB-9 Tampico photographed at Lydd, Kent.

1988 SOCATA TB-10 Tobago on final approach to Henstridge, Somerset in August 2007.

SOCATA TB-20 Trinidad N5ZY taking off from its home base at Henstridge, Somerset in April 2014.

1989 SOCATA TBM700 F-WKDL (the third prototype) on the approach to land at Farnborough, Hampshire.

2006 SOCATA TBM850 F-HBGA at Farnborough, Hampshire in July 2006.

SOCATA TBM series. The TBM700 and TBM850 are single-engine pressurized turboprops in the same general class as the Piper Meridian, carrying two crew and four or five passengers. The TBM 700 first flew in July 1988 and is the result of collaboration between SOCATA at Tarbes and the American company Mooney (resulting in the TBM designation).

The TBM850 has a more powerful PT6A engine rated at 850hp in the cruise, but flat rated to 700hp at takeoff. The TBM900 has various improvements, including winglets and a five-blade propeller. 324 TBM700 and 338 TBM850 have been built and production of the TBM900 continues.

Sopwith Triplane replica N500/G-BWRA photographed taking off from Henstridge, Somerset in May 2009.

Sopwith

Sopwith is a famous British First World War manufacturer of (predominantly) fighter aircraft. Small numbers of original aircraft are preserved, mainly as museum exhibits. Many flying replicas of Sopwith aircraft from the First World War have been built, including the Camel, Pup, One and a Half Strutter, and Triplane. Many SE5A replicas are plans built from the Replica Plans design, but Sopwith replicas tend to be one-off designs at either sub- or full-scale, and have differing degrees of fidelity. All these designs are represented by the Sopwith Triplane replica shown above.

Sorrell

The Sorrell SNS-7 Hiperbipe, which appeared in 1973, is a reverse-stagger high performance two-seat homebuilt biplane. In April 2014, there were nineteen listed on the U.S. civil register and one in the UK.

G-HIPE (now G-ISMS) is the only Sorrell Hiperbipe in the UK, seen at Cranfield, Bedfordshire in July 1996.

1930 Southern Martlet G-AAYX on the flight line at The Shuttleworth Trust, Old Warden, Bedfordshire.

Southern Aircraft

The Southern Martlet aerobatic biplane was designed in 1929 by F.G. Miles and first flown in July 1929. Seven aircraft, powered by a number of different engines, were built. G-AAYX, the fourth Martlet, survives and has been restored to flying condition.

Spartan Aircraft Ltd. (UK)

The two-seat Spartan Arrow was development of the Simmonds Spartan. A three-seat version was also built as the Spartan Three-seater. The Arrow, was first flown in May 1930, was less successful than the Simmonds design (forty-nine of which were built). Fifteen Spartan Arrows and twenty-six Spartan Three-seaters were built. The Three-seater was more successful than the Arrow because it was ideally suited to joyriding, thus increasing its market.

The surviving Spartan Arrow G-ABYX photographed at Abingdon, Oxfordshire in May 2004.

NC705N is a 1929 Spartan C3-165, photographed at Oshkosh, Wisconsin.

Spartan Aircraft Co. (U.S.)

Spartan C3. The Spartan C3 was a successful three-seat open cockpit biplane, first flown in October 1926, of which some 122 were built with a number of different types of engine ranging from 120hp to 225hp. Five appeared on the U.S. civil register in April 2014, but only one is believed to be active.

Spartan 7 Executive. The Spartan Executive is a clean five-seat low-wing monoplane first flown in January 1936 and sold for private and business use. Thirty-five were built and in April 2014, twenty were listed on the U.S. civil register, but not all are active.

1940 Spartan 7W Executive NC17667 photographed at Oshkosh, Wisconsin.

N10TS is a 1976 Spencer Air Car 12E photographed at Lake Hood Airstrip, Anchorage, Alaska in May 1983.

Spencer

The Spencer Air Car is a four-seat single-engine amphibious flying boat. The Air Car is similar in configuration to, but smaller than, the Republic Seabee. The prototype was first flown in 1970 and the type is designed to be homebuilt from plans. Although as many as fifty are said to have been built, only three appeared on the U.S. civil register in April 2014.

Spezio

Spezio Sport Tuholer. The Tuholer is a two-seat open cockpit strut-braced low wing homebuilt monoplane. The type was first flown in May 1961; twenty-eight appeared on the U.S. civil register in April 2014.

Spezio Sport Tuholer N113DM photographed at Oshkosh, Wisconsin.

Sportavia RF4D D-KALC photographed at Popham, Hampshire in July 2014.

Sportavia-Pützer

Sportavia-Pützer was created by the merger of Alpavia of France with Pützer of Germany to build the RF-4D, an improved version of the Fournier RF-3. The company went on to develop and manufacture the two-seat RF-5 and to develop further variants of both types. Their final product was a four-seat development of the Fournier RF-6 initially known as the RF-6C, but subsequently produced in a modified form as the RS-180 Sportsman.

Sportavia RF-4D. The RF-4D motor glider is similar to the RF-3 and can be distinguished by the rounded profile to the lower rear fuselage compared with the flat surface of the RF-3. Three RF-4 were built in France, followed by some 155 production aircraft built at Dahlemer-Binz in Germany.

Two RF-4D developments were produced by Sportavia, the RF-7 and the SFS-31 Milan. The RF7 was a higher performance RF-4D combining a six-foot reduction in span with the more powerful 67hp SL1700E engine of the two-seat RF-5. The SFS-31 Milan (SFS standing for Scheibe Flugzeugebau Sportavia) combined an RF-4D fuselage with the wings of the SF-27M glider; the Milan was also provided with a feathering propeller to enhance its engine-off performance. Wingspan is increased by some twelve-feet to four-nine feet and two inches (fifteen meters).

Sportavia SFS-31 Milan D-KIRL being readied for a test flight before being delivered to the UK as G-AYRL.

1972 Sportavia RF5G-AZRK taxies at Popham, Hampshire in July 2014.

Sportavia RF-5. The RF-5 is a lengthened two-seat development from the RF-4 with increased span (forty-five feet), folding outer wing panels and a 67hp Limbach SL1700 E engine. The prototype first flew in January 1968 and 127 were built in Germany and ten by Aero Jéan in Spain.

RF5 variants

Sportavia built two developments of the RF-5, the RF-5B Sperber and the Sportavia S.5. The RF-5B, which flew in May 1971, emphasized engine-off glide performance and featured a ten foot nine inch increase in span and a cut-down rear fuselage and revised

canopy for maximum all-round view. Ninety-nine were built by Sportavia and by Helwan in Egypt.

The Sportavia S-5 was a one-off quiet aircraft adaptation of the RF5 for the German Government. It used a Lycoming 115hp engine driving a three-bladed propeller. The exhaust was heavily silenced, being led into boxes on either side of the fuselage, where cooling air was also admitted. The exhaust finally exited aft of the rear cockpit. The prototype was under construction in the spring of 1971 and was flying by the summer. It was extremely quiet; noise measurements revealing that, at the same distance, the S-5 was quieter than a K-7 glider with its airbrakes out.

Prototype RF-5B D-KHEK under test in July 1971 at Dahlemer-Binz externally ballasted for aft CG trials.

D-EAFA is the one-off Sportavia S.5 at Dahlemer-Binz, Germany in summer 1971.

1979 Sportavia RS-180 Sportsman G-VIZZ photographed on the approach to Dunkeswell, Devon.

Sportavia RS-180 Sportsman. The RS-180 Sportsman is a four-seat development of the Fournier RF-6, initially designated RF-6C. First flown with a low-set tailplane, the RF6C, of which four were built, encountered handling problems and the production machine, the RS-180, emerged with a mid-set tailplane mounted part-way up a large fin. The RS-180 was powered by a 180hp Lycoming O-360 and a total of eighteen were produced.

Stampe/SNCAN

The Stampe et Vertongen SV4 aerobatic training biplane first flew in 1933. Thirty-five aircraft were built in Belgium pre-war, but the vast majority were built post-war by SNCAN (Nord) who built 700 examples as civil and military trainers. Some 150 were also built in Algeria and a further sixty-five civil, and military aircraft were built post-war in Belgium by Stampe & Renard. Many still operate and in May 2014, forty-eight appeared on the UK civil register.

G-BAKN is a 1946 SNCAN-built Stampe SV4C photographed at Henstridge, Somerset.

1950 Starck AS.57 F-PCIM photographed at Brienne-le-Chateau, France.

Starck

André Starck designed and built a number of aircraft including the one-off AS.20, flown in October 1942 and a series of single-seat low wing monoplanes, known as the AS.70 Jac, of which twenty-three were built with various engines and designations. Next came a two-seat enlarged version, the AS.57, of which eleven were built. The last significant type was the AS.80 Lavadoux or

Holiday of 1947, which was a wooden tandem seat high wing aircraft for which plans were made available for home construction. In May 2014 there were the following Starck aircraft on the French register: AS27 (1), AS.70 (5), AS80 (4), AS.57 (1), AS.37 (1). One AS.80 was listed on the UK register.

1940 Starck AS.80 Lavadoux G-BJAE photographed at Dunkeswell, Devon.

1990 Star-Lite SL-1 G-FARO photographed at Henstridge, Somerset in April 2014.

Star-Lite

The Star-Lite SL-1 is a small single-seat all composite homebuilt aircraft designed by Mark Brown of Star-Lite Aircraft. The type was supplied for kit-building, but kits are no longer available. Aero Designs developed a two-seat derivative known as the Pulsar, which is described earlier in this book. In June 2014, three were registered in the UK and twenty-nine were listed on the U.S. civil register.

Stearman

Stearman is a name that many associate with the Stearman A75 and PT-13/PT-17 built by Boeing during the Second World War. Prior to this, however, the then independent Stearman Aircraft had built a number of designs at Wichita, including 170 Stearman C3 and 41 Stearman Model 4 Speedmail biplanes. In May 2014, twenty-two Stearman C3s and thirteen Stearman Model 4 Speedmail aircraft were listed on the U.S. register, not all being active.

Stearman C3-B NC6438 photographed over Wyoming. *Xavier Meal*

G-CBYJ is a 2004 Steen Skybolt, photographed at Sandown, Isle of Wight in June 2014.

Steen

The Steen Skybolt is an aerobatic two-seat biplane designed to be homebuilt. The Skybolt first flew in October 1970 and has been highly successful, reflected by the numbers flying worldwide; in May 2014 there were 287 on the U.S. register, sixteen in the UK, two in France, ten in Australia and twenty-seven in Canada.

Stephens

The Stephens Akro is a single-seat mid-wing aircraft designed for competition aerobatics. The Akro first flew in July 1967 and was very influential, giving rise to, or influencing, several other designs, including the Laser Z200 and 230, Haigh Superstar and Extra 230/Extra 300.

1976 Stephens Akro N81AC (later G-RIDE) photographed at Compton Abbas, Wiltshire.

1980 Stewart Headwind N1053N photographed at Oshkosh, Wisconsin.

Stewart

The Stewart Headwind is a single-seat homebuilt aircraft reminiscent of the Aeronca C-2. The prototype Headwind first flew in March 1962. The Stewart Aircraft website indicates that, 'over 100 are in service worldwide.' Eighteen were listed on the U.S. civil register in May 2014.

Stinson

The Stinson Aircraft Company had immediate success with its first product, the SM-1 Detroiter, which was a single-engine high wing commercial monoplane. In the commercial aviation field, the company went on to build two three-engine airliners, the low wing Model A and the high wing Model T or SM-6000.

Its first product for the private owner was the 1928 SM-2 Junior, which was a scaled down four-seat Detroiter. The aircraft sold well and was rapidly developed through a series of variants including the 1930 SM-7 and SM-8. The Stinson Junior S of 1931 had a fully cowled engine; the final model being the Junior R of 1932 with a deeper fuselage and a stub wing mounting the undercarriage and wing struts.

A total of 321 Stinson Junior were built; in May 2014, forty-three were listed on the U.S. civil register, most of these being Stinson SM-8A or Stinson Junior S models – not all are active.

The next major Stinson family is the Stinson Reliant. The first model was the Stinson SR of 1933; a development of the Junior R with a bulged fairing on the lower fuselage providing the attachment for the undercarriage and wing struts. The Reliant was developed through a succession of models from the SR-1 of 1933 through to the SR-10 of 1938. The 1936 SR-7 introduced a new wing with tapered outer sections, a single wing strut and a revised undercarriage; this and subsequent models are known as 'gull-wing' Reliants. A curved, rather than faceted windscreen was introduced with the SR-9 and the helmeted engine cowling of the earlier models was replaced with a smooth cowling on the 1938 SR-10C. The final model was the SR-10J, or Vultee V-77 of which 500 were supplied to Britain during the War under Lend Lease and used as Royal Navy AT-19 navigation trainers. Total production was 762 SR series Reliants and 500 V-77. Many remain in operation.

Wartime saw the production of two observation and liaison aircraft, the L-1 Vultee-Stinson Vigilant and the L-5 Sentinel. 324 L-1 were built but few remain active. The L-5 was a development of the Model 10 Voyager (see below) for military use. More than 3,900 were built and many remain active with private owners as a popular entry-level warbird.

The final Stinson large-scale production model was the Voyager family. This was a smaller and more affordable aircraft for the private owner initially produced pre-war as the two-seat HW-75 and Model 10, and post-war as the 108 Voyager. 277 HW-75 and 775 Model 10 were built up to 1942. The 108 Voyager was a larger four-seat development that was produced in four versions; the 108, 108-1, 108-2 and 108-3. The 108-3 introduced a larger fin with a long curved dorsal extension, distinguishing it from the other models. The 108 Voyager was very successful and 5,266 were built, many of which are still flying.

Stinson's final design for the private owner was the twin engine, twin fin, Twin Stinson, which was subsequently developed into the Piper PA-23 Apache.

1930 Stinson SM-8A Junior photographed at Cape Cod in 1991. *Jim Smith*

1931 Stinson Junior.S NC12143, photographed taxying at Oshkosh, Wisconsin.

1933 Stinson JR SR Reliant NC13477 photographed at Lake Hood, Anchorage, Alaska in May 1983. This aircraft is now displayed in the Museum of Flight at Seattle, Washington.

VH-UXL is a 1936 SR8C Reliant photographed at Avalon, VIC, Australia. *Jim Smith*

N9570H is a 1942 Stinson V-77, subsequently registered as G-BUCH, photographed at Wroughton, Wiltshire.

N63230 is a 1941 Vultee Stinson L-1 Vigilant photographed in the 'Movieland of the Air' collection at Orange County Airport, Anaheim, California; this aircraft is now part of the Kermit Weeks collection in Florida.

N57598 is a 1943 Stinson L-5 Sentinel photographed at Oshkosh, Wisconsin.

G-AFYO is a 1939 Stinson HW-75 photographed at Abingdon, Oxfordshire in May 2004.

G-BPTA is a 1947 Stinson 108-2 Voyager photographed landing in a stiff crosswind at Henstridge, Somerset.

VH-ROA is a 1949 Stinson 108-3 Voyager, photographed at Echuca, VIC, Australia in April 2013.

Stits SA-3B Playboy N4076K photographed at San Clemente, Arizona in October 2013. *Peter Davison*

Stits

Ray Stits designed a series of homebuilt aircraft, a selection of the more numerous types being illustrated below.

Stits SA-3A Playboy. The Playboy first flew in 1953 and is a single-seat monoplane with a strut-braced low wing; the SA-35 is similar, but seats two side-by-side. In May 2014, nineten Playboys were listed on the U.S. civil register.

SA-6B Flut-R-Bug. The Flut-R-Bug is a single-seat (SA-6A) or two-seat (SA-6B) mid-wing adaptation of the SA-3A Playboy with a tricycle undercarriage. In May 2014, seven were listed on the U.S. civil register.

N10BM is a 1984 Stits SA-6B Flut-R-Bug photographed at Oshkosh, Wisconsin in July 1985.

N4685S is a 1965 Stits SA-7D Sky Coupe photographed in Florida in April 1990. *Jim Smith*

Stits SA-7 Sky Coupe. The Sky Coupe is a two-seat side-by-side high wing monoplane marketed in kit form for home completion.

Stits SA-11 Playmate. The Playmate is a three-seat low wing strut-braced monoplane developed from the SA-3. Distinguishing features include the tricycle undercarriage, blown canopy and sharply-swept tail fin. The Playmate was first flown in September 1963 and eleven were listed on the U.S. civil register in May 2014.

N4523 is a 1974 Stits SA-11 Playmate photographed in Arizona.

G-BODI is a 1988 Glasair III Model SH-3R photographed at Cranfield, Bedfordshire.

Stoddard Hamilton

Stoddard Hamilton Glasair. The two-seat Glasair is a very high performance all-composite kit-built homebuilt aircraft that was first flown in 1979. The type can be built with a fixed tailwheel undercarriage, or a fixed, or retractable, tricycle undercarriage. The Glasair II has a wider cockpit and various construction improvements. The Glasair III has a stretched fuselage and retractable tricycle undercarriage. Fitted with a 300hp Lycoming IO-540, the Glasair III offers cruise speeds of more than 280 mph. Tubocharged and turbine powered models have also been built. Over 1,000 Glasair aircraft have been built worldwide.

Stoddard Hamilton GlaStar and Sportsman 2+2. The GlaStar is a composite kit-built high wing monoplane that was first flown in November 1994. It is equipped with folding wings and can be equipped with a tailwheel or tricycle undercarriage. A four-seat development, the Glasair Sportsman 2+2, was introduced in 2005. In May 2014, some 300 GlaStars were listed on the U.S. register, with fourteen in the UK, fifty-eight in Canada, and twenty-one in Australia.

VH-XPF is a four-seat Sportsman 2+2, which replaced the Glastar in production; it was photographed in April 2013 at Echuca, VIC, Australia.

N40D (now G-IIIM) is a 1974 Stolp SA-100 Starduster photographed at Henstridge, Somerset.

Stolp

The Stolp-Adams family of homebuilt aircraft comprises a series of single-seat and two-seat aerobatic biplanes and a single-seat parasol monoplane, as described below.

Stolp SA-100 Starduster. The SA-100 Starduster is a small single-seat aerobatic biplane that was first flown in 1957. In May 2014, forty were listed on the U.S. civil register.

Stolp SA-300 Starduster Too. The Starduster Too is an enlarged and more powerful two-seat version of the SA-100 Starduster. The aircraft is fully aerobatic and is extremely popular. In May 2014, there were more than 200 on the U.S. civil register, sixteen in Canada and sixteen in the UK.

G-KEEN is a 1971 Stolp SA-300 Starduster Too photographed at Finmere airfield, Buckinghamshire.

1973 Stolp SA-500 Starlet G-AZTV taxying at Compton Abbas, Wiltshire.

Stolp SA-500 Starlet. The Starlet is a homebuilt single-seat parasol monoplane. It has been less successful than the Starduster biplane series, but nevertheless, eleven aircraft are listed in the Starduster Registry at http://starduster.aircraftspruce.com/registry.html

Stolp SA-750 Acroduster II. The Acroduster II is a Starduster Too development which has been optimized for aerobatics and features a strengthened airframe, reduced span and length and larger ailerons. Some forty aircraft are listed in the Starduster Registry and sixteen were listed on the U.S. civil register in May 2014.

Stolp SA-750 Acroduster II photographed at Oshkosh, Wisconsin. This is believed to be the factory demonstrator N750X.

G-BLAF is the only UK registered Stolp SA-900 V-Star, photographed at Cranfield, Bedfordshire.

Stolp SA-900 V-Star. The V-Star is a small single-seat homebuilt biplane, which has something of the appearance of a biplane version of the SA-500 Starlet. In May 2014, thirteen were listed on the U.S. civil register.

Sukhoi

The Sukhoi Design Bureau is famous for its high performance fighter aircraft – notably the Su-27 Flanker family. In the sporting aircraft field, Sukhoi has produced some remarkable aerobatic aircraft, these being the Su-26, Su-29 and Su-31, which are illustrated below. The Su-26 first flew in June 1984, the type winning the World Aerobatics Championship in 1986. The Su-29 is a two-seat aircraft with a stretched fuselage and a large bubble canopy. The 1992 Su-31, which was initially designated Su-29T, is a single-seat aircraft with a more powerful engine and a cut down rear fuselage fitted with bubble canopy.

Sukhoi Su 26M '06' at Bristol Airport after arriving prior to the 1986 World Aerobatic Championships at South Cerney, Gloucestershire.

Sukhoi Su 29 '01' photographed at the Farnborough Air Show, Hampshire in September 1992.

Jurgis Kayris flies an aerobatic demonstration in Su 31 LY-LJK at Avalon, VIC, Australia.

G-PIXY RK855 is a Spitfire Mk 26 photographed at its home base of Henstridge, Somerset.

Supermarine Aircraft

Supermarine Spitfire Mk.26. The Supermarine Spitfire Mk.26 is a sub-scale (80%) replica Spitfire for home construction. Originating in Australia and first flying in 1994, the Spitfire Mk.26 can seat two in tandem. The Mark 26b is enlarged (90% scale) and is a more practical two-seat aircraft. Eleven were registered in the UK in May 2014, one being a Mk.26b.

Swallow

Swallow Airplane Manufacturing took over from Laird Aviation in 1923 and produced two main types of aircraft, the Swallow (some 350 built) and the TP trainer (112 built). In May 2014, nine Swallows and six TPs aircraft were listed on the U.S. civil register.

Swallow TP C8761 on display at San Diego. This aircraft remains listed on the FAA civil register with the Yanks Air Museum at Chino, California.

The first Swearingen SX300 N300SX photographed at Oshkosh, Wisconsin in 1985.

Swearingen

Swearingen is known for the SA26 Merlin and SA226 Metro twin engine turboprops and the Sino Swearingen SJ 30 executive jet. In the light aircraft field, the company developed the two-seat high performance 300hp SX300. The first aircraft flew in July 1984 and in May 2014, twenty-nine were listed on the U.S. civil register.

SZD

The SZD 45 Ogar is a two-seat side-by-side self-launching motor glider built in Poland from 1973. The Ogar has a high wing with a pod and boom fuselage and a high-mounted 65hp SL1700 Limbach engine driving a pusher propeller. Some 230 were built.

1976 SZD 45 Ogar G-BEBG photographed at Wroughton, Wiltshire.

Jabiru-powered Taylor Monoplane G-OBJM photographed at Henstridge, Somerset in April 2012.

John Taylor (UK)

Taylor Monoplane. The Taylor Monoplane is a single-seat low wing wooden homebuilt aircraft. The prototype G-APRT was built by John Taylor in Ilford, and first flown in July 4, 1959. At the time of the twenty-fifth Anniversary of its first flight, about 100 of these aircraft had been built and flown, including a significant population of the type in New Zealand. In May 2014, twenty-eight examples were listed on the UK civil aircraft register.

Taylor Titch. The Titch is a higher performance wooden single-seat aircraft distinguished from its predecessor by its finer lines, closed cockpit and tapered wing planform. The prototype was first flown in January 1967. The Titch has been constructed worldwide including several in the United States.

Taylor Titch G-ATZH 'Catch 22' in racing trim at Popham, Hampshire in July 2014,

N41RG is a 1987 Taylor Coot, photographed in Arizona.

Moulton Taylor (U.S.)

Molt Taylor is noted for his innovative flying car, the Aerocar, and the Taylor IMP and Mini-IMP (single-seat aircraft with a pusher propeller and inverted V tail). He also designed the Taylor Coot amphibious homebuilt flying boat. The Coot first flew in 1969 and some seventy have been built. Around nineteen were listed on the U.S. civil register in May 2014.

Taylorcraft

CG Taylor was responsible for the Taylor E-2 Cub (see Piper). After splitting from Piper, he set up the Taylor-Young Airplane Co, which was renamed as Taylorcraft Aviation Corp in 1938. Its first product was the side-by-side high wing 40hp Taylorcraft Model A. Some 606 Taylorcraft A were built before the Model B was introduced in 1938. Similar in appearance, pre-war Model Bs had an engine with exposed cylinder heads, post-war examples (see below) having a fully cowled engine. Installed power ranged between 50hp and 65hp, dependent on the engine fitted.

1938 Taylorcraft BF-60 NC21287, with a 60hp Franklin 4AC150-A engine at Oshkosh, Wisconsin.

1940 Taylorcraft BL NC24312, with a 50hp Lycoming O-145 engine photographed in Texas.

Taylorcraft DF-65 (L-2 Grasshopper) G-BRIY 42-58678 (originally built as a TG-6 glider) at Wroughton, Wiltshire.

Taylorcraft L-2 (O-57) Grasshopper. The tandem seat Taylorcraft Model DC, DF and DL were adapted for use by the USAAF as an observation and liaison type as the O-57 or L-2 Grasshopper. 250 were also completed as the TG-6 glider. 2,119 were supplied to the USAAF. The L-2A had an open cowling, with the L-2M (900 built) had an enclosed cowling.

Taylorcraft DCO. Post-war, many L-2 Grasshoppers were modified for civilian use and are generally designated Taylorcraft DCO-65. Examples can be found with either open or closed cowlings under the same designation. In May 2014, some 365 Taylorcraft DC/DCO were listed on the U.S. civil register.

N50839 is a 1945 Taylorcraft DCO-65 photographed at San Jose, California.

C-FJGO is a 1946 Taylorcraft BC-12D photographed in the Montreal, Quebec, Canada area.

Taylorcraft BC-12D. The most numerous of the side-by-side Taylorcraft models is the BC-12D, of which more than 2,800 were built post-war. The aircraft is operated in considerable numbers in the U.S. and Canada with more than 1,400 listed in May 2014 on the U.S. civil register, together with 180 in Canada and sixteen in the UK.

Taylorcraft F19 Sportsman, F21 and F22. The F19 Sportsman is an updated BC-12D powered by an O-200 engine and flown in 1973. 120 were built. The F21 is similar with a 118hp Lycoming; the F-22 being a nosewheel variant of the F21. In May 2014, the U.S. civil register listed 104 F19; thirty-four F21; and twelve F22.

Taylorcraft F19 D-EBAU photographed at Balen Keiheuvel, Belgium in May 1989.

Taylorcraft F21B N4417B photographed at Oshkosh, Wisconsin.

Taylorcraft F22 N44191 photographed at Oshkosh, Wisconsin.

Tecnam

Tecnam is an Italian aircraft manufacturer making light aircraft some of which meet full certification requirements, others meeting VLA (Very Light Aircraft) or LSA (Light Sport Aircraft) regulations. The range includes high wing and low wing light aircraft with fixed or retractable undercarriages and light twin-engine aircraft. A representative selection of Tecnam designs is illustrated below.

Tecnam P92. A high wing two-seat light aircraft that is sold in several versions including the P92 Echo and Echo Super, the P92 Eaglet with a modified wingtip shape, and the P92 2000 RG with retractable undercarriage. The P.92 first flew in March 1993 and more than 2,000 are flying worldwide. In May 2014, seventeen appeared on the UK civil aircraft register, with fifty-seven P92s (of all variants) being listed on the U.S. register.

2003 Tecnam P92-EM Echo G-CBDM taking off from Henstridge, Somerset in April 2009.

Tecnam P92 Eaglet VH-SHH photographed at Avalon, VIC, Australia. *Jim Smith*

Tecnam P92-2000RG 24-4263 photographed at Avalon, VIC, Australia in March 2007.

24-4520 is a Tecnam P96 Golf 100 photographed at Temora, NSW, Australia. *Jim Smith*

Tecnam P96 Golf. The P96 Golf is a low wing companion model to the P92, offering comparable performance and sharing some component parts with its high wing relative. The Golf has not been as successful as the P92, although the type is operated in some numbers in Europe and Australasia.

Tecnam P2002 Sierra. The Sierra is a two-seat side-by-side low wing monoplane that is sold in a number of versions, with either fixed (P2002 JF) or retractable undercarriage (P2002 JR), or as the kit-built P2002 EA or RG. Tecnam say that more than 1,000 P2002 are in service worldwide, with large training fleets in many countries, including Russia. In May 2014, twenty-six P2002s were registered in the UK, with fifty listed on the U.S. civil register.

2010 Tecnam P2002 Sierra Deluxe G-OTEC climbs away from Henstridge, Somerset in April 2014.

Tecnam P2006T VH-OWW, photographed at Temora, NSW, Australia in April 2011. *Jim Smith*

Tecnam P2006T. The P2006T is a light twin engine four-seat high wing aircraft with a retractable undercarriage. The type first flew in September 2007. A multi-role adaptation for military applications is designated the Tecnam MMA. More than 100 Tecnam P2006T had been built by the end of 2011. In May 2014, eleven were listed on the U.S. civil register, with three in Canada, five in the UK and four in Australia.

Tecnam P2008. The two-seat high wing P2008 mixes metal wing construction with an aerodynamically refined carbon composite fuselage. The type was first flown in September 2009 and is currently in production. In May 2014, fourteen were listed on the U.S. civil register, with two in Australia.

Tecnam P2008 VH-MSF, photographed at Temora, NSW, Australia in April 2011. *Jim Smith*

N70VB is a 1977 Ted Smith Aerostar 600 photographed at Blackbushe, Hampshire in April 2010.

Ted Smith

Ted Smith designed the Aero Commander series of twin engine aircraft and subsequently produced the high performance Ted Smith Aerostar. The Aerostar features a mid-set straight wing and swept tail surfaces. The Aerostar 600 (282 built) first flew in October 1967, production subsequently concentrating on the turbocharged Aerostar 601 and the pressurized 601P. In 1978, production was taken over by Piper Aircraft and produced as the PA-60 and PA-61. 1,010 Aerostars were built, over half by Piper, production being completed in 1984.

Temco

Temco (Texas Engineering & Manufacturing Corporation) were the primary manufacturer of the Globe GC-1 Swift.

Temco TE-1 (T-35) Buckaroo. The Buckaroo is a tandem two-seat trainer developed from the Swift. A total of twenty aircraft were built, ten being supplied to Saudi Arabia (other production numbers are also quoted). In May 2014, three Buckaroo aircraft appeared on the U.S. register.

N909B is a 1953 Temco T-35A Buckaroo in Saudi Air force colors photographed at Oshkosh, Wisconsin.

1997 Thorp T-211 G-BXPO photographed at Thruxton, Hampshire.

Thorp

The designer John Thorp contributed to the design of several notable aircraft including the Lockheed Neptune and the Piper Cherokee.

Thorp T-211. The Thorp T-11 Sky Scooter of 1946 was adapted to become the Thorp T-211 two-seat light aircraft. The type has been produced both as a production aircraft and kit for home assembly. The number of aircraft that have reached flight status is unclear, but is at least thirty. The Thorpedo is a Jabiru-powered derivative certificated under LSA requirements. Forty-eight T-211s or Thorpedos were listed on the U.S. civil register in May 2014, although it is not clear how many of these were active.

Thorp T-18. The T-18 is a high performance single-engine all metal homebuilt aircraft. First flown in 1963, the T-18 is typically powered by a 150hp to 180hp engine giving cruise speeds of around 180 mph. More than 1,500 sets of plans have been sold and at least 400 aircraft have been flown. In 1976, T-18 N445DT became the first homebuilt aircraft to be flown round the world.

Clive Canning's Thorp T-18 VH-CMC was flown from Australia to and from the 1976 PFA Rally at Sywell, Northamptonshire in the UK. The photograph shows VH-CMC in October 2006 at Moorabbin, VIC, Australia.

Thruxton Jackaroo G-APAM photographed at Thruxton, Hampshire. Flown by aviatrix Sheila Scott as "*Myth*", G-APAM flew from 1959 to 1984 as a Jackaroo, before being converted back to a Tiger Moth.

Thruxton Jackaroo

The Wiltshire School of Flying developed a four-seat Tiger Moth variant with a wider fuselage and enclosed cockpit, which was produced at Thruxton by Jackaroo Aircraft Ltd as the Thruxton Jackaroo. The Jackaroo made its first flight in March 1957. A total of nineteen conversions were completed. Four aircraft remain registered in the UK.

Thurston

David Thurston, who designed the Colonial Skimmer and the Lake LA4 went on to produce the Thurston TSC-1A Teal, which first flew in June 1968. The Teal had a pylon-mounted engine driving a tractor propeller and a T-tail. A total of thirty-eight were built, split between Thurston, Schweizer and Teal Aircraft. The TSC-1A1 had increased all up weight and fuel capacity. The TSC-1A2 Teal II had an improved flap system, permitting a further increase in maximum weight.

N87857 is a 1977 Thurston TSC-1A2 Teal II photographed at Lake Hood Airstrip, Anchorage, Alaska.

1941 Timm Aerocraft 2SA NC34912 photographed at Oshkosh, WI.

Timm

Timm Aerocaft 2SA. The Aerocraft 2SA is a tandem two-seat trainer developed as a modification of the two-seat side-by-side Kinner Sportwing. The 2SA was first flown in 1941 and only six were built.

Timm Tutor. The Timm N2T-1 training monoplane was built for the U.S. Navy as a training aircraft. Its construction made use of resin-impregnated plywood using the 'aeromold' process. Initially flown as the PT-160K in May 1940, 262 examples of the production version (PT-220C) were ordered by the U.S. Navy in 1943 as the N2T-1. In May 2014, twelve N2T-1s were listed on the U.S. civil aircraft register.

1943 Timm N2T-1 N61864 photographed at Oshkosh, Wisconsin.

The author's 1938 Tipsy B G-AFSC photographed at its then home base of Henstridge, Somerset.

Tipsy

The Belgian designer EO Tips was responsible for the pre-war single-seat Tipsy S2 and two-seat Tipsy B.

Tipsy B. The Tipsy B was produced in the UK by Tipsy Aircraft Co. Ltd. and featured side-by-side seats in an open cockpit, the two-seats being slightly staggered to provide shoulder clearance in the relatively narrow fuselage. British built aircraft had an enlarged, mass balanced rudder, one piece elevator, wash out of the wing tips and, from the sixth aircraft, letter box slots in the leading edge ahead of the ailerons. A total of eighteen were built in the UK and four in Belgium. In May 2014, four aircraft were registered in the UK (where they are also known as the Tipsy Trainer).

Tipsy BC and Belfair. Twenty-three examples of a cabin version of the Tipsy B were built before the War in Belgium, known as the Tipsy BC. Three aircraft were also assembled post-war in the UK (from Belgian manufactured components) at Sherburn-in-Elmet. These enclosed aircraft are known in the UK as the Tipsy Belfair. In May 2014, one example remained registered in the UK.

Tipsy BC (or Belfair) G-APIE photographed at Abingdon, Oxfordshire.

Tipsy Nipper

Tipsy Nipper. The single-seat aerobatic Tipsy Nipper first flew in December 1957, the first production machine flying in February 1959. Fifty-nine aircraft and seventy-nine kits were built by Avions Fairey in Belgium; a second Belgian company, Cobelavia, producing a further eighteen. Nipper Aircraft Ltd. produced the Nipper Mk.III in the UK, both as a factory-built aircraft, and in kit form. Some thirty-two Nipper Mk.III airframes were manufactured under contract by Slingsby Aviation Ltd. At least 110 Nippers were built, with thirty-seven registered in the UK in May 2014, these being a mix of factory and home-built aircraft.

TL Ultralight

TL Ultralight of the Czech Republic manufacture a series of modern light aircraft including the TL-96 Star, TL-2000 Sting S3 and S4. These clean low wing monoplanes are of all-composite construction and are Rotax-powered. The StingSport conforms to US LSA (Light Sport Aircraft) requirements; the TL-2000 RG has a retractable undercarriage; and the TL-2000 Carbon Sting is of all CFRP construction. The TL-3000 is a high wing monoplane from the same company. Some 150 aircraft in the TL-96 and TL-2000 series are reported to have been sold. In September 2014, fifteen Sting aircraft were listed on the UK civil aircraft register, all being of the Carbon Sting model. At the same time, some sixty-two were registered on the U.S. civil register, the majority of these being of the StingSport variant.

2013 TL Ultralight TL-2000UK Carbon Sting S4 G-ZIZY takes off from Henstridge, Somerset in September 2014.

1981 Prototype Trago Mills SAH-1 G-SAHI badged as an FLS Sprint at Farnborough, Hampshire.

Trago Mills

Trago Mills SAH-1 and FLS Sprint. The SAH-1 was a private venture trainer to replace the Bulldog developed at Bodmin, Cornwall, by Sydney A Holloway with funding from Trago Mills. The prototype first flew in August 1983. Design rights passed to FLS Aerospace, who re-launched the type as the FLS Sprint. In May 2014, four were listed on the UK register (one SAH-1 and three FLS Sprint).

Travel Air

Travel Air was set up in 1925 by the great pioneers Clyde Cessna, Walter Beech and Lloyd Stearman, each of whose surnames features in this work. The company built a range of commercial aircraft and aircraft for the private owner. The company was absorbed into Curtiss-Wright in August 1929, resulting in a change of designation of some models.

The Travel Air A, B and BH were single-engine biplanes that were later re-designated Travel Air 2000, 3000 and 4000. All were three-seat single-engine single bay biplanes, with the two passengers sat side-by-side in the front cockpit. Production spanned the take-over by Curtiss-Wright, who marketed the types as the Sportsman and Speedwing. Around 1,300 aircraft of this family were built, including some 600 Travel Air 2000 and a similar number of Travel Air 4000, with a wide range of different engines.

The Travel Air 5000 was a high wing six-seat monoplane. First flying in March 1926, a total of ten were built.

The Travel Air 6000 was a luxury development of the 5000, intended for the private owner. The type became popular with small airlines and fulfilled a similar role to the Stinson Detroiter, Curtiss Robin, Fairchild FC-2 and Bellanca Pacemaker. The Curtiss-Wright 6B Sedan was a further development of the type following Travel Air's acquisition by Curtiss-Wright. Although totals are not clear, some 100 Travel Air 6000 and C-W 6B Sedan were built. Travel Air built a series of five racing monoplanes known popularly as 'Mystery Ships' due to the secrecy surrounding their construction. The first of these flew in August 1929.

The CW-12 and CW-16 Sport Trainer and Light Sport were single-engine biplanes that were in development at the time of the Curtiss-Wright take-over. The CW-12 had two-seats, while the CW-16 carried two passengers and the pilot. A total of forty-one CW-12s and around thirty CW-16s were built.

A selection of Travel Air types are illustrated below, the captions identifying each model and where it was photographed.

NC174V is a 1929 Travel Air B-4000 photographed in the Kermit Weeks collection at Polk City, Florida.

NC9084 is a 1930 Travel Air S-6000-B photographed in 1995.

NC11715 is a 1931 Curtiss-Wright Travel Air 12W at Pearson Field, Vancouver in June 2010. *Peter Davison*

Tri-R KIS

The Tri-R KIS is a kit-built homebuilt aircraft that was first flown in 1991. A four-seat development is known as the KIS Cruiser or Pulsar Super Cruiser.

In May 2014, a combined total of thirty aircraft of these models were listed on the U.S. civil aircraft register, with six in the UK and two in Australia.

G-TKIS is a 1995 Tri-R KIS, photographed at Henstridge, Somerset.

G-BRIO is a 1992 modified Turner Super T-40A photographed at Cranfield, Bedfordshire.

Turner

The Turner T-40 is a wooden two-seat side-by-side low wing monoplane designed for home construction and incorporating a folding wing design. The type is distinguished by its bubble canopy and, in the case of the Super T-40A, a comparatively small, sharply swept fin. The type was first flown in April 1961. Tail wheel or tricycle undercarriage configurations are available.

Ultravia Pelican PL PH-JLM photographed at Old Sarum, Wiltshire in August 2013.

Ultravia

Ultravia produced a range of two-seat high wing light aircraft kits for home construction. An initial single-seat microlight design, Le Pelican, was followed by the two-seat Pelican, Flyer SS, Pelican PL and Sport; the changes in designations reflecting the design rights passing from Ultravia to New Kolb Aircraft and then Ballard Sport. 127 Ultravia aircraft were listed on the Canadian civil register in May 2014.

United Consultants

The UC-1 Twin Bee is a conversion of the Republic Sea Bee to a twin engine configuration. The type was first flown in 1962. Twenty-three conversions were carried out and nine aircraft were listed on the U.S. civil register in May 2014. Production was split between United Consultants (3) and STOL Aircraft (20).

1972 Universal UC-1 Twin Bee N123RB photographed at Winter Haven, Florida.

Valentin Taifun 17E OZT photographed at Avalon, VIC, Australia in March 2013. *Jim Smith*

Valentin

The Valentin Taifun is a two-seat side-by-side German motor glider which first flew in February 1981. With a seventeen-meter wingspan, the Taifun offers good engine-off performance with a glide ratio of around thirty. A total of 136 Valentin Taifuns were built.

Valmet

Finnish company Valmet has built a number of military trainers such as the Valmet L-70 Vinka and the L-90 TP Redigo, together with license manufacture of the Fouga Magister and BAe Hawk. The Valmet (or Valtion) Viima was a two-seat trainer similar to the Focke Wulf Steiglitz that was first flown in 1935. Two prototypes were followed by around twenty production Viima IIs.

1939 Valmet Viima II G-BAAY/VI-3 photographed at Badminton House Airstrip, Gloucestershire.

Van's Aircraft

Van's Aircraft, founded by Richard 'Van' VanGrunsven, advertises itself with some justification as 'The world leader in kit aircraft.' In mid-May 2014, 8,671 Van's designs had been completed and flown. The main types are described below, together with the numbers of each that had been completed within the total given above.

Vans RV-3. The RV-3 is a single-seat high performance low wing monoplane with a nineteen-foot eleven-inch wingspan that was first flown in 1971. The pilot sits beneath a streamlined canopy and maximum all-up weight is 1,100lbs. Up to mid-May 2014, 280 had been flown. The RV-3B is fitted with a wing spar of revised design.

Vans RV-4. The RV-4 is a two-seat development of the RV-3. First flown in August 1979, the RV-4 has a wingspan of twenty-three feet. By mid-May 2014, a total of 1,367 RV-4 had been built and flown.

Vans RV-6/6A. The RV-6 is a two-seat side-by-side development of the RV-4. It can be built with a tailwheel (RV-6) or tricycle undercarriage (RV-6A). This convention of an 'A' suffix for tricycle undercarriage also applies to the RV-7, RV-8 and RV-9 models. The RV-6 first flew in June 1986; wingspan remains twenty-three feet and maximum weight is 1,600lb. As with most of the other aircraft in the family, the RV-6 is cleared for aerobatics. By mid-May 2014, no less than 2,528 RV-6 or -6A had flown.

Vans RV-7/7A. The RV-7 has replaced the RV-6 and is a similar design, with its wingspan increased to twenty-five feet; fuel capacity and rudder area are also increased. The RV-7 first flew in 2001 and has a maximum weight of 1,800lbs. and is aerobatic up to 1,600lb. In mid-May 2014, 1,359 RV-7 or -7A had been flown.

Vans RV-8/8A. The RV-8 is an improved RV-4 with a roomier cockpit and can be distinguished by its canopy frame rollover protection, rather than the aft pylon structure used in the RV-4. First flown in 1995, the RV-8 operates at the same weights as the RV-7 and has a twenty-four foot wingspan. 1,235 had flown by mid-May 2014.

Vans RV-9/9A. The RV-9 is similar to an RV-7, but is designed to be more docile and has an increased span (28ft.) and wing aspect ratio; the RV-9 is non-aerobatic. First flown in December 1997, 911 had been flown by mid-May 2014.

Vans RV-10. The RV-10, which only has a tricycle undercarriage, is a four-seat touring design with thirty-one-foot nine-inch span and 2,700 pound maximum weight. First flown in May 2003, 667 had been flown by mid-May 2014.

Vans RV-12. The RV-12 is an LSA-certified two-seat side-by-side monoplane powered by a 100hp Rotax 912 engine. Wingspan is twenty-six foot nine-inch and maximum weight is 1,320lb. First flown in November 2006, 323 had been flown by mid-May 2014.

Vans RV-14. The RV-14 is a two-seat design derived from the four-seat RV-10, with twenty-seven foot span and 2,050 pound maximum weight. The type was first flown in July 2007 and only the single prototype had been flown up to mid-May 2014.

VH-EXP is a Vans RV-3 photographed at Illawarra Regional Airport, NSW, Australia in March 2008.

1999 Vans RV-4 G-RVIV photographed climbing away from Henstridge, Somerset in April 2014.

G-CFDI is a 1999 Vans RV-6 seen departing its home base of Henstridge, Somerset in April 2010.

2010 Vans RV-7 VH-TQQ was photographed at Echuca, VIC, Australia in April 2013.

2001 Vans RV-8 G-BZWN photographed at Henstridge, Somerset in April 2009.

2004 Vans RV-9A G-RUVY landing at its home base of Henstridge, Somerset in March 2009.

2010 Vans RV-10 G-XRVX photographed at Dunkeswell, Devon in November 2013.

Vans RV-12 19-7516 photographed at Temora, NSW, Australia in April 2011. *Jim Smith*

G-VARG is a 1980 Varga 2150A Kachina photographed at Compton Abbas, Wiltshire.

Varga

The Varga Kachina has its origins in the 1948 Morrisey 1000 Nifty, being essentially an all-metal version of the earlier wooden aircraft. Morrisey built two Morrisey 2000, the next version being the Morrisey 2150 with a Lycoming O-235 engine. Production rights were sold to Shinn, who built thirty-five with the 150hp O-320 engine. Large-scale production was then undertaken by Varga Aircraft, who built 121 examples as the Varga 2150A Kachina.

Victa/AESL/Glos Air/NZAI

The Victa Airtourer originated with the wooden Millicer Airtourer, the winning design in a Royal Aero Club light aircraft design competition, which first flew in April 1959. Victa Ltd. built an all-metal version, the Victa Airtourer 100, flown in December 1961. The type was offered as the Airtourer 100 and 115, a total of 169 being built. Rights then passed to Aero Engine Services Ltd. in New Zealand (later renamed NZ Aerospace Industries and then Pacific Aerospace). AESL continued

to build the type and introduced the 150hp Airtourer Super 150, also supplying twenty-three partly knocked-down kits to be assembled and completed by GlosAir Ltd. in the UK and marketed as the Glos-Airtourer. GlosAir completed twelve Glos-Airtourer 115s (T2), one T4 Airtourer 150, seven T7 Super 150s (T6) and three T6/24 Super 150s. AESL built thirty T1s (115hp), and a total of fifty T2 to T6s with 130hp to 150hp, these figures including those supplied to GlosAir. The T6/24 had minor improvements including electrically operated flaps and trim; four were supplied to the NZAF.

The type was further developed and put into production as the Pacific Aerospace CT/4 Airtrainer. The fully aerobatic Airtrainer has a rear-hinged bubble canopy, a strengthened airframe and a 210hp IO-360 engine. A total of 113 were built for military and civil users. In May 2014, thirty CT/4As were listed on the Australian civil register, with fourteen Airtourers of different types registered in the UK.

Prototype Millicer Airtourer VH-FMM photographed at the RAN FAA Museum at Nowra NSW, Australia in March 2008.

1964 Victa Airtourer 100 G-ASYZ photographed at Compton Abbas, Wiltshire.

1968 GlosAir Airtourer 115 G-AWDE on display at the Biggin Hill Air Fair, Biggin Hill, Kent.

1970 AESL GlosAir Airtourer Super 150 G-AZOF at Henstridge, Somerset in April 2009.

1972 AESL Airtourer T6 photographed at Camden, NSW, Australia in March 2008.

VH-MCT A19-046 is a 1975 NZAI/Pacific Aerospace CT/4A photographed at Echuca, VIC, Australia.

1985 Viking Dragonfly G-BKPD photographed at Cranfield, Bedfordshire.

Viking

The Viking Dragonfly is a tandem wing composite aircraft of similar configuration to the Quickie Q2, albeit with a greater wingspan and lower power. The type flew for the first time in June 1980 and received the 'outstanding new design' award at that year's EAA Convention. Normally, a converted Volkswagen engine of 55hp to 65hp is used. Some aircraft have mainwheels beneath the foreplane (Dragonfly Mk. II), rather than at the wingtips. The type has also been built with a fixed tricycle undercarriage as the Dragonfly Mk.III. Some 500 aircraft are believed to have flown.

1973 Volmer VJ-22 Sportsman G-BAHP taxying at Cranfield, Bedfordshire.

Volmer

The Volmer VJ-22 Sportsman is a wooden two-seat amphibious flying boat. The engine is mounted on a pylon structure above the wing center section and may be fitted with a pusher or tractor propeller. The design uses the wings from an Aeronca Champ aircraft. The type first flew in December 1958. Around 100 examples have been flown, with forty listed on the U.S. civil register in May 2014.

Vultee

The Vultee BT-13 Valiant was an intermediate trainer of the Second World War. The type was first flown in 1939 and was normally powered by the 450hp Pratt & Whitney R-985 engine. The type was used by both the USAAC (BT-13, BT-13A and BT-15) and by the U.S. Navy (SNV). A total of 7,832 were built and a number remain in operation with private owners. In May 2014, some 283 of all variants were listed on the U.S. civil register.

N69605 is a 1941 Vultee BT-15 photographed at its base of Midland, Texas.

Waco 10 N4453Y at Lakeland Forida, in April 1988. *Jim Smith*

Waco

Waco of Troy, Ohio, was a prolific manufacturer of high quality open and cabin biplanes from the late-1920s to the 1940s. Waco used a somewhat Byzantine designation system, based on a three letter code to identify engine model, airframe version and design family, resulting in designations such as INF, ARE, CTO, YKS and so on.

The explanation of the designation system is rather complex and for details, the reader s recommended to look at at http://www.aerofiles.com/wacodata.html. In putting together this chapter, the author has referred to the data provided in Aerofiles at http://www.aerofiles.com/_waco.html together with reference material such as the Juptner series and information on Wikipedia and elsewhere.

The photographs below, mainly from the author's own collection, are presented in approximate chronological order of the models concerned, together with a brief explanation of what distinguishes each type. This presentation is by no means comprehensive, but does give an indication of the variety of the surviving aircraft from this popular family of classic and upmarket light aircraft, fully justifying their advertising slogan, "Ask Any Pilot."

Waco 9 and 10. The three-seat Waco 9 and 10 open cockpit biplanes were originally Curtiss OX-5 powered and were developed into a range of variants with different engine types and design features. The Waco 10 was re-designated Waco GXE after 1928, but most developments form the Waco 'O' family – ASO, CTO, KSO, etc. Including all these derivatives, a total production figure of 1,623 aircraft is widely quoted.

1928 Waco ATO N6930 photographed at Oshkosh, Wisconsin.

Waco ATO. The ATO is a version powered by the 220hp Wright J-5 radial. Appearing in 1928, fifty-four were built. Twenty-six were listed on U.S. civil register in May 2014, although not all are active.

Waco CTO. The CTO is a taperwing development of the Waco CSO. 29 civil and thirty military variants were built. Normally powered by a 225hp Wright J-6 engine, the CTO is a popular airshow performer sometimes having increased power for higher performance. Seventeen were listed on the U.S. civil register in May 2014.

1930 Waco CTO N665N photographed on take-off at Oshkosh, Wisconsin in 1980.

NC605Y is a 1930 Waco INF photographed in the Ottawa area; this aircraft is now registered CF-CJR.

Waco INF. the INF is a 1930 three-seat biplane fitted with a 125hp Kinner B-5 A total of fifty were built, of which nine were listed on the U.S. civil register in May 2014; that photographed below being sold onto the Canadian register.

Waco QCF. The QCF is a three-seat biplane dating from 1931 and powered by a 165hp Continental A-70., thirty-one were built and twenty-seven were still listed on the U.S. civil register in May 2014, although not all these aircraft will be active.

NC11468 is a 1931 Waco QCF photographed at Oshkosh, Wisconsin.

N12453 is a 1932 Waco IBA photographed at Oshkosh, Wisconsin.

Waco IBA. The 1932 IBA was a two-seat biplane powered by a 125hp Kinner B-5. Only three were built, that shown below being the sole example still registered in May 2014.

Waco UIC. The 1933 Waco UIC is a four-seat cabin biplane with 210hp Continental R-670. A total of eighty-three were built, with fifteen listed on U.S. civil register in May 2014.

NC13409 is a 1933 Waco UIC photographed at Palmer, Alaska.

N14128 is a 1934 Waco YMF photographed at Orlando, Florida.

Waco YMF. The 1934 Waco YMF is a three-seat open cockpit biplane with 225hp Jacobs L-4. 18 were built and the type was revived in 1990 as YMF-5 Super from Classic Aircraft Corp (see below).

Waco YKS-6. The 1934 Waco YKS-6 is a four-seat cabin biplane with unequal span wings. Built in a series of variants as the YKC, YKC-S and YKS-6; with totals of sixty YKCs: twenty-two YKC-Ss: and sixty-five YKC-6s, for a grand total of 147 aircraft. Fifteen Waco YKS-6s were listed on the U.S. civil register in May 2014.

1936 Waco YKC-6 NC16517 photographed at Oshkosh, Wisconsin.

1939 Waco YKS-7 NC20905 taking off from Denton, Texas.

Waco YKS-7. The 1937 Waco YKS-7 is a four or five-seat cabin biplane powered by a 225hp Jacobs L-4. Eighty-six were built and twenty-five were listed on the U.S. civil register in May 2014.

Waco ARE. The 1939 Waco ARE is a four-seat cabin biplane with unequal span wings powered by a 300hp Jacobs L-6 engine. Only four were built, that shown below was the only example listed on the U.S. civil register in May 2014.

1939 Waco ARE photographed at Oshkosh, Wisconsin.

1939 Waco AGC-8 NC66206 photographed at Echuca, VIC, Australia in April 2013.

Waco AGC-8. The 1937 Waco AGC-8 is a four to five-seat unequal span cabin biplane with 300hp Jacobs L-6 engine. A total of seventeen were built, with four listed on the U.S. civil register in May 2014.

Waco UPF-7. The 1937 Waco UPF-7 is a two to three-seat open cockpit biplane with 220hp Continental R-670 and a sweeping dorsal fin. More than 600 were built and as a result, the UPF-7 is one of the most often seen today. No less than 205 were listed on the U.S. civil register in May 2014.

An immaculate 1940 Waco UPF-7 N30113 photographed at Denton, Texas.

1941 Waco YPF-7 N32077 photographed at Oshkosh, Wisconsin.

Waco YPF-6 and YPF-7. The 1935 Waco YPF-6 is a three-seat biplane with a pilot's cockpit enclosure and 225hp Jacobs L-4. Five were built, three of which were re-designated as Waco YPF-7 in 1937. One YPF-6 and two YPF-7 were listed on the U.S. civil register in May 2014.

Waco YMF-5 Super. The 1990 YMF-5 Super is a Waco by association. An updated version of the 1934 YMF built by Classic Aircraft Corporation, the YMF-5 Super is powered by a Jacobs R-755B engine. The type has proved popular, with nearly 100 listed on the U.S. civil register in May 2014.

1990 Classic Aircraft YMF-5 Super N7P at Bryce Canyon Airport, Utah in May 1992.

WAR (War Aircraft Replicas)

WAR have designed a wooden plans-built aircraft, whose common basic structure can be adapted using moulded foam blocks, supplied by WAR, and composite skins to produce sub-scale replicas of a wide range of Second World War aircraft (mostly single-seat fighters).

The first type to fly, in 1974, was the WAR Focke Wulf 190. Since then, completed aircraft include the P-47 Thunderbolt, Curtiss P-40E, Sea Fury, F4U Corsair, P-51 Mustang and Mitsubishi Zero. There is even a scale Lockheed P-38 Lightning. A selection of WAR replicas is illustrated below.

2003 WAR Focke-Wulf 190 '9' G-CCFW photographed at Henstridge, Somerset.

1979 WAR Chance Vought F4U replica N404CW at the Valiant Air Command Museum, Titusville, Florida.

1979 WAR Republic P-47 Thunderbolt replica N25GH taking off from Oshkosh, Wisconsin.

1986 WAR Hawker Sea Fury replica G-BLTG/WJ237 at Cranfield, Bedfordshire, parked next to Isaacs Spitfire replica G-BBJI.

1961 Wassmer WA-40 Super IV Sancy F-BKAB photographed at Brienne-le-Chateau, France.

Wassmer Aviation

Wassmer manufactured significant numbers of Jodel D112 and D120 aircraft before developing and manufacturing their own powered aircraft. (Wassmer was also a significant manufacturer of wooden and composite gliders).

Wassmer WA-40 Super 4 Sancy. The five-seat Wassmer WA-40 Super 4 Sancy first flew in June 1959. The type had a retractable undercarriage, wooden wings and a fabric-covered steel tube fuselage. The first fifty-two aircraft were built with an unswept fin. In May 2014, 9 WA-40 were listed on the French civil aircraft register.

Wassmer WA-40A Super IV. From the fifty-third aircraft, the WA-40 was built with a swept fin and re-designated WA-40A Super IV. Fifty-seven WA-40As were built. The Wassmer WA-4/21 Prestige was a more powerful variant, of which some thirty were built. The Cerva CE-43 Guepard was an all-metal version of the WA-4/21 that was first flown in May 1971. Forty-four were built. In May 2014, fifteen WA-40As were listed on the French civil aircraft register.

OO-GRH is a Wassmer WA-40A Super IV photographed at Balen Keiheuvel, Belgium in May 1989.

G-ATZS is a 1966 Wassmer WA-41 Baladou photographed at Thruxton, Hampshire. *Jim Smith*

Wassmer WA-41 Baladou. The Wassmer WA-41 Baladou is a simpler version of the WA-40A with a fixed undercarriage. The Baladou was introduced in March 1965; a total of 58 were built. In May 2014, twenty-two WA-41s were listed on the French civil aircraft register, with a further three registered in the UK.

Wassmer WA-51 Pacific and WA-52 Europa. The four-seat 150hp WA-51 Pacific is the production version of the all-composite WA-50 prototype. First flown in May 1969, thirty-nine were built. The WA-52 Europa is a 160hp version of the WA-51. A total of fifty-nine were built. In May 2014, nine WA-51/-51As were listed on the French register, together with one WA-51A in the UK. Nineteen WA-52s were registered in France, with a further three in the UK.

G-EFVS is a Wassmer WA-52 Europa photographed at Sandown, Isle of Wight in June 2014.

D-EELC is a 1977 Wassmer WA-54 Atlantic photographed at Innsbruck, Austria in August 1980. *Jim Smith*

Wassmer WA-54 Atlantic. The WA-54 is a WA-52 with a 180hp Lycoming engine and increased gross weight. The WA-54 was first flown in February 1973 and fifty-five were built, seventeen appearing on the French register in May 2014.

Wassmer WA-80 and WA-81 Piranha. The WA-80, which was first flown in October 1975, was a 100hp two-seat all composite training aircraft that was first flown in November 1975. The WA-81 was a variant with a third seat. Production comprised six WA-80s and eighteen WA-81s. In May 2014, two WA-80s and eight WA-81s appeared on the French register.

F-GAIF is a 1977 WA-81 Piranha, photographed at Brienne-le-Chateau, France.

2003 Wheeler Express S2000 photographed at Illawarra Regional Airport, NSW, Australia. *Jim Smith*

Wheeler

The Wheeler Express is a high-performance long range four-seat homebuilt aircraft. Installed power is typically 300hp to 350hp, providing cruise speeds of 185 kt to 200kt. The type was first flown in July 1987 and is of all-composite construction. After the closure of Wheeler, design rights passed to later Express Design Inc., and then Composite Aircraft Technologies. Variants have been marketed as the Express CT, Express S90, Express 2000FT and the Express 2000RG with retractable undercarriage. In May 2014, sixty-six Express aircraft were listed on the U.S. civil aircraft register.

Wittman

Steve Wittman designed the pioneering Buster and 'Chief Oshkosh'/Bonzo midget racers in the early 1930s. His Wittman Tailwind is a highly successful two-seat homebuilt aircraft that has been built worldwide. The Tailwind first flew in 1953 and more than 350 have been flown, the most common variants being the original W-8 and the updated W-10. In May 2014, 131 were listed on the U.S. civil register, with twelve in the UK and six in Canada.

G-BMHL is a 1986 Wittman W-8 Tailwind photographed at Eggesford, Devon.

1985 Wolf Boredom Fighter N65GS photographed at Oshkosh, Wisconsin in 1985.

Wolf

The Wolf W-11 Boredom Fighter is a single-seat homebuilt biplane that was first flown in August 1979. In general configuration, the Boredom Fighter resembles a First World War SPAD fighter and is often painted with an imagined SPAD color scheme. In May 2014, ten examples were listed on the U.S. civil register. Photographs of around thirty examples can be found at http://www.adap.com/Builders.htm.

Woody Pusher

The Woody Pusher is a tandem seat open cockpit high wing wooden homebuilt aircraft with an engine driving a pusher propeller mounted at the wing center section. In overall configuration, the type resembles the Curtiss Junior. By 1977, twenty-seven aircraft were reported to have been flown, with eighteen listed on the U.S. civil register in May 2014.

Woody Pusher G-BSFV photographed at Henstridge, Somerset.

Czech-built 1956 Yak C.11 G-BTUB photographed at Cranfield, Bedfordshire in July 1994.

Yakovlev

Yakovlev Yak-11. The Yak-11 is a two-seat advanced training aircraft based on the Yak-3 fighter. The type first flew in November 1945 and was produced in quantity in both Russia and Czechoslovakia (C.11), with a combined total of some 4,566 aircraft. In May 2014, some ten Yak-11 aircraft were listed on the U.S. civil register, with a further five in the UK.

Yakovlev Yak-12. The Yak-12 is a high wing short take-off and landing multi-role liaison aircraft. First flown in 1947, nearly 5,000 were built (excluding Chinese production). The Yak-12 was license-built in Poland, where it was further developed as the PZL-101 Gawron, of which 325 were built. The type was also produced in China as the Shenyang Type 5. The main production variant is the Yak-12M.

PZL-built Yak 12M LY-FKD.

Yak 18T HA-YAV Eggesford, Devon in May 2009.

Yakovlev Yak-18T. The 1946 Yak-18 was a tandem two-seat basic trainer that served throughout the communist bloc, some 8,700 being built. Single-seat aerobatic variants were produced including, for example, the Yak-18PM and -18PS. These aircraft anticipated the later Yak-52 and the single-seat aerobatic Yak-50, -54, and -55 (see below). The Yak-18T is an extensively modified four-seat cabin tourer with a 360hp Ivchenko M-14P engine. In May 2014, six Yak-18Ts were registered in the UK, with sixteen listed on the U.S. register.

Yakovlev Yak-50. The Yak-50 is a single-seat aircraft designed for competition aerobatics. It first flew in September 1975 and replaced the Yak-18PS in the competition role, twice winning the World Aerobatic Championships. 314 Yak-50 were built and the type is now popular with Western private owners. In May 2014, twenty-one were registered in the UK and thirty-six were listed on the U.S. civil register.

1980 Yak 50 '49' G-YAKU Henstridge, Somerset in May 2014.

Yak-52s G-YAKE and G-YAKN of the Yakovlevs Display team at their home base of Henstridge, Somerset in June 2013.

Yakovlev Yak-52. The Yak-52 is an aerobatic two-seat trainer developed from the Yak-50. The type first flew in 1979 and mass production was undertaken in Romania. More than 1,600 have been built and many are operated with private owners in Europe, the U.S., UK and Australasia. In May 2014, forty-eight were registered in the UK, forty-seven in Australia, together with 154 listed on the U.S. civil register.

Yakovlev Yak-54. The two-seat Yak-54 mid-wing aerobatic aircraft was derived from the single-seat Yak-55 (see below) and flew for the first time in December 1993. In May 2014, four were listed on the U.S. civil register.

The as-yet unflown prototype of the Yak 54 photographed at the Paris Air Show in June 1993. This aircraft was not flown until December 1993.

Yak 55M RA01333 photographed at Cranfield, Bedfordshire in July 1998.

Yakovlev Yak-55. The single-seat Yak-55 is designed for competition aerobatics and first flew in May 1981. The design was very successful in the 1982 World Aerobatics Championships. The later Yak-55M has a thinner wing section and appeared in 1989. More than 200 have been built. Six Yak-55s and fifty-six Yak-55Ms were listed on the U.S. civil aircraft register in May 2014.

Heintz Zenith 100 LR F-PVQS Paris Air Show, Le Bourget, Paris in June 1977.

Zenith/Zenair

Chris Heintz designed the HR series of aircraft for Robin before designing a series of homebuilt aircraft drawing on that experience. Initially working in France, he emigrated to Canada in 1973, setting up Zenith Aviation (Zenith being an anagram of his surname), which later became Zenair.

Zenith CH-100. While still in France, Heintz produced the first of his homebuilt designs, the two-seat Heintz Zenith CH-100, which was first flown in March 1970.

Around fifteen examples were built in France designated Heintz Zenith -90, -100, -115, -120, -125 and -130 dependent on installed power.

Zenith CH-150 Acro Zenith. The CH-150 was a one-off aerobatic development that led the way to the CH-180 Super Acro (see below). It was developed from the non-aerobatic single-seat CH-100 Mono-Zenith. In May 2014, two examples were listed on the U.S. civil aircraft register.

Zenith CH150 C-GCGW photographed at Oshkosh, Wisconsin.

Prototype Zenith CH-180 Super Acro-Z C-GZEN 'J-Bird' photographed at Oshkosh, Wisconsin in 1985.

Zenith CH-180 Super Acro-Z. The CH-180 was a development of the CH-150 suitable for unlimited aerobatics. The CH-180 first flew in July 1981. In May 2014, three CH-180 aircraft were registered in Canada, with one further example in the U.S.

Zenair Zenith CH-200. The CH-200 is a two-seat low wing homebuilt developed from the Heintz Zenith 100, originally flown in France (see above). This model was very successful, with numerous examples having flown in Canada, USA and the UK. In May 2014, nine were listed on the U.S. civil register and thirty-four in Canada

1977 Zenith CH200 C-GQEF photographed at Oshkosh, Wisconsin.

1983 Zenair CH250 G-GFKY photographed at Cranfield, Bedfordshire in July 1994.

Zenair Zenith CH-250. The CH-250 is a development of the CH-200, with increased fuel and baggage capacity and additional side cockpit glazing. The canopy itself is forward sliding, rather than side-hinged. In May 2014, twenty-two were registered in Canada, nine in the U.S. and two in the UK. Like the CH-200, the aircraft can be built with tailwheel or tricycle undercarriage.

Zenair CH-300 Tri-Z. The CH-300 is a further development of the CH-200, configured as a three-seater (or two plus two); it was first flown in July 1977. This type was subsequently evolved into the Zenair CH-2000, first flown in 1993. In May 2014, five CH-300s were listed on the U.S. civil register with ninety-six examples of the later CH-2000; the Canadian register listed forty-four CH-300s and six CH-2000s.

1980 Zenair CH300 TD Tri-Z N80WB photographed at Oshkosh, Wisconsin.

2004 Zenair CH-601UL Zodiac G-CDAL on take-off from Henstridge, Somerset in April 2014.

Zenair CH-601 Zodiac. The CH-601 is a Rotax-powered kit-built and factory-built two-seat light aircraft that is one of the most successful designs from Zenair. First flown in 1984, the Zodiac has been built in a number of variants. The original variant was the VW-powered CH-600; the -601 introduced Rotax power; the -601HD (Heavy Duty) was an upgraded version; the -601HDS has a reduced wingspan with tapered tips and increased gross weight; the -601UL (1991) meets Canadian and European ultralight regulations at a lighter weight; the -601XL (also 1991) is an improved HD with a revised canopy and other changes including a thinner wing; the CH-650 has an enlarged canopy, increased power options and a swept fin. The Zodiac XL meets U.S. Light Sport Aircraft regulations. More than 1,000 have been built with some hundreds flying in the U.S., and seventy-nine were listed on the UK register in May 2014.

Zenair STOL CH-701. The CH-701 kit-built high wing two-seat STOL aircraft was introduced in 1986. Zenair say that more than 500 are flying worldwide. With its thick wing, full span slats and effective flaps the aircraft is designed to operate from short unprepared strips. The larger CH-801 is a four-seat aircraft to the same design concept. The CH-750 is similar to the CH-701, but meets LSA certification requirements.

2004 Zenair STOL CH-701SP takes off from East Pennard airstrip in June 2014.

1997 Zivko Edge 540 G-EDGY demonstrating the power available as it climbs steeply directly after takeoff.

Zivko

The Zivko Edge 360 and Edge 540 are high performance Unlimited Class competition aerobatic aircraft, from Zivko Aeronautics. The Edge 540 is best known for its successful participation in the Red Bull Air Race World Series, which combines aerobatics with pylon racing around a pre-defined course. A two-seat variant of the Edge 540 is designated the 540-T. In June 2014, four Edge 360s or 540s were registered in the UK, with thirty-three Edge 540s or 540-Ts listed on the U.S. civil register.

Zlin

Zlin Trener series. The Czechoslovakian (Morovan) Zlin 226 Trener and 326 and 526 Trener Master revolutionized the world of competition aerobatics. In a step that has since been followed by designers of other competition machines from the U.S. to France, Russia and elsewhere, the Zlin sought characteristics that would allow the easy performance of maneuvers that would score highly under the competition Aresti scoring system. The type was also capable of new maneuvers that had not been seen before, such as the lomcovak with its nose over tail rotations.

The type has its origins in the Zlin 26 of 1947. The Zlin 126 and 226 Trener have a fixed undercarriage, whereas the Zlin 326 and 526 Trener Master have retractable mainwheels. Single-seat variants carry an A suffix and are known as the Akrobat. The Zlin was the dominant aerobatic aircraft of the 1960s; in the first two FAI World Aerobatic Championships, more than half the contestants flew the Zlin 226. 1,488 aircraft were built in the Zlin 26 to Zlin 726 series, 1,125 of these being Zlin 226, 326 and 526 Trener/Trener Master.

1958 Zlin 226T Trener D-EJGO (later G-EJGO) photographed at Cranfield, Bedfordshire.

1962 Zlin Z326 Trener Master G-BKOB landing at Popham, Hampshire in July 2014.

Zlin 526A Akrobat (single-seat Trener Master) G-AWAR photographed at Redhill Aerodrome, Surrey. This aircraft was successfully forced landed by Neil Williams in June 1970 by means of an inverted approach to land after an in-flight structural failure of the port wing spar.

Three Zlin Z-50LS aircraft of the Czech aerobatic team at the World Aerobatic Championships, South Cerney 1986. *Jim Smith*

Zlin Z-50L. The single-seat Zlin Z-50L aerobatic aircraft was designed to continue the tradition for competition aerobatics for which the Trener and Trener Master had become famous. The first Zlin Z-50L flew in July 1975 and was rapidly adopted in international competitions, being highly placed in the World Championships in 1976, 78, 80 and 82. The Zlin Z-50LS increased power from 260hp to 300hp, winning the World championships in 1984 and 1986. Some seventy-eight Zlin Z-50 series aircraft were built.

Zlin Z-42 family. The Zlin Z-42 family comprises five related types, the Zlin Z-42, Z-142, Z-43, Z-143 and Z-242. The Zlin Z-42 is a two-seat side-by-side low wing monoplane powered by a 180hp M-137A inverted six cylinder engine. This is the production version of the 1966 Zlin Z-41, designed as a training aircraft to replace the Zlin Trener.

The Zlin Z-42 flew for the first time in October 1967. The Zlin Z-42M has revised tail surfaces and a constant speed propeller. The Zlin Z-142 has a revised cockpit with sliding canopy and a 210hp Walter M337 engine and flew for the first time in December 1978.

The Zlin Z-43, which flew in December 1968, is a four-seat touring aircraft based on the Z-42 and featuring enlarged tail surfaces as well as the necessary fuselage modifications. Eighty Zlin Z-43s were built. Re-engining of the Zlin Z-43 with a 235hp Lycoming O-540, and the Z-142 with a 200hp Lycoming AEIO-360 engine, results respectively in the Zlin Z-143L and the Zlin Z-242L. In May 2014, there were 7 Z-142, six Z-143Ls and thirty-one Z-242Ls listed on the U.S. civil register with five Z-142s and fourteen Z-242Ls registered in Canada.

Zlin Z-42M D-EWNT at Berlin Gatow, Germany in September 2011.
Johann Visschedijk

Zlin Z-142 OK-RNN Paris Air Show 1987

Zlin Z-143L OK-XYJ Paris Air Show 1993.

Zlin Z-242L photographed at Point Cook, VIC, Australia in October 2006.

Zlin Savage Cub. The Zlin Savage Cub is one of several Light Sport aircraft designs that resemble the Piper Cub. The type started life in Italy, before production was moved to Zlin in the Czech Republic. The type is produced in several variants including the Cub-S, Savage Cub, Savage Bobber, Cruiser and Classic. By December 2012, more than 250 Zlin Savage aircraft had been delivered. In May 2014, twenty-two Zlin Savage types were listed on the U.S. civil aircraft register.

Zlin Savage Cub 24-7775 photographed at Echuca, VIC, Australia in April 2013.

BIBLIOGRAPHY

Eyre, David. *The Illustrated Encylopedia of Aircraft in Australia and New Zealand.* (Child & Associates Publishing, NSW, Australia, 1988).

Gaillard, Pierre. *Les Avions Francais de 1944 a 1964.* (Editions EPA, Paris, 1990).

Gaillard, Pierre. *Les Avions Francais de 1965 a 1990.* (Editions EPA, Paris, 1991).

Green, William and Pollinger, Gerald. *The Aircraft of the World.* (Macdonald, London 1953, 1955 and 1965).

Jackson, AJ. *British Civil Aircraft Since 1919, 2nd Edition, Volumes 1 thru 3.* (Putnam, London 1973 and 1974).

Juptner, Joseph P. U.S. *Civil Aircraft Volumes 3 thru 8.* (Aero Publishers Inc., Fallbrook, California, 1966-1980)

Lambert, Mark and Munson, Kenneth and Taylor, Michael JH. *Jane's All the World's Aircraft 1990-91.* (Janes Information Group Ltd, Coulsdon, Surrey, 1990).

Ord-Hume, Arthur WJG. *British Light Aeroplanes.* (GMS Enterprises, Peterborough, 2000).

Simpson, Rod. *Airlife's General Aviation.* (Airlife Publishing Ltd, England, 1991).

Simpson, Rod. *Airlife's World Aircraft.* (Airlife Publishing Ltd, UK, 2001).

Smith, Ron. *British Built Aircraft.* (5 volumes, Tempus Publishing and The History Press, Brimscombe, 2002 to 2005).

Smith Ron. *Piper Cherokee: A Family History.* (Amberley Publishing, Stroud, 2012).

Taylor, John WR. *Jane's All the World's Aircraft.* (Sampson Low, Marston & Co. Ltd, London). Various editions thru to 1973-74

Taylor, John WR, Munson, Kenneth. *Jane's All the World's Aircraft.* (Macdonald and Janes Publishers Ltd, London, 1978-79).

Taylor, John WR, Munson, Kenneth. *Jane's All the World's Aircraft 1985-86.* (Janes Publishing Co. Ltd, London, 1985).

Underwood, John W, with Bowers, Peter M. *The Vintage and Veteran Aircraft Guide.* (Collinwood Press, Glendale, California, 1974).

Underwood, John and Collinge, George. *The Lightplane Since 1909.* (Heritage Press, Glendale, California, 1975).

INDEX

Adam 7
Aermacchi Lockheed 7
Aero (Czechoslovakia) 8
Aero Boero 8
Aero Commander 9
Aero Designs 17
Aeromot 17
Aeronca (and successors) 18
Aerosport 28
AISA 28
Alon 29, 144
Alpi 29
American Aviation (and successors) 30
American Eagle 32
Anderson 33
Andreasson 33
ANEC 34
Antonov 34
Arctic Aircraft 35
Arion 35
Arrow Aircraft (UK) 36
Arrow Aircraft and Motors (US) 36
ARV Aviation Ltd 37
Auster Aircraft Ltd and Taylorcraft Aeroplanes (England)
Ltd, Beagle-Auster Aircraft Ltd 38
Avia 48
AviaMilano 48
Aviation Traders (Engineering) Ltd 49
Avid 49
AV Roe & Co Ltd 50

Beagle Aircraft Ltd 51
Bede 53
Beech Aircraft Corporation 55

Bellanca Aircraft Corporation (and successors)... 66
Binder 68, 259
Blackburn 68
Blériot 70
Boeing (Stearman Aircraft Division of Boeing Aircraft
Co, Wichita) 70
Boisavia 72
Bölkow (and Messerschmitt-Bölkow-Blohm) 72
Bowers 74
Brandli 75
British Aircraft Manufacturing Co Ltd 75
Brochet 76
Brugger 77
Brunner-Winkle (and successors) 77
Bücker (factory and license-built) 78
Buhl 80
Bushby Long 81
Butler 82

CAARP 83
CAB 86
Callair 87
CASA 87
Cassutt 88
Caudron 88
Celerity 89
Centre Est 89
Cerva 92
Cessna 92
CFM (Cook Flying Machines) 105
Chilton 105
Chrislea 106
Christavia 106
Christen (later Aviat) 107

Christena 107

Cirrus.. 108

Clutton Tabenor.. 108

Colomban.. 109

Commonwealth (Rearwin) 109

Commonwealth Aircraft Corporation
     (CAC) (Australia)... 110

Comper.. 111

Corben.. 111

Corby 112

Cozy Aircraft 112

Croses 113

Culver 116

Cunningham hall.. 117

Currie.. 117

Curtiss and Curtiss-Wright.................................. 118

CZAW 119

Daphne Airplanes 120

Dart Aircraft Co 120

Dart Aircraft Ltd.. 121

Davis.. 121

De Havilland Aircraft Co Ltd................................ 122

De Havilland Canada 130

Denney.. 132

Deperdussin.. 132

Desoutter.. 133

Dewoitine 133

Diamond.. 134

Dormoy.. 135

Dornier.. 135

Dan Rihn 136

Driggs.. 137

Druine.. 137

Dyke.. 139

DynAero.. 140

EAA.. 141

Edgley Aircraft Co. Ltd (and successors).............. 142

Emigh.. 143

English Electric Ltd 143

Engineering & Research Corporation (Erco)
     (and related designs)...................................... 144

Escapade.. 145

Europa Aircraft Co 145

Evans.. 146

Evektor – Aerotechnik.. 147

Extra Flugzeugebau 147

Fairchild 150

Fairchild Aircraft Ltd.. 152

Fauvel.. 153

FFA (Flug & Fahrzeugwerke AG)........................ 153

Fiat Aviazione.. 154

Fieseler 154

Fleet Aircraft 155

Flight Design 157

Focke Wulf 157

Fokker.. 158

Foster-Wikner 158

Found Brothers Aviation 159

Fournier.. 160

Fuji 163

Funk Aircraft 164

Gatard 165

Gazuit-Valledeau.. 165

General Avia 166

Gere 167
GippsAero 167
Globe (Temco) 168
GlosAir 168, 378
Granger 168
Granville Brothers 169
Great Lakes 170
Grindvals 171
Grob 171
Groppo 172
Grumman 173
Gyroflug 176

Harlow 177
Hatz 177
Hawker Aircraft Ltd 178
Heath 179
Helio Aircraft 179
Helton 181
Hindustan Aeronautics Ltd (HAL) 181
Hirth 183
Hoffmann 183
Holste 184
Hovey 185
Howard 186
Hummell 186
Hunting 187

IAR 188
Ikarus 189
Ilyushin 190
Iniziative Industriali Italiane 3I 190
Interstate 191
Isaacs 191

Jabiru 193
Janowski 194
Javelin 194
Jeffair 195
Jodel 195
Johnson 201
Jurca 201

Kaminskas 203
K&S 203
Kappa 204
Kelly 204
Klemm 205
Kreider Reisner 206

L-13 Inc. 207
Laird 207
Lake 208
Lancair 209
Lancashire Aircraft 210
Laser 211
Laverda 211
Leopoldoff 212
LET (Omnipol) 212
Levier 213
LightWing 214
Lincoln 215
Lockheed 215
Luscombe 217
Luton Aircraft 219

Malmo MFI 221
Marquart 221
Mauboussin 222

Maule 222

Meyers 145 223

Meyers OTW 224

Mignet and related types 224

Miles Aircraft 226

Mong 231

Monnett and Sonex 231

Monocoupe 235

Mooney 236

Morane Saulnier 238

Morgan Aeroworks 239

Murphy Aircraft 240

Nanchang 241

Nardi 241

Naval Aircraft Factory 242

Neiva 242

Nesmith 243

New Standard 243

Nicollier 244

Noorduyn 244

Nord Aviation 245

North American Aviation 247

Oberlerchner 249

Oldfield 249

Orlican 250

Parker 251

Partenavia 251

Pazmany 253

Percival 255

Pereira 256

Piaggio 257

Piel 259

Pietenpol 264

Pilatus 264

Piper 265

Pitcairn 279

Pitts 279

Pober 281

Porterfield 281

Potez 282

Pottier 283

Procaer 284

Pützer 284

PZL 285

Quickie 286

Rand 288

Rans 289

Rearwin 291

Replica Plans 293

Republic 293

RFB 294

Riley 294

RLU 295

Robin 296

Robinson 302

Rollason 302

Rose 303

Rutan 303

Ryan 306

SAAB 309

SAI (Skandinavisk Aero Industri) 309

Scheibe 312

Schleicher	313
Scottish Aviation	314
SeaRey	314
SIAI-Marchetti	315
SIAT	317
Silence	318
SIPA	318
Sisler	319
Skyfox	319
Skyote	320
Slepcev	321
Slingsby	321
SMAN	322
Smith	323
Smyth	323
SOCATA	324
Sopwith	329
Sorrell	329
Southern Aircraft	330
Spartan Aircraft Ltd (UK)	330
Spartan Aircraft Co (US)	331
Spencer	332
Spezio	332
Sportavia-Pützer	333
Stampe/ SNCAN	335
Starck	336
Star-Lite	337
Stearman	337
Steen	338
Stephens	338
Stewart	339
Stinson	339
Stits	345

Stoddard Hamilton	347
Stolp	348
Sukhoi	350
Supermarine Spitfire Mk 26	352
Swallow	352
Swearingen	353
SZD	353
John Taylor (UK)	354
Moulton Taylor (US)	355
Taylorcraft	355
Tecnam	358
Ted Smith	359
Temco	359
Thorp	362
Thruxton	363
Thurston	363
Timm	364
Tipsy	365
TL Ultralight	366
Trago Mills	367
Travel Air	367
Tri-R KIS	369
Turner	370
Ultravia	371
United Consultants	371
Valentin	372
Valmet	372
Van's Aircraft	373
Varga	378
Victa / AESL / Glos Air / NZAI	378

Viking.. 380

Volmer... 381

Vultee... 381

Waco... 382

WAR.. 390

Wassmer Aviation................................ 392

Wheeler... 395

Wittman.. 395

Wolf.. 396

Woody Pusher...................................... 396

Yakovlev.. 397

Zenith / Zenair...................................... 401

Zivko... 405

Zlin... 405

CLASSIC LIGHT
AIRCRAFT